FREEDOM

A SHARED SACRIFICE!

New York's African American Civil War Soldiers

To Kim
I hope you'll Enjoy
Marjory Allen Perez

MARJORY ALLEN PEREZ

ISBN 978-0-9891209-7-5

Cover Design by George Perez
Photograph in background of cover: Beaufort National Cemetery,
South Carolina. Credit George Perez.
Printed in United States of America by McNaughton & Gunn,
Saline, Michigan

Published by Herons Bend Productions

 Herons Bend Productions

Dedication

To the extraordinary people whose stories

fill the pages of this book

and

to my family, friends and fellow researchers

who have made this journey possible

Preface

We've all heard the expression that "all politics is local." I've always believed that "all history is local." My journey for this particular project began when I decided to research the African American soldiers from Wayne County, New York who served in the Civil War. It seemed so simple when I first started out. Find the names, identify their units, tell what happened to them.

What I did not expect was that I would spend the next four decades collecting not only the stories of men from Wayne County, but would reach out to tell a much larger story about soldiers from Western New York and in turn a story about the Civil War.

The title for this book grew out of a realization that those who fought for the preservation of the Union, regardless of race, fought to free the nation from the bonds of slavery. I am sure that many did not see that as their goal at the time, but that is the truth. The shared sacrifice of the nation during the four years of civil war was just one step in fulfilling the promise of the founding fathers (and mothers) to form a "more perfect union." The road to that "more perfect union" has been strewn with obstacles, with racism proving to be the hardest legacy of slavery for us to overcome.

I have no illusions that this is a complete story. Any researcher knows that "just down the road" is another piece of the story, waiting to be uncovered or in many cases, rediscovered. I admit that even as I started writing, I was not able to stop myself from straying back into research mode, to follow another clue or idea, and in the end, greatly expanding my original outline. The lack of photographs to assist in illustrating the stories of the soldiers is one of my main regrets. The hope is that this effort will generate additional stories and photographs, which will find their way into the next edition.

TABLE OF CONTENTS

Introduction

America's Civil War broke out in April 1861. The initial call to arms by President Abraham Lincoln brought eager volunteers, but not all volunteers were welcomed. There was no place in the Union Army for African Americans who were anxious and able to serve. A letter to the editor appeared in the May 1861 issue of, *Douglass' Monthly* stating "it seems to me extremely proper that the descendants of Africans should take a prominent part in a war which will eventually lead to a general emancipation of the race." Frederick Douglass, the editor, responded that "...we do most earnestly urge our people everywhere to ... organize themselves into societies and companies, purchase arms for themselves, and learn how to use them. The present war ... will in all probability reach a complexion when a few black regiments will be absolutely necessary." [1]

Frederick Douglass used his newspaper in September 1861 to once again urge the recruitment of black soldiers under the headline "Fighting Rebels with Only One Hand." [2] Douglass took his mission advocating for enlistment of black soldiers to New York City in February 1862, with a speech before the Cooper Institute. He reminded his audience that "Colored men were good enough to fight under Washington ... good enough to fight under Andrew Jackson ... good enough to help win American independence, but they are not good enough to help preserve that independence..." [3]

In the summer of 1862 the Civil War had been raging for over a year and it was painfully clear that more manpower would be required by the Union Army. A call for an additional 300,000 men by President Lincoln issued in July was followed the next month with instructions for states to create a militia of an additional 300,000 men, which could be called upon if conscription became necessary to fill the ranks. The threat of a draft was a very unpopular option and in order to keep from

1

enforcing it and to meet these quotas, states, counties and municipalities began to offer bounties for volunteer enlistments. Yet, there was one source of manpower that the Union continued to bar from army service. African American volunteers were rejected at every turn.

The one concession made in the summer of 1862 was Congress' authorization to accept "persons of African descent" into military service in a limited role as non-combatants to be used mostly as laborers. This was not the role advocated by Frederick Douglass. That hope was finally fulfilled with the issuing of the Emancipation Proclamation on January 1, 1863, which not only declared all slaves held in states "in rebellion" were "forever free", but also stated that African American men were to become part of the regular army of the United States of America and be used in combat. The change of heart had little to do with a new appreciation for the black soldier but was rooted in the facts that North was losing the war and white soldiers were no longer lining up as eager recruits. The harsh reality of the Civil War had made it acceptable to turn former slaves and free black men into soldiers.

The proclamation was met with great excitement among the African Americans of New York State, but actual implementation of Lincoln's declaration regarding black soldiers was slow to gain momentum in the North. Recruitment for the Union Army rested with each State and only two northern states – Massachusetts and Rhode Island – immediately stepped forward to request permission of the Secretary of War to organize regiments with black soldiers. Both states received permission, but only Massachusetts followed through. By the end of May 1863, the 54th Massachusetts was ready to leave camp for assignment in South Carolina and the formation of the 55th Massachusetts was almost completed.

TO COLORED MEN!

FREEDOM,

Protection, Pay, and a Call to Military Duty!

On the 1st day of January, 1863, the President of the United States proclaimed FREEDOM to over THREE MILLIONS OF SLAVES. This decree is to be enforced by all the power of the Nation. On the 21st of July last he issued the following order:

PROTECTION OF COLORED TROOPS.

"WAR DEPARTMENT, ADJUTANT GENERAL'S OFFICE,
Washington, July 21.

"*General Order*, No. 233.

"The following order of the President is published for the information and government of all concerned:—

EXECUTIVE MANSION, Washington, July 30.

"'It is the duty of every Government to give protection to its citizens, of whatever class, color, or condition, and especially to those who are duly organized as soldiers in the public service. The law of nations, and the usages and customs of war, as carried on by civilized powers, permit no distinction as to color in the treatment of prisoners of war as public enemies. To sell or enslave any captured person on account of his color, is a relapse into barbarism, and a crime against the civilization of the age.

"'The Government of the United States will give the same protection to all its soldiers, and if the enemy shall sell or enslave any one because of his color, the offense shall be punished by retaliation upon the enemy's prisoners in our possession. It is, therefore, ordered, for every soldier of the United States, killed in violation of the laws of war, a rebel soldier shall be executed; and for every one enslaved by the enemy, or sold into slavery, a rebel soldier shall be placed at hard labor on the public works, and continued at such labor until the other shall be released and receive the treatment due to prisoners of war.

"'ABRAHAM LINCOLN.'"

"'By order of the Secretary of War.
"'E. D. TOWNSEND, Assistant Adjutant General.'"

That the President is in earnest the rebels soon began to find out, as witness the following order from his Secretary of War:

"WAR DEPARTMENT, Washington City, August 8, 1863.

"SIR: Your letter of the 3d inst., calling the attention of this Department to the cases of Orin H. Brown, William H. Johnston, and Wm. Wilson, three colored men captured on the gunboat Isaac Smith, has received consideration. This Department has directed that three rebel prisoners of South Carolina, if there be any such in our possession, and if not, three others, be confined in close custody and held as hostages for Brown, Johnston and Wilson, and that the fact be communicated to the rebel authorities at Richmond.

"Very respectfully your obedient servant,

"EDWIN M. STANTON, Secretary of War.

"The Hon. GIDEON WELLES, Secretary of the Navy."

And retaliation will be our practice now—man for man—to the bitter end.

LETTER OF CHARLES SUMNER,

Written with reference to the Convention held at Poughkeepsie, July 15th and 16th, 1863, to promote Colored Enlistments.

BOSTON, July 13th, 1863.

"I doubt if, in times past, our country could have expected from colored men any patriotic service. Such service is the return for protection. But now that protection has begun, the service should begin also. Nor should relative rights and duties be weighed with nicety. It is enough that our country, aroused at last to a sense of justice, seeks to enrol colored men among its defenders.

"If my counsels should reach such persons, I would say: enlist at once. Now is the day and now is the hour. Help to overcome your cruel enemies now battling against your country, and in this way you will surely overcome those other enemies hardly less cruel, here at home, who will still seek to degrade you. This is not the time to hesitate or to higgle. Do your duty to our country, and you will set an example of generous self-sacrifice which will conquer prejudice and open all hearts.

"Very faithfully yours,

"CHARLES SUMNER."

Recruitment poster, produced in late summer of 1863, assuring African American soldiers of protection and equal pay. https://www.archives.gov/files/education/lessons/blacks-civil-war/images/recruitment-broadside.gif.

The rapid filling of the ranks of the 54th and 55th Massachusetts was accomplished with the able assistance of a network of African American leaders working throughout New England, New York and beyond. Many of those who joined were from Western New York. There were multiple reasons for the black men to enlist, but at the core were two goals - to prove that they could fight for their country and to put an end to slavery.

Meanwhile in New York State there were no official efforts to organize regiments of African American soldiers. State elections in the fall of 1862 resulted in the election of Democrat Governor Horatio Seymour, who opposed not only the Emancipation Proclamation, but also the enlisting of black troops, and legislation calling for conscription. Once the flurry of recruitment that had accompanied the organization of the 54th and 55th Massachusetts had died down, African American men in New York, wishing to enlist, were in limbo.

Conscription became a reality with the passage of Civil War Military Draft Act on March 3, 1863. The volunteer army, even with the bounty system, was not sufficient to win the Civil War. Northern states were now required by law to identify and register all men, black and white, who were of draft age beginning in the summer of 1863. With draft looming on the horizon, there was still no clear-cut path for the African American men who were subject to the new law.

African American leaders in New York issued their own call to action on July 1, 1863, organizing a "Grand Mass Convention of Colored Citizens" which would "show the Government and People their willingness to aid in the suppression of the Rebellion by organizing a large force of Colored Volunteers for the War." The Convention was held in Poughkeepsie, New York on July 15th and 16th for the expressed purpose of developing a plan to assist both state and federal governments in the organization of the colored troops in New York State. They proposed that the appointment of "trusty able men of color" who would be authorized to "canvas the entire State for recruits: that such persons be enabled to call meetings, address and enlist men."[4] There is no record that the officials of New York State actually responded to the offer expressed so eloquently by the men at the Poughkeepsie meeting, but in fact continued to drag their feet.

As the draft proceeded during July and August, the New York government remained passive in regard to the organization of black regiments. Many of the men whose names were drawn in the draft throughout Western New York were funneled into the 8th United States Colored Troops (USCT), being formed at Camp William Penn near Philadelphia. In mid-summer 1863, the Rhode Island Adjutant-General's Office had resurrected its plan to raise a regiment of black soldiers. Connecticut joined the movement in late November when it began recruiting for the 29th Connecticut Infantry (Colored). The two states were faced with the same problem as Massachusetts when it came to raising a full regiment from its relatively small African American population, so once again the network of African American leaders in New York State went into action. And once again the men of Western New York answered the call.

The logjam in New York State was finally breeched in late November 1863 when the Union League Club of New York City resolved to "adopt and prosecute such measures as they shall deem most effectual for aiding the Government in raising and equipping the quota of volunteers to be raised in the State of New York." The Union League pressed forward and wrote directly to the Secretary of War and on December 3, 1863 the Adjutant General's Office notified the club that "you are hereby authorized ... to raise one regiment of Infantry to be composed of colored men... designated as the Twentieth Regiment United States Colored Troops."[5]

The committee immediately "put themselves into communication with the prominent colored men in this city and solicited their co-operation" and also "sought an interview with a Committee appointed at a public meeting held at the Cooper Institute, who were moving to raise a colored regiment" without authorization from the War Department."[6] The plans generated by the Convention of Colored Citizens, held in Poughkeepsie in July come into play. Throughout December 1863 and January 1864, hundreds of New York's black men arrived in New York City to fill the ranks of the 20th United States Colored Infantry regiment. So many came that the War department quickly authorized the formation of two more New York State regiments.

It would be difficult to accurately determine the total number of African American soldiers who served in the Civil War from New York. The War Department set the amount at about 4,100 men, which may not include soldiers serving in units organized outside of New York State. We know that a sizable portion of those African American soldiers were from Western New York.

What follows is an attempt to tell the story of some of the African American soldiers who served in the Union army between 1863 and 1865. The focus has been on men from Western New York who served in the 54th Massachusetts, 55th Massachusetts, 5th Massachusetts Cavalry, 8th USCT, 14th Rhode Island Regiment Heavy Artillery (also known as 11th USCHA), 20th USCT, 26th USCT, and 31st USCT. There is also a section including men from the region who served in other miscellaneous units.

The African American Community of Western New York State before the Civil War

The area, referred to in this book as Western New York, encompasses twenty-nine counties stretching from Oneida County on the east to Erie County on the west; and from Jefferson county in the north to the Pennsylvania state line. This is the same geographical area identified by historian Whitney R. Cross as the Burned-over District - "the storm center" in which religious fervor produced the social reform movements of the nineteenth century.[7] (See Fig. 1)

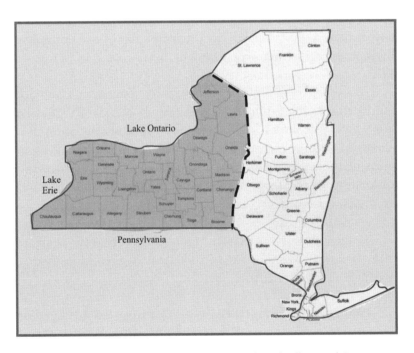

Fig. 1. Shaded area represents counties within the "Burned Over District" as described by Whitney R. Cross and the counties included in this study.

The African American community of the region was not immune to the religious revivals and social reform movements discussed in *The Burned-over District*. Beginning in the 1820s, the black communities formed organizations to advocate for civil rights, participate in the anti-slavery movement, protect slaves seeking freedom, and promote temperance efforts. The Geneva (New York) Colored Anti-Slavery Society held its third annual meeting in January 1839 and among the issues discussed "whether they can innocently or consistently use the products of slave labor." Three months later, some of the same persons attending the Anti-Slavery meeting met in Geneva to form the "Moral and Mental Improvement Society", with the object "to maintain our political rights, to encourage education amongst us, to assist in getting each member into profitable employment in trades or agriculture, to suppress intemperance, licentiousness among our people, and support the cause of universal liberty."[8]

In the 1840s and 1850s, a series of New York Colored Men's Conventions were held in New York State, in which the extension of suffrage to black men was a main agenda item. Local black leaders were instrumental in hosting two of the National Colored Men's Conventions, held in Buffalo in 1843 and Rochester ten years later, in 1853. African American women of the region were also active in religious and social reform group. The Geneva Ladies' Anti-Slavery Society advertised in September 1848 that they had secured Frederick Douglass as speaker at their October meeting.

The demand for equal rights and suffrage were dominant themes within the African American community prior to the Civil War. In 1821 the New York Constitution had removed property requirements for white male voters but imposed a requirement that to qualify as a voter, a black man must possess property valued at a minimum of $250. In 1846 New York voters rejected a proposal to remove the property requirement for black males by a margin of 71% to 29%, thereby denying voting rights to more than 90% of the black male citizens in the state. The black suffrage issue was on the ballot in 1860 and again New York State voters rejected the proposal to remove the property requirements for black males. The margin of defeat was slightly lower than in 1846, with 63% (as compared to 71%) of New York voters marking "no" on the ballot. In the region of Western New York, the tally was fifteen counties against and fourteen counties for the amendment.[9] (Fig. 2) The African American community of Western New York had fought hard for their rights, but again were pushed back. Within three years these same men, who were denied the right to vote, would be asked to fight in the Civil War.

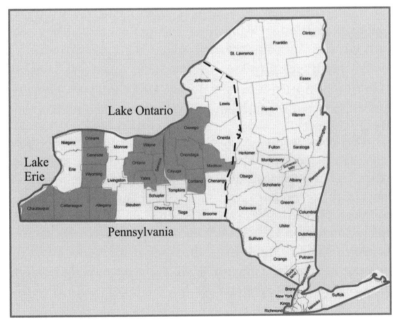

Fig. 2. Black suffrage vote in Western New York, 1860. Shaded counties voted Yes to expand universal suffrage to black males.

In 1860, the region was home to a little under one and a half million persons, which represented thirty-eight percent of the New York state's total population. The census takers of 1860 recorded 9,274 persons as being black or mulatto within the region – less than one percent of the region's total population and only nineteen percent of the state's total black population.[10] (Fig. 3)

The African American population was fairly evenly distributed between urban and rural communities within the region. Twenty percent were residents of one of the largest cities in the region – Buffalo, Rochester, Syracuse, Utica and Oswego. An additional thirty percent were living in smaller villages, mostly located along major transportation routes, such as the Erie Canal and near railroad hubs. (Fig. 4) The balance was scattered among rural farming areas of the region. Rural residents most often listed their occupations as farmer and farm laborer. City and village dwellers had more variation in their occupations, including barber, cook, sailor, day laborer, whitewasher, carpenter, domestic servant, hostler, mason, and teamster.

One more statistic is also important to the subject of this book. The region included less than 1,900 African American males between the ages of 15 and 40, the ages that would be considered of military age in 1863. The overall African American population and the number of military age males of this region was relatively small on the eve of the Civil War. It is appropriate to think that the social and civic activism demonstrated by the community would be a source of support and strength for their soldiers.

County	African American Population	Total County Population
Allegany	264	41,881
Broome	464	35,906
Cattaraugus	151	43,886
Cayuga	451	55,767
Chautauqua	205	58,422
Chenango	263	40,934
Chemung	572	26,917
Cortland	16	26,249
Erie	878	141,971
Genesee	84	32,189
Lewis	39	28,580
Jefferson	209	69,825
Livingston	184	39,547
Madison	300	43,545
Monroe	567	100,618
Niagara	517	50,399
Oneida	638	105,202
Onondaga	555	90,686
Ontario	639	44,573
Orleans	131	28,717
Oswego	335	75,958
Schuyler	100	18,840
Seneca	213	28,138
Steuben	475	66,690
Tioga	248	28,748
Tompkins	297	31,409
Wayne	270	47,762
Wyoming	52	31,968
Yates	157	20,290
Total	**9,274**	**1,455,617**
NYS State Totals	**48,005**	**3,880,735**

Fig. 3. 1860 Population –Western New York Counties

	County	African American Population	Total Population
Buffalo	**Erie**	809	81,129
Rochester	**Monroe**	410	48,204
Syracuse	**Onondaga**	321	28,119
Utica	**Oneida**	213	22,529
Oswego	**Oswego**	100	16,716
Lockport	Niagara	209	13,523
Auburn	Cayuga	210	10,986
Owego	Tioga	100	8,935
Elmira	Chemung	370	8,682
Seneca (Town)	Ontario	308	8,448
Binghamton	Broome	319	8,325
Watertown	Jefferson	49	7,572
Canandaigua	Ontario	171	7,075
Ithaca	Tompkins	218	6,843
Niagara Falls	Niagara	242	6,603
Corning	Steuben	78	6,003
Bath (Town)	Steuben	135	5,129
	Total	**4262**	**294,821**

Fig. 4. 1860 Population – Western New York Cities, Villages and Towns with population over 5,000 residents.

Go East Young Men

Massachusetts Welcomes New York Recruits:
The 54th, 55th Massachusetts Infantry and
5th Massachusetts Cavalry

On January 1, 1863, Abraham Lincoln formally issued the Emancipation Proclamation, officially declaring that African American men could join the regular army of the United States of America and engage in combat. While most northern states were slow to respond, Massachusetts did not hesitate. Massachusetts' Governor John A. Andrew was able, finally, to put into action his plan to raise a regiment of African American men – his goal from the earliest days of the war. An ardent abolitionist, Governor Andrew was convinced that a black regiment, formed in the North, would advance the cause against slavery and dispel the myths about the inferiority of black soldiers on the battlefield. Within two weeks of the issuance of the Emancipation Proclamation, Andrew had received permission from Secretary of War, Edwin S. Stanton, to recruit black soldiers for the 54th Massachusetts Infantry Regiment. It was Andrew's plan to attract the best and the brightest young African American men to this elite regiment – the first to be raised by a northern state.

Since the black population of Massachusetts alone would not be able to fill the ranks of a regiment (about 1,000 men), a committee was established in early February 1863 with the goal of raising funds to support the regiment's recruitment efforts. George L. Stearns was appointed agent to oversee recruitment and he established a network of recruiters, reaching all the way to St. Louis, Missouri. One of his most successful recruiters was Frederick Douglass, of Rochester, New York, who, in March, 1863, used his newspaper *Douglass' Monthly* to rally the troops with an impassioned editorial entitled **"MEN OF COLOR, TO ARMS!**[11] Douglass, who for many years had crisscrossed upstate New York speaking against slavery, once again took to the roads, this time on a mission to enlist his fellow New Yorkers "to fly to arms, and smite with death the power that would bury the government and your liberty in the same hopeless grave." He lamented that New York State had not yet called upon the black man to fight, but that "Massachusetts now welcomes you to arms as soldiers."

Recruitment efforts spread across Western New York, resulting in the enlistment of over one hundred soldiers between early March and the end of April of 1863. At Elmira more than twenty-five men signed on to serve in the 54th Massachusetts. Buffalo became a central recruitment center, relaying volunteers from its community, Canada, Ohio, western Pennsylvania and further west on to Boston. On April 14, 1863, Batavia, New York's *Republican Advocate* carried an article that had appeared previously in the *New York Evening Post*, reporting that Sergeant Albert D. Thompson, of Buffalo, had made four trips from Buffalo to Boston, ferrying nearly two hundred enlistees for the 54th Massachusetts Regiment.[12]

Syracuse and Rochester also proved to be fertile grounds, with a combined total of another thirty recruits. When the first regiment was filled, the overflow was assigned to the 55th Massachusetts Infantry and later the 5th Massachusetts Cavalry. Each man who joined the regiments committed to becoming part of something bigger than themselves, yet it is the stories of the individuals that made the unity of purpose possible.

Two of the recruits had particularly close ties to Frederick Douglass. His twenty-two-year-old son, Lewis F. Douglass, enlisted in Company F of the 54th on March 23rd and within two days he had been promoted to Sergeant Major and assigned to Regimental Field and Staff duties. Douglass' younger son, Charles R. Douglass, enlisted on April 18th and was made a corporal in Company F. The military record of Charles Douglass took several twists and turns in the first months after enlistment and, because of illness, he was never able to assume his duties with the 54th. In March of 1864 he was healthy enough to rejoin the army and was assigned as Sergeant of Company I in the newly formed 5th Massachusetts Cavalry.[13]

A third recruit from Rochester may also have been associated with Douglass through his newspaper business. Samuel J. Robinson, of Rochester, New York, enlisted on March 18th and was mustered into Company D with the rank of Corporal on March 30th. The *Company Descriptive Book* shows that he was a relatively small man, being only five feet two inches tall, twenty-two years old, born in Toronto, and occupation was "printer." It is very possible that he worked for Douglass in his newspaper. Robinson's time with the 54th was brief, as on May 27th, Corporal Robinson was transferred to the 55th Massachusetts and promoted to rank of First Sergeant. A month later he was again promoted, achieving the rank of Sergeant Major and assigned to Non-Commissioned Staff of the regiment. Robinson continued to rise in the ranks of the 55th Massachusetts and on November 14, 1863 he was made Quarter Master Sergeant, a prestigious rank with significant responsibilities.

Robinson's good fortune took a turn, when he was reduced to the ranks for drunkenness, while at Folly Island, South Carolina, and assigned to Company D on March 10, 1864. A month later he was again on the way up, when he was appointed to the rank of Corporal in the company. His last fall to the ranks occurred on June 11, 1864 when he was found guilty of forgery. What he had forged is not stated in his *Compiled Military Records*, but it must not have been too serious as there is no indication Robinson spent any time in the Guard House. He was mustered out of the service with his regiment on August 29, 1865 at Charleston, South Carolina.[14]

The men who signed on represented many occupations. There were multiple boatmen, sailors, waiters, porters, day laborers, cooks, farmers and barbers. From Buffalo there was a confectioner, a gunsmith and an upholsterer. There was a weaver from Elmira, a fireman from Rochester and a cabinet maker from Ithaca. The age span was also varied, with the youngest recruit claiming to be sixteen years old, while the oldest set his age at forty-one years.   John Shorter was so anxious to join the army that he tacked three months on to his age when he enlisted on April 9, 1863, giving his age as sixteen. John Shorter's widow told the pension examiner that her husband had run away from a farm in Michigan, where he had been apprenticed, to join the army.

The Shorter family had deep roots in Western New York. John's grandparents, Charles and Sally Ann Shorter moved to the pioneer village of Cayuga, located at the north end of Cayuga Lake, about 1815.   Their only son, Charles Jr., married a girl from the neighborhood, named Mariah, about 1830 and they began to raise their family, which eventually included seven children. John Shorter, the youngest child, was born in Clyde, New York on June 20, 1847.   Shortly after John's birth, his parents and the younger children moved to Michigan. Mariah Shorter is said to have died about 1855 in Toledo, Ohio, the whereabouts of the children's father after 1850 is not known.   By 1860 the four older children – Sarah, Charles, Jane and Alfred - were residents of Wayne and Cayuga counties in New York and the three youngest boys – Hezekiah, William and John – were living in the household of James and Catherine Smith in Amboy, Hillsdale County, Michigan.   John was still living in Michigan when he enlisted and that was where he returned immediately after a disability discharge on June 3, 1865.

Private Shorter did not have an easy time of it while serving with the 54th Massachusetts. Beginning in September 1863, his medical records indicate he was being treated for dysentery, and on December 26th he was admitted to the hospital in Beaufort, South Carolina, with diagnosis of chronic diarrhea. Shorter remained in the hospital until May 2, 1864, when he was issued a convalescent furlough, which allowed him to travel to Michigan for a six-week visit.   On May 26th, Private

17

Shorter finally returned to duty in Company G. His luck took another bad turn when he was wounded in the hand at Honey Hill, South Carolina on November 30, 1864 and once again was admitted to the hospital, where he remained until his discharge which evaluated his disability to one-fourth, qualifying him for a pension. The soldier returned to Michigan, where he immediately applied for a pension, which was issued on August 5th. He remained in Michigan for two years, moving to Boston in September of 1867, where he worked in hotels as a waiter for the next eighteen years. He died at the age of thirty-eight years on October 18, 1885, leaving a wife, Rebecca Highsmith Shorter, and no children.[15]

Miles Moore, Drummer, of Elmira, New York.
Used with permission of Massachusetts Historical Society.

Another young recruit, Miles Moore, also added months – as many as twelve months – on to his age, when he enlisted in Elmira, New York in late April 1863. Census records and his civil war pension file put him at only fifteen years old at the time of enlistment. His height of five feet tall, also indicates he may not have reached his full height, with the normal growth spurt that young men experience in their mid to late teens. Assigned to Company H, Private Moore was detailed as a drummer and musician between May 1863 and August 1865 by order of Col. Robert G. Shaw at the organization of the Regiment. Miles Moore (also known as David M.), the son of David and Elizabeth Moore, gave his birthplace as Ithaca, Tompkins County, New York on his enlistment papers and the census records indicate that the family moved frequently between the late 1840s and 1860, before settling in Elmira, New York. In the 1865 New York census, Miles' mother, Elizabeth, was listed as a widow, mother of nine children, with two sons in the service.[16]

Private Miles Moore was one of the few soldiers that chose to continue to serve in the army after the Civil War. He enlisted in Company E of the 39th U.S. Colored Infantry in May 1868 at Fort Columbus, located on Governors Island in New York Harbor, serving as a drummer in the regimental band. He transferred to Company F, 25th U.S. Infantry in April 1870 and was discharged while at Fort Clark, Texas, on August 30, 1870.[17]

After his discharge Miles moved to New Orleans, perhaps drawn there by the presence of his older brother William A. Moore, who had served in the 14th Rhode Island Heavy Artillery (later called the 11th USCHA), which had been stationed in the vicinity of New Orleans in 1864 and 1865. William Moore deserted from his regiment in September 1865, one month before it was scheduled to be mustered out and transported to Rhode Island for final discharge ceremonies. William's reason for not returning north with his unit may have been that his future bride, Louisa Rosemire, lived in New Orleans. Miles Moore settled into life in New Orleans and in 1875 married Ardelle Rosemary, probably a sister or relative of his brother's wife. The two Moore families were living together on Washington Street in New Orleans in the summer of 1880. About 1888 Miles brought his family north to Saratoga Springs, New York. Miles died there in 1904 and Ardelle died in 1925. Both were buried in Greenridge Cemetery.[18]

Among the older recruits was Cornelius Harding, of Utica, New York, who sometimes went by the name of Hardin. Mr. Harding's origins are hard to pin down, as various census records place his birth in New York, Virginia, and South Carolina. He told the enlisting officer he was forty-one-years old and was born in Hagerstown, Maryland. His obituary states he was born in Orange County, New York on the 11th day of the 11th month in the year 1811. Harding was also vague about his age, with different documents placing his birth year anywhere between 1810 and 1830. Like young John Shorter and Miles Moore, he was not truthful about his age in 1863, but in this instance made himself at least ten years younger to remain eligible for service.

Private Harding's pension record does little to untangle his biography. He waited until 1889 to begin the application process, giving his age as eighty-two years old and stated he suffered from "malarial poisoning and rheumatism" contracted while "digging trenches and sleeping on the ground" while at Morris Island in July 1863. According to his statement "he has not been able to follow his occupation as a barber at any time since his discharge." His claim was supported by Charles W. Lloyd, also of Utica, who stated the two men had enlisted together and had been tent mates. Lloyd also noted that Harding's poor health meant that he was often "left in camp when going on force[d] marches." The two men must have made an interesting pair. Lloyd was only twenty-years-old when he enlisted, while, according to his pension application, Private Harding was fifty-six-years old.[19]

Five men, all giving their ages as thirty-eight and thirty-nine years old, enlisted at Elmira and were mustered into Company F on May 12, 1863. Wesley R. Armstrong and Levi Carter were brothers-in-law, working as a blacksmith and laborer, respectively. Andrew Miller gave his occupation as blacksmith, John P. Price worked as a barber and William R. Lee was a weaver by trade. None of the five was born in New York State, but migrated to Elmira, New York sometime in the late 1840s and 1850s, as the city became a major transportation hub, linking commercial interests of Pennsylvania and New York.

While the bulk of the enlistments of men from Western New York started in early March, this was not always the case. Among the first western New Yorkers to enlist in the 54th was George H. Lee, who enlisted at New Bedford, Massachusetts, where he was working as a hostler. Born in Geneva, New York in 1842, Lee answered the call to arms on February 22nd and two weeks later joined with fifty-two other recruits, assembled at New Bedford's City Hall, for ceremonies that would launch him into his military career. From there the men marched to the depot and boarded trains that took them to Camp Meigs, located in Readville, Massachusetts, outside of Boston[20].

Private Lee was described in the Company Books as twenty-one years old, five feet, eight and one-half inches tall, with a brown complexion, black eyes and black hair. Lee assumed a leadership role in Company C, with his appointment to rank of Sergeant on March 30th.[21] On May 18th, the regiment received news that it was to be sent immediately to the Department of the South. The young soldier made a quick trip to New Bedford, where on May 26th, he married Caty M. Smith, the eighteen-year-old daughter of William H. and Catherine Smith, just two days before his regiment left Camp Meigs for the duty in South Carolina.[22]

George Lee's journey to becoming a soldier in the 54th Massachusetts began in the small village of Geneva, New York, located at the north end of Seneca Lake in the Finger Lakes region. His grandparents, Willis and Katy Lee, along with several of their children, enslaved by John Nicholas, were brought to upstate New York from Virginia about 1800. By 1810, Willis and Katy Lee were manumitted by Nicholas and had set up their own household near the Nicholas family. Over the next ten years they accumulated about twenty-five acres of farmland and continued to raise their family. Their youngest son, Thomas, born about 1813, was the father of George H. Lee.[23]

Thomas Lee moved his family to Boston, Massachusetts sometime between 1855 and 1860, where they remained until the death of Thomas' wife, Mary Lucinda, in 1880. During their time in Massachusetts, they often took in visitors from their home town of Geneva and thereby maintained close ties with old neighbors and relatives. Thomas Lee returned to his home town of Geneva, New York in the early 1880s. His only living sibling, Hannah (Lee) Atkins, was a resident of Olean, Cattaraugus County at the time, but it is likely he still had many relatives living in and around Geneva. In November of 1884 he was admitted to the Ontario County Poor House because of age and sickness. His record included information that his parents had both been slaves and that Thomas Lee was a "Jack of All Trades." He died in the Poor House on May 31st, 1886. George H. Lee grew up in the midst of a family that was intimately connected to the ravages of slavery. He died in Boston on February 23, 1900.[24]

Not all the recruits that had arrived at Camp Meigs from Western New York, marched out of camp on May 28th, 1863. Eighteen-year-old Walter Gayton, of Geneva, New York, had arrived at Readville on March 29 and was slated to be assigned to Company E. Gayton was the son of Thomas and Harriet (Hardy) Gayton, and grandson of Thomas Gayton, who had been enslaved by Robert S. Rose and manumitted in 1822. Walter's father, Thomas, died in November of 1859 of consumption, leaving a widow and three children - Henrietta, age 15, Walter, age 14 and Eva, age 4. In the 1860 census, the Gayton family was living with George and Mary A. Allen (sister and brother-in-law of Harriet Gayton) and Walter was learning the trade of barbering, under the tutelage of his uncle.

The *Company Descriptive Book* indicate that Walter Gayton was just a half-inch shy of six feet tall, with a dark complexion and black eyes and hair. He listed his occupation as barber. In the remarks section of the book it states that Gayton deserted from Camp Meigs on April 18th, which would have been five days before the company was officially mustered into the regiment. It is only natural to question why Gayton would have deserted. There were two other desertions from Company E on that date – Nathan Brown and William Boyd. Did they travel together? Is it possible that Gayton did not realize that he was officially in the army, even without being mustered into the company? Had he heard from his widowed mother, that she needed him to come home? What became of Walter Gayton immediately after his desertion is not known, but in September of 1869, he was living with fellow Geneva, New York natives, Thomas Lee and his son George H. Lee, at 24 Parkman St. in Boston's third ward. Gayton died at the Lee home of consumption after an illness of one year, the same disease that felled his father ten years earlier. His body was returned to his hometown of Geneva, New York for burial.[25]

There were two desertions and three transfers to the 55th Massachusetts in the days immediately preceding its removal from Camp Meigs on May 28th, all involving men from Western New York and all from Company D. The desertions occurred on May 20th, eight days before the regiment sailed for the south. Edwin Lukes, a twenty-eight-year-old boatman, enlisted in Steuben County on March 18th, was mustered into Company D on March 30th. John F. Harrison, described as being eighteen years old, five feet four inches tall with light complexion, blue eyes and brown hair, enlisted in Buffalo, New York and had worked as a sailor at the time of enlistment. Neither man had supplied a place of birth on their enlistment records, so other than their place of enlistment, there are few clues to their past or their future. An African American family with the surname of Lucas has deep roots in Steuben County, but Edwin Lukes does not seem to be connected. There is one possible sighting of Harrison after his desertion, with the draft record of a twenty-five-year old man identified as John Harrison, registering in Buffalo in July 1863, described as black, married and a sailor. Other than that, both men seem to just disappear from the records, with no obvious census records for them before or after 1863.[26]

In the days just prior to the 54th Massachusetts leaving Camp Meigs there were also three Western New York soldiers transferred to the newly formed 55th Massachusetts. In addition to Samuel J. Robinson, mentioned earlier, there were John E. Davis and Oscar Sesor. Oscar Sesor (sometimes spelled Sessor), age twenty-four and a native of Rochester, New York, was working as a sailor at the time of his enlistment in Portsmouth, New Hampshire on March 17, 1863. When he was mustered into Company C of the 55th Massachusetts on May 31, 1863, he was promoted to rank of First Sergeant, which was to be a short-lived status. For reasons unknown, Sesor deserted his post on July 11, 1863, while still at Camp Meigs. His regiment was in the final stages of preparing to move to the

Department of the South when he abandoned his unit. Sesor apparently had second thoughts for on October 20th, he surrendered to authorities in Elmira, New York and was put under arrest at the Conscript Camp in that city. He was returned to his Company, then located at Folly Island, South Carolina, on November 11, 1863.

Lt. William Gannett, Commanding Officer of Company C, wrote a letter to Lt. Colonel Hartwell, Commander of the 55th Massachusetts, dated November 11, 1863, requesting that Sesor be granted a pardon and restored to serve in the company, without trial. He gave two reasons why Sesor should be restored to the company. First, he had given himself up and had not fled to Canada as some had advised. Second, the Lieutenant said Sesor was "a valuable man to the Company and is spoken of highly by officers of this regiment both as to his behavior and discipline before he left his regiment. It is believed that he will endeavor to do his duty as a soldier & a man." Four days later Special Order #605 was issued, stating that "Private Oscar Sessor [sic]... is hereby relieved from arrest as a deserter and restored to duty without trial..." Sesor had to forfeit all pay from time of his desertion until date of his reinstatement on November 15, 1863. Perhaps it was his musical talent that saved him from additional punishment, as the service records show that he was detailed to the Regimental Band between January and June 1864. It appears that Private Sesor served the remainder of his time in the army without incident and was mustered out with the regiment in October 1865.[27]

It was not entirely clear sailing for Oscar Sesor after the war ended. In May, 1866 he was arrested for burglarizing the jewelry store of Captain William D. Downey in Honeoye Falls, New York. On May 15, 1866 the Rochester *Union and Advertiser* reported that he had been convicted in Monroe County court of "mail robbery" and sentenced to six years at

Auburn State Prison. It may have been that Downey's jewelry store was also the post office. The 1870 census for the prison includes listing for inmate Oscar Sesor, age 32, mulatto, born in New York, occupation Sailor. He was discharged from Auburn on May 15, 1871, with a commutation shaving off one year of his sentence. Eight months later, Sesor reenlisted in the Army at St. Louis, Missouri and became a member of the 25th Infantry. Not finding this a suitable occupation, he once again chose to desert, making his escape at San Antonio, Texas on September 6, 1872. His last desertion may explain why no record has been found that he applied for a Civil War pension.[28]

John E. Davis enlisted at Niagara, New York on March 18, 1863 and was mustered into Company D of the 54th Massachusetts. His transfer to the 55th Massachusetts was recorded on May 27th. Davis, twenty-eight-years old, gave his occupation as cook. He may have been unwell for much of his time in the service as he was detailed once as an officer's servant and another time as a groom for an officer. He died at Folly Island, South Carolina on June 5, 1864 at the Regimental Hospital. Cause of death was consumption.[29]

By June 22, 1863, the 55th Regiment was complete with a full contingent of ten companies mustered into service. The number of Western New Yorkers in the ranks was much smaller than had been the case for the 54th Massachusetts. Brothers Alberto and Laban Robbins of Peterboro, New York, both enlisted on June 3rd and were mustered into Company F on June 15th. Charles H. Wesley of Elmira joined on June 5th and was mustered into Company G. as a sergeant ten days later. Ephriam Freeman, a thirty-eight-year-old farmer, born in Buffalo, enrolled on June 8 and became a member of Company I on June 22, 1863.[30]

Seeing Action in South Carolina

The service record of the 54th Massachusetts Infantry has been well documented in numerous books, articles and in the movie "Glory." The regiment marched through Boston on May 28, 1863 to board transports which took them to St. Simon's Island off the Georgia coast, joining the command of Colonel James Montgomery. In early July the regiment was moved to Folly Island, South Carolina, readying for an attack on Fort Wagner, located on Morris Island, guarding the entrance of Charleston Harbor. The 54th Regiment suffered its first losses in battle on James Island in the early morning hours of July 16th. Companies B, H and K were on picket duty when they were surprised by an attack by Confederate forces. Company H suffered the brunt of the casualties, with six deaths, five wounded and ten captured. Company K lost two killed and six wounded. Company B, which was being held in reserve, reported one soldier wounded and one taken prisoner.[31]

Among those who died during the action on James Island were twenty-six-year-old Anthony Schenck and twenty-seven-year-old Henry Dennis. Private Schenck enlisted in Buffalo, New York, on April 29, 1863. Corporal Dennis enlisted in Ithaca, New York on the same day. Both men, mustered into Company H on May 13, 1863 at Camp Meigs, drowned as they attempted to swim across a creek during the engagement. Nothing is known about Schenck, beyond the *Company Descriptive Book*, which indicated he was single, born in Cleveland, Ohio, 5' 5" tall with a light complexion, brown eyes and black hair, and worked as a laborer in civilian life. Corporal Dennis left a more extensive record, thanks in part to the pension application of his dependent mother, Catharine Simons Dennis, of Ithaca, New York. Mrs. Dennis identified herself in a deposition dated March 15, 1864 as the widow of Charles Dennis and the mother of Henry Dennis, Corporal in Company H of the 54th Massachusetts. She claimed that her son, Henry, had been her sole support at the time of his enlistment and for several years prior, her husband having died on February 18, 1848. At the time of her application she had three living sons - two had families of their own and were unable to contribute to her support and one was then in the army. At enlistment, Henry Dennis was described as being single, five feet and eight inches tall, of dark complexion with brown eyes and black hair, born in Ithaca, New York, and a barber, which at the time was one of the few trades open to African Americans.[32]

Two days later, the men of the 54th Massachusetts Regiment were once again facing the enemy, when they were assigned to lead the assault on Fort Wagner. The ten companies formed into two lines – five in front from left to right were companies K, C, I, A, and B. In the second line, left to right were companies H, F, G, D and E. Western New York soldiers were concentrated in companies D, E, and F, part of the second line of attack. Next in line came the 6th Connecticut, followed by 48th New York Volunteers. When the orders were given to march forward, the 54th was about sixteen hundred yards or about a mile from Fort Wagner. Try to imagine marching that distance with all the necessary military equipment required for battle, through soft sand, over dunes and into shell craters.

The Union generals on the ground were certain that their strategy would win the day, but looking back, most came to realize that the battle plan was doomed. The vulnerability of Fort Wagner was grossly overestimated and its strength equally underestimated. The failure to take Fort Wagner was not for lack of trying on the part of the men of the 54th Massachusetts. In fact, the bravery and determination of the soldiers on that fateful night became legendary. Nevertheless, the toll on the unit was terrible. Trying to tally the living, the dead, the wounded and the missing took weeks, and even then, the actual numbers continued to shift as names were moved from missing to dead, or missing to captured, and wounded to dead. Caught in the confusion of the aftermath of the assault on Fort Wagner were many of the soldiers who had enlisted in Western New York.

Thomas P. Riggs, Nathaniel Hurley, and George W. Moshroe were all listed as missing in action on initial reports. It took months to determine that Hurley and Moshroe were prisoners of war and that Private Riggs had died in the attack. At home the messaging was also muddled. Sarah Riggs, mother of Thomas Peter Riggs, did not know that her oldest child had enlisted in the army until the early summer of 1863 and it took longer to learn of his death. Thomas or "Tommy" as he was called by his mother, had left home, in Georgetown, Canada West with his friend, John Wilson Moore, in December of 1862 to find work in the warehouses of Hamilton, Canada. In March 1863, the two men crossed the Niagara River and traveled to Buffalo, New York, where on March 20th they enlisted in the 54th Massachusetts regiment.

According to the voluminous material found in the pension file of Sarah Riggs, she first learned that her son was in the army when she received a letter from Tommy's friend, John Moore, that the two were on their way south, but gave no specifics as to their status. She surmised from the paper used, that they must be in the army. Sometime in the late summer of 1863, Moses Jackson, a Sergeant in Company E of the 54th Massachusetts, wrote to a family friend in Hamilton, Canada to report that Thomas Riggs had been killed in the assault on Fort Wagner and asked that someone inform Thomas' mother of his death. Jackson had known the family for several years prior to his enlistment and almost thirty years after the death of his friend, would provide a deposition in support of Sarah Riggs' pension appeal.

It was not until the early 1870s that Sarah Riggs, began the process of applying for a pension, based on her claim that she was a dependent mother, who had been supported through the work of her son for almost nine years prior to his enlistment. The file contains numerous depositions attesting to this fact, outlining in great detail the fact that Thomas' father, Primus Riggs, was a chronic drunkard, who did not provide for his wife and family.

One of the most telling parts of the pension papers is the last deposition provided by Sarah Riggs, as she attempted to get her pension reinstated. The original certificate had been issued in 1874, while Mrs. Riggs lived in Detroit, Michigan. In 1881, a pension examiner reviewed the file and judged that the mother had not been dependent on her son for support and that she had no claim on a pension. It would be ten years before the pension was reinstated. In reading over this final statement, the abject poverty of this family and the effect of her husband's alcoholism on its stability is palpable. It also painted a picture of a woman who possessed enormous resourcefulness and commitment to her family.

Sarah Thompson was only fifteen years old when she married Primus Riggs at Schenectady, New York in 1838. Over the next forty years she led what could only be described as an itinerant life within New York state and Ontario, Canada. After the war the Riggs family moved back to the United States, stopping in Niagara Falls and Buffalo, New York, before moving on to Sandusky, Ohio and finally Detroit, Michigan, where they lived about ten years. Sarah Riggs made her last move about 1881, when she settled in Chicago, Illinois.[33]

a constant turmoil & I could not live in peace
with my husband for any length of time, He
would either get drunk & leave me, or would get
to acting so badly that I would be forced to leave
him & go out to look for work to support my
children. At first when he would go away from
me, he would write to me in a short time asking
me to join him, and on his promise to do better I
being young, felt I must go to him - but as the
years would go by & I found there was no dependence
to be placed in him, I would have lived apart
from him if I could, but when I would get
a place to work & my children provided for
in some kind of a Home, along he would come
& he would leave to take them in. Maybe he would
do first rate for awhile & then he would get so
bad that I would be forced to leave him &
look for work at some other place
     I had eight children, the letter of their birth.
I cannot give but the 1st Thomas, was born at
Schenectady N.Y. The Second a still born child
was born at Albany N.Y. The 3rd Margaret
was born at Schenectady, the 4th Napoleon was
born at Rochester N.Y. The 5th John was born
at Syracuse N.Y. The 6th Sarah was born at
Brooklyn Canada. The 7th Hubert was born at
St Pols Canada & the 8th Emma was born at
Ogdensburg N.Y. You see from that we were
constantly changing about, After the birth of
my last child we went from Ogdensburg to
Hamilton Canada where we remained a couple
of years, from there we went to Toronto Canada where
we lived about two years. Then we moved to Guelph
Canada, & lived there nearly two years, & from there
we went to Georgetown Canada where we lived at
the time Thos. left home to enlist,

An excerpt from the pension file of Sarah Riggs, outlining the turmoil of her married life and the multiple moves she undertook as she tried to support her family and escape from her abusive husband.

Thomas P. Riggs was twenty-three years old when he enlisted in the 54th Massachusetts, and he had been the main support of his mother and six siblings for at least nine years. Deposition after deposition described him as a "good boy", industrious, hard-working, and devoted to his mother. Thomas left behind no letters that would explain his decision to join the army, but it may well have been a combination of motives. To secure steady income to continue to support his family? To have a chance to escape the responsibilities he had shouldered for so many years? To fight for a cause? To find adventure? His death occurred just four months after his enlistment, putting an end to any dreams he might have had for himself or his family.

Private George W. Moshroe enlisted in Elmira, New York on April 8, 1863 and was mustered into Company F on April 23rd. The twenty-three-year-old was described as being five feet, eight inches tall, with a light complexion and brown eyes. Although Private Moshroe gave his birthplace as Steuben County, New York, no evidence has been located for any person with this name in New York or Pennsylvania prior to 1863. Perhaps he enlisted using an alias when signing up for the army. After being listed as "missing since assault on Fort Wagner", his status was updated on August 31, 1863 to "prisoner of war." Moshroe was included in a large exchange of prisoners in North Carolina on March 4, 1865. His military records indicated that he was absent and sick in the General Hospital at Fortress Monroe, Virginia at the time the regiment was mustered out on August 20, 1865. His muster out date was recorded one month later on September 30th in Boston, Massachusetts. What happened to George W. Moshroe after his discharge is unknown. No one ever applied for a pension in his name.[34]

Nathaniel Hurley, of Rochester, New York, did not survive his prisoner of war experience. The nineteen-year-old was a strapping five feet nine inches tall at the time of his enlistment, but he could not withstand the ill treatment he suffered first at Andersonville Prison in Georgia and later at Florence Prison in South Carolina. Beginning in early February of 1865, the Confederate leaders initiated the process of releasing and exchanging prisoners held at Florence, South Carolina, but it was too late for Private Hurley. He died at Florence on February 15, 1865. As is the case with so many of the soldiers of the 54th Massachusetts, nothing has been located that would tell the story of Nathaniel Hurley prior to his enlistment. Although he claimed to have been born in Rochester, New York and is thought to have been living in that city at the time of his enlistment, there is no Nathan or Nathaniel Hurley in the 1850, 1855 or 1860 census in the Rochester area. With no one applying for a pension based on his service, Nathaniel Hurley is one more mystery soldier.[35]

In November, the tally of enlisted casualties was estimated at nine killed, 147 wounded and 100 men missing. It does not appear the record accounted for the deaths from wounds received during the assault, which included five men from Western New York. Charles Kane enlisted in Buffalo on March 27th and was assigned to Company A. Other than the basic information provided on his enlistment form, nothing more is known about this soldier. The twenty-eight-year-old gave his birth place as Kaskaskia, Illinois, a small community, located on the banks of the Mississippi River. The birthplace is an intriguing clue to the possible origins of Charles Kane. In December of 1816, a sixteen-year-old, mulatto servant named Rebecca, was indentured to Elias K. Kane of Kaskaskia for a term of forty years. In the 1850 census of Kaskaskia, Rebecca

Kane, a 50-year old black woman, had living in her household a twenty-year-old black man with the name of Charles Owen. If research could connect Rebecca Kane and Charles Owen to Charles Kane, the mystery of who Charles Kane was might be revealed.[36]

George Washington and Charles K. Reason enlisted in Syracuse, New York and were mustered into Company E on April 23rd. While both men gave their birthplace as Syracuse, that is most likely not the case. No census record has been located for George Washington, but a widow's pension filed by Mary F. Washington (nee Henry) stated that a Methodist clergyman married the couple in Oswego, New York on August 1, 1854. George Washington, aged twenty-nine years, died on August 3, 1863, of wounds received during the assault on Fort Wagner and was buried in Beaufort, South Carolina. A pension certificate dated November 2, 1867 established that the widow was entitled to $8.00 per month as of August 3, 1863. Charles K. Reason was described as being twenty-three years old and over six feet tall, with a dark complexion. In the 1860 census a farm laborer with the name of Charles Reason, was listed in the household of Asa and Polly Fyler, in the town of Onondaga, New York, with a birthplace listed as Alabama. Private Reason died on July 27, 1863, nine days after he was shot at Fort Wagner. No one applied for a pension based on his service.[37]

Elmira, New York was the place of enlistment for two men who died of wounds received at Fort Wagner. Thirty-eight-year old William R. Lee and thirty-one-year-old George Holmes were both married men and left behind families. William Richard Lee, born in Baltimore, Maryland married Sarah Dunham in Elmira on October 26, 1854 and four children were born to the couple prior to his entering the army – Estella Frances, Elva Josephine, Mary Ann and William Freeman. Private Lee was in the hospital at Beaufort, South Carolina for over two months before he was transferred to the Hospital Steamer *Cosmopolitan* in the first days of October 1863 for transport to New York. He did not make it home, dying on board the steamer on October 4th.[38]

George Holmes died in the hospital at Beaufort, South Carolina on August 15, 1863. His widow, Mary A. (Jackson) Holmes, started her pension application in November 1863, stating that she was then twenty years old and had married George Holmes in Elmira on January 15, 1855. The couple had two children – Rebecca, age seven and John, age four. She was awarded a pension of twelve dollars a month, commencing on the day of her husband's death. Mary A. Jackson remained a widow until her marriage to Acker Smith in February 1874.[39]

The day following the assault on Fort Wagner was difficult for the survivors of the 54th. Captain Luis Emilio described July 19th as "the saddest in the history of the Fifty-fourth, for the depleted ranks bore silent witness to the severe losses of the previous day. Men who had wandered to other points during the night continued to join their comrades until some four hundred were present."[40] The day also marked the beginning of the siege of Fort Wagner and preparations for the bombardment of Fort Sumter. The goal was to remove the Confederate forces from both strongholds and to pave the way for the taking of Charleston, South Carolina. In early August the men of the 55th Massachusetts joined their "brother soldiers", having left Camp Meigs on July 20th for North Carolina. With the new plans to take Fort Wagner, their destination was altered and they were stationed at Folly Island, a narrow strip of sand, separated from Morris Island by a channel called Lighthouse Inlet.

It was also during the summer of 1863 that the Commonwealth of Massachusetts received permission to organize a third regiment of black soldiers to be called the 5th

Massachusetts Cavalry. The rush to enlistment by African American men from the Northern States had slowed, so once again Governor John Andrew called upon George L. Stearns to activate his network. Stearns reached out to Frederick Douglass, who had been so successful in his efforts to bring men into the 54th Massachusetts. Douglass responded with a harsh letter, dated August 1, 1863, outlining why he could not participate in any more recruitment efforts. His chief objection lay with the failure of the Federal government to protest against the mistreatment of the black soldiers taken prisoner by the Confederacy, especially after the assault on Fort Wagner. He saw the failure as a betrayal, making it impossible for him to continue to recruit additional soldiers, without assurances that the President would "demand justice and humanity, for black soldiers."[41]

The siege of Fort Wagner lasted fifty-eight days and the men of the 54th and 55th endured almost two months of constant fatigue duty under the most inhospitable conditions. The regimental history of 55th Massachusetts describes the toll taken by the fatigue duty which went on day and night and engaged on average 350 men each twenty-four- hours from the unit. Details were employed in cutting timber, building wharves, loading and unloading stores, artillery and ammunition, hauling heavy guns to the front and working in trenches – much of the time while under enemy fire.[42] In addition the regiments were also doing picket and guard duty.

Over the next few months, many of those wounded during the assault on Fort Wagner returned to duty and the arrival of new recruits in mid-January of 1864 began to fill the ranks of the 54th Massachusetts to near full strength. On January 29th, the two regiments began preparations to be transported to Florida, traveling first to Hilton Head, where the regiments bivouacked with other troops, including the 8th USCT, newly arrived from the North. An additional fifty recruits were added to the ranks of the 54th Massachusetts on February 1st and on February 5th the assembled troops began boarding ships headed for the mouth of St. John's River, leading to Jacksonville, Florida. The goals of the expedition were four-fold – secure access to needed products, such as cotton, lumber and turpentine; cut off Confederate access to those same products; obtain recruits for the Colored Troops regiments; and restore Florida to the Union.

The Florida Expedition

As is often the case with war, the plans as laid out do not always result in victory. The 54th Massachusetts was once again caught in a military operation commanded by General Truman Seymour – the same general that had commanded the attack on Fort Wagner, just six months earlier – and it did not end well. With a total force of about 5,500 men, General Seymour felt very confident that he would have the local Confederate troops within his grasp in very short order. Confederate General Joseph Finegan's army consisted of close to 5,000 men and he was also confident that he would defeat his opponent. Shortly after arriving in Florida, Seymour began pushing into the interior. Meeting little resistance, he was able to establish a few outposts. The Commander of the Department of the South, General Quincy A. Gillmore, visited Jacksonville on February 14th, and left with the understanding that no additional advances were to be made, without orders from headquarters. Seymour either did not understand the order or he ignored Gillmore's directions.

On February 18th, Seymour ordered an advance with the objective of destroying the railroad. The next evening, the 54th Massachusetts arrived at Barber's Station and camped in the woods near the 1st North Carolina (35th USCT). The 55th Massachusetts was left behind to protect Jacksonville. In the morning, the troops began to depart from camp, with the 54th

Massachusetts being part of the third brigade. The Battle of Olustee began about 1:30 in the afternoon as the leading troops were surprised by the Confederate forces. The 54th joined the fray late in the afternoon and took up position on the left flank. The battle was one of the bloodiest of the Civil War. The Union losses were estimated at 1,850 killed, wounded or captured. Confederate losses were put at 950. The 54th Massachusetts went into battle with 497 men and 13 officers. The casualty lists for the regiment included 66 wounded, thirteen dead and eight missing.[43]

Two of the wounded were standouts in the regiment. The bravery of Acting Sergeant Major Stephen A. Swails, during the Battle at Olustee, won him special mention from his commanding officer, Colonel Edward Hallowell. On March 1, 1864, the Colonel wrote in his battle report that Swails "deserves special praise for his coolness, bravery and efficiency during the action; he received a severe but not mortal wound in the head."[44] Sergeant Swails enlisted on April 8, 1863 in Elmira, New York, where he worked as a boatman. Upon enlistment he was appointed First Sergeant in Company F. In November 1863, Swails assumed the rank of Acting Sergeant Major and was serving in that role when he was wounded, while relaying information to Col. Hallowell concerning the conditions on the left flank of the regiment's position. On March 11, 1864, just eleven days after Hallowell singled him out for his actions at Olustee, Swails received a commission as 2nd Lieutenant from Governor John Andrew of Massachusetts. Since the United States Army did not allow African Americans to become officers, it was ten months before he was mustered in with that rank. Meanwhile he performed all the duties of a Lieutenant in his company and regiment.

On January 16, 1865, Stephen A. Swails was discharged for promotion and the next day mustered in as 2nd Lieutenant of company D, 54th Massachusetts, becoming the first black soldier to become an officer in the United States Army. There was one more promotion for Lt. Swails. On June 3, 1865 he was mustered in as 1st Lieutenant, joining Company C. Lt. Swails was mustered out with his regiment in Charleston, South Carolina on August 20, 1865.

Lt. Stephen Atkins Swails
1832 - 1900

The newly discharged Lieutenant may have returned to his home in Elmira, but he did not stay. The 1865 census showed his wife Susan (also known as Sarah) and two children – Susan and Stephen, ages three and two - boarding with Jesse Swails, his brother. In 1866 Stephen A. Swails married in South Carolina to Susan Acrum Aspinwall. It is not known if Swails and his first wife divorced or just separated. His first wife identified herself as a "widow" of James A. Swails as late as 1897. Swails and his second wife settled in Kingstree, South Carolina, where he became actively involved in the political life of the community during the Reconstruction Era. He edited a Republican newspaper and in 1867 was elected a state senator on the Republican Party's ticket. The 1870 census lists his occupation as "County Auditor." The list of his accomplishments included being admitted to the bar, opening a law firm, and serving as a member of the Electoral College.

The withdrawal of federal troops from the South in 1877, marking the end of Reconstruction, was a death knell against equality for the African American community throughout the former Confederacy. An attempted assassination forced the former Lieutenant to resign from office as State Senator and leave his adopted home. By 1879 Swails moved to Washington, D.C. where he was able to find employment with the government and practice law. He did not give up on working to secure equality for his former constituents. In 1888, Swails was one the signers of a letter to the Governor of South Carolina, urging that in the spirit of fairness, at least one Republican Commissioner of Elections should be appointed in each county and that one Republican manager should be present at each of the voting precincts. The Governor responded that "to the eternal honor of our State and the Democratic party, it can now be said that our elections are the freest and fairest in the world." It is doubtful that the black voters of South Carolina shared that view. Stephen A. Swails died in 1900 and was buried in the Humane and Friendly

Society Cemetery in Charleston, South Carolina. Throughout his life, Mr. Swails exhibited the bravery and coolness under fire that had won him the admiration of his commanding general at Olustee.[45]

Also wounded on February 20, 1864 was Sergeant Albert D. Thompson of Company D, whose company was situated at the farthest left edge of the battle line occupied by the 54th Massachusetts. The danger of the unit being flanked by the enemy forces put his company in an especially precarious position. With a severe wound to his left arm, Thompson was admitted to the hospital in Beaufort, South Carolina on February 24, 1864 where he remained a patient until mid-August, when he was permitted a thirty-day furlough which allowed him a brief visit home to Buffalo. Upon his return, the hospital retained his services as clerk, but he was anxious to return to duty with his regiment. It was noted in his military record that he was granted his wish and returned to his company on October 9th.

Albert D. Thompson, the oldest child of Nimrod D. and Elizabeth (Meyers) Thompson, was born in Oswego, New York in 1845. The family had moved to Buffalo about 1848, where his father established himself as a successful caterer. Nimrod Thompson played a prominent role in the New York State Colored Men's Conventions that advocated for equal rights for African American citizens. His son had been a promising student at the Vine Street School, a segregated public school in Buffalo.

When the Civil War broke out, Albert had been sorely disappointed that because of his color and age, he was excluded from joining the army. Barely eighteen years old in March, 1863, he was among the first to rush to the Buffalo recruiting office set up by Major George L. Stearns for the 54th Massachusetts where he was promptly appointed to the rank of

First Sergeant. During the next few weeks Sergeant Thompson became one of the most active recruiters in the city of Buffalo and surrounding towns. His military record shows that on July 17, 1865, the Sergeant was promoted to rank of First Lieutenant, but that he was never mustered to that rank. A second attempt to move the Sergeant into the officer corps was dated August 12, 1865, assigning him the rank of Second Lieutenant, but when mustered out with his regiment on August 20th, his rank remained that of First Sergeant.

Following the ceremonies which officially dismissed the 54th Massachusetts from service, Albert D. Thompson returned to Buffalo, New York where in December 1868, he married Mary E. Nelson. He was quickly immersed in civic and business activities of his community. About 1870 Thompson made a dramatic decision, which would take him far from home into the heart of Mississippi. His mission was the education of the newly freed slaves. He may have been inspired by the example of his former principal at the Vine Street School, the Reverend Benjamin F. Randolph, who had served the school in Buffalo from 1858 to 1863. Rev. Randolph had left his post in Buffalo in November 1863 to become chaplain of the 26th USCT, one of the first New York State sponsored black regiments. At the war's end Randolph chose to remain in South Carolina to work with the Freedmen's Bureau in Charleston, focusing on education and securing equal political rights for the African American population. Rev. Randolph was assassinated in October 1868, becoming an early victim of the Ku Klux Klan's violence.

Albert D. Thompson was assigned to teach in the largest school at Hernando, Mississippi, located about thirty miles south of Memphis, Tennessee. He met with opposition from the Ku Klux Klan and at one point he and his family were forced to flee their home and to remain hidden in the woods for some time. Thompson was moved to another school at Brookhaven,

Mississippi, located about 240 miles south of Hernando. While in Brookhaven the former soldier made an application for pension based on his disability due to the gunshot wound to his left arm. He was awarded a pension of two dollars a month, dated to December 22, 1877.

In the summer and early fall of 1878, a yellow fever epidemic swept through the Mississippi River Valley from New Orleans to Memphis, Tennessee, eventually encompassing eight states. On September 4, 1878, while on a visit to his brother-in-law in Hernando, Thompson penned an appeal to the "Masonic Fraternity and Friends of Humanity Everywhere" describing the "utter destitution of hundreds" and that "pestilence and famine are still at work among them." One month later, the thirty-three-year old was dead from the same disease that claimed over 16,000 lives in less than three months.[46]

Among the missing after the Battle of Olustee was Isaac Hawkins, a thirty-year-old corporal, from Ridgeway, Orleans County, New York, who had joined the regiment as a new recruit at Morris Island in mid-January. It is safe to say, that he was not a well-trained recruit, but perhaps nothing could have prepared him for the confusion and chaos that characterized this battle. It would be many months before it was known that Corporal Hawkins had not only been wounded in battle, but that he had been a prisoner of war since the day of the battle, confined at Andersonville, located in southern Georgia and several other prisons. Hawkins was part of a prisoner exchange that took place at North East Bridge, North Carolina on March 4, 1865.

He arrived at Camp Parole, Maryland on March 14th and four days later he was on his way home for a thirty-day furlough. Waiting at home was his wife Sarah, three young daughters, his parents Richard and Caroline Hawkins, and several siblings. Not at home were three brothers who were still serving in the army. Henry G. Hawkins enlisted in the 26th USCT in December 1863. Augustus C. and Charles R. Hawkins, both enlisted in November 1864, serving in the 2nd and 3rd USCT respectively.

Isaac Hawkins' furlough was scheduled to end on April 18, 1865, but while at home he was diagnosed with typhoid pneumonia. Dr. S. F. Benjamin of Medina wrote to Camp Parole authorities in a letter dated April 15th that Hawkins is "in my opinion unfit for duty and unable to travel ... he will not be able to resume his duties for the period of thirty days." Yet on May 2nd he was furnished transportation from Rochester to Annapolis. Two weeks later he was discharged from the army at Camp Parole, Maryland with a certificate of disability.[47]

From information in pension file of Isaac S. Hawkins, it appears that he did not return to his family in Orleans County after his discharge, but remained in Annapolis, Maryland, where he started a new life. In April 1866 he enlisted for a one-year term in "the Naval School on board US Frigate *Marion*" as a Landsman. In June he was promoted to Steerage Cook and transferred to the U.S. Frigate *Savannah*. In April 1867 Hawkins reenlisted and was assigned to the U.S. Monitor *Tonawanda* at the Naval Academy and later detailed as a servant in the Steam Engineering Building before his discharge in May 1868. By 1870 he moved to Washington, D.C. and was working as a cook in a restaurant owned by Joseph Platz.

About 1870 Hawkins married Charity Wells, a young woman he may have met in Annapolis, her home town. About the same time, his wife in Orleans County, New York, believing her husband was dead, also remarried. Charity died in January 1877, leaving at least two children, who were then raised by her mother, Arianna Wells, in Annapolis, Maryland. Hawkins married for a third and last time in December 1880 to Ella M.

Nolan and the couple lived at 124 2nd Street, S.W. Isaac Hawkins died August 24, 1902 in Washington, D.C. and was buried in Arlington.[48]

The veterans of the assault on Fort Wagner, acquitted themselves well at the Battle of Olustee, but their losses were grave and morale must have been at a low point. As the last regiment to leave the field of battle, the 54th Massachusetts formed part of the rear guard during the retreat. The retreat was initially chaotic and among the biggest challenges was the removal of the wounded to safety. Captain Emilio, in his regimental history, included a description of the heroic efforts of men of the 54th Massachusetts that saved many from certain death or imprisonment. According to a report by Dr. M. M. Marsh, of the U.S. Sanitary Commission, many of the wounded had been loaded on to railroad cars, that:

> *through eagerness to escape the supposed pursuing enemy, too great pressure of steam was employed, and the flue collapsed; and here the immortal Fifty-fourth (colored) did what ought to insure it higher praise than to hold the field in the face of a victorious foe,*
> *- with ropes it seized the engine (now useless) and dragged it with its doomed freight for many miles ...*
> *They knew their fate if captured; their humanity triumphed. Does history record a nobler deed?'*[49]

The regiment was able to make the 120-mile trip from the battlefield to Jacksonville in a little over two days, where they quickly prepared for possible additional advances by the Confederate forces. Fortunately, there were only a few skirmishes with minor casualties during the following months. By the middle of April 1864, the Massachusetts' regiments were headed back to the barrier islands off of Charleston, South Carolina. Morris, Folly and James Islands were once again home to the men of the 54th and 55th.

Return to South Carolina and the Siege of Charleston

"Hurry up and wait ... and wait some more" is a phrase often associated with life in the army. After returning to Morris and Folly Islands in April 1864, camp life for the 54th and 55th Massachusetts regiments was dominated by tedious picket duty, exhausting fatigue duty and the issue over equal pay for black soldiers. Life on any island on the Atlantic coast may seem idyllic to present day vacationers, but that was far from the reality for the troops occupying the sand bars. Dealing with constantly blowing sand which invaded every container of food and every piece of clothing; blazing sun with no shade (after denuding the landscape of every piece of timber for fuel, building platforms for tents, etc.); daily work schedules that included building wharves and battery sites, digging trenches, unloading stores, dragging heavy equipment through soft sand; and the vagaries of tropical storms stirring up the sea, sending waves over the tops of dunes, designed to protect the camp sites – all bore down on the men trying to maintain war readiness and discipline.

Add to the physical conditions faced by the men of the 54th and 55th Massachusetts, the fact that the promise of pay, equal to that of white troops, had been a mirage. A white private was being paid thirteen dollars per month, plus a clothing allowance of $3.50. An African American private's pay was set by the United States government at ten dollars per month, of which $3.00 was withheld monthly for clothing. The 54th Massachusetts was the first of the North's black units to be confronted with this blatant discrimination and their reaction was to refuse to accept any pay, until the inequity was rectified. Even when the Governor of Massachusetts tried to "fix" the pay gap by having his state make up the difference, the troops of the 54th Massachusetts held fast to their principled stand.

Although standing on principle is a noble position, the longer the stalemate went on, the more desperate the situation became for the soldiers and their families at home. Sergeant Joseph H. Walker, of Company B, 55th Massachusetts, wrote to the *Weekly Anglo-African* on March 26, 1864 from Florida:

> *Will you please let us know what action has been taken in Congress in relation to our pay. Eleven months have now passed away and still we are without pay. How our families are to live and pay house-rent I know not. Uncle Sam has long wind, and expects as much of us as any soldiers in the field; but if we cannot get any pay what have we to stimulate us?"*[50]

Two months later in "A Soldier's Letter" dated May 29th, 1864 written by a sergeant in the 55th Massachusetts from Folly Island to *The Christian Recorder* summarized the hardship experienced by his fellow soldiers. He wrote:

> *When we enrolled ourselves into the ranks of the Union army we did so with the understanding that we should be allowed the same pay, rations, clothing and treatment as the white troops. We were even promised this by Governor Andrews [sic] himself, who stated, at the same time, that he had authority direct from Washington … Do you call it fair? Do you notice a semblance of justice in the fact that while many of our families, our poor wives and children, are at home crying for bread and the necessaries of life, their husbands and fathers are out upon the field battling in defence [sic] of the Union, without receiving a cent of pay? … We have been told some monstrous falsehoods, and have been deceived and hoodwinked in various ways, and yet our officers reprimand us for complaining …*[51]

To say that the morale of the soldiers was at a low point that summer of 1864 would be an understatement. Adding insult to injury was the heavy burden of fatigue duty. Alberto Robbins, of Co. F, 55th Massachusetts, was a healthy and strong, twenty-two-year old from Peterboro, New York when he enlisted, but by September 15th he was discharged on account of physical disability. Captain James D. Thurber wrote on August 27, 1864 that the soldier was unfit for duty for over two months, having been "taken sick while performing fatiguing work on this Island [Folly]." Dr. W. S. Brown wrote that the soldier suffered from general debility, indolent scrofulous ulcers on both legs, anasarca and partial deafness and summed up his diagnosis with the words "of no use as a soldier."[52]

Rumors, speculations and false promises also added to the declining morale of the men. On June 13, 1864 Congress passed an Army appropriations bill, which contained a clause that was aimed at equalizing the pay between black and white soldiers. Unfortunately, it was a bit murky relative to how it would affect those who enlisted prior to January 1864, based on their status of freedom on or before April 19, 1861 – the commencement of the Civil War. John Collins, Orderly Sergeant in Co. H. of the 54th wrote to *The Christian Recorder* on July 7, 1864 that "Day after day we await the arrival of each mail in anxious expectancy to see whether Congress has taken any steps to pay us off, for you know that men cannot live without something to nourish them at times."[53]

Finally, on August 1, 1864 the War Department issued General Orders, No. 120, instructing that officers commanding regiments of "colored troops" to identify all men who had enlisted prior to January 1, 1864 and to determine who among them were "Free, on or before April 19th, 1861" and for that information to be noted on the next company muster rolls.

Those "free" prior to the start of the war were to receive "full pay allowed by law at the same period to white soldiers." The soldiers were required to make a verbal oath to establish their right to full and equal pay.

Many considered the requirement of having been "free" prior to the start of the war to be an insult, but the commander of the 54th Massachusetts came up with a solution that met the letter of the law – what is often referred to as "the Quaker oath." Soldiers were asked to affirm "You do solemnly swear that you owed no man unrequited labor on or before the 19th day of April, 1861. So help you God."[54] It was a battle won by the black soldiers and the men of the 54th and 55th Massachusetts had set the tone and provided the leadership.

Pay days for the 54th Massachusetts came on September 28th and 29th. Luis Emilio quoted one officer's observations that

We had been eighteen months waiting, and the kaleidoscope was turned, - nine hundred men received their money; nine hundred stories rested on the faces of those men, as they passed in at one door and out of the other ... Two days have changed the face of things, and now a petty carnival prevails. The fiddle and other music long neglected enlivens the tents day and night...[55]

Of the $170,000 paid to the soldiers of the 54th Massachusetts, $100,000 was forwarded home to their families. The 55th Massachusetts first saw the paymaster on September 30th, but he did not have sufficient funds to pay the entire unit. Finally, on October 7th, every man in the regiment had received their wages through August 31, 1864. The non-commissioned officers of the 55th Massachusetts planned a special celebration for Monday, October 10th, featuring speeches, toasts and music.[56]

The fall season also brought a spate of requests for furloughs. Levi Carter and Andrew Miller, members of Company F in the 54th Massachusetts and both from Elmira, New York, were given furloughs in October 1864. Private Carter, aged thirty-nine years, left camp on October 18th for his thirty-day leave. Waiting at home was his wife Mary and three children – sons Joseph and John H., aged ten and three respectively and daughter Jane Mary, six years old.[57] Corporal Miller's furlough started on October 28th and he too traveled to Elmira, New York. While at home the corporal took the opportunity to marry Phebe Ann Van Cleaf on November 24th, just a few days before he was due back in camp. The marriage was very brief, as Corporal Andrew Miller was shot in the head during the battle of Boykin's Mills in South Carolina on April 18, 1865. He died of his wounds two days later. Miller's widow began the process of applying for a pension in December of 1865 and was granted a certificate on April 14, 1866.[58]

From Honey Hill to Boykin's Mills

On November 15, 1864, General William T. Sherman, left the conquered city of Atlanta, Georgia and began his "March to the Sea," with the goal of taking the city of Savannah, while wreaking havoc along the 285-mile trek. The Union forces stationed along the coast of South Carolina were called upon to assist Sherman's army by cutting the railroad connection between Charleston and Savannah. On November 28th the two Massachusetts regiments boarded boats that would take them first to Hilton Head, South Carolina and then up the Broad River to a landing spot, called Boyd's Neck, site of an abandoned plantation.

Unfortunately, the bad luck that had plagued the 54th Massachusetts in other battle situations, once again raised its ugly head. Heavy fog had delayed the boats movement up the river and interfered with the speed of debarkation of the troops, resulting in it being late in the afternoon of November 29th before all troops had landed. Instead of a quick march from the river to the town of Grahamville, located on the Charleston and Savannah Railroad, skirmishes with the enemy and bad maps resulted in the troops wandering across the countryside for hours, before reaching Bolan's Church, a crossroads well shy of their target, giving the defenders at Grahamville, plenty of time to gather their forces. The 55th Massachusetts, left behind at Boyd's Landing, started their march from camp about 7 a.m. on November 30th, meeting up with the larger force shortly after noon.

The enemy forces took up a defensive position on a ridge of high ground, called Honey Hill, with a clear view of main road to Grahamville. The 55th Massachusetts went into action first, making two attacks against the enemy. The 54th Massachusetts entered the battle as the 55th was leaving the field. The Confederate line did not give way and the Union forces began their retreat about dusk. Once again, the brave men of the 54th and 55th showed courage and determination, while suffering extreme losses, because of poor leadership at the highest levels of command.

The Union forces suffered total losses of 746 – 89 killed, 629 wounded, and 28 missing or captured. The 55th Massachusetts is said to have sustained a loss of about 100 killed and wounded, while from the 54th Massachusetts there were two killed, 38 wounded and four missing at the end of the day. Wounded at Honey Hill were seven men from the Western New York contingent of the 54th Massachusetts. Alexander Renkins, a sailor from Buffalo, New York and corporal in Company D, suffered his second serious wound during the Battle of Honey Hill, when a minié ball passed through his left hand, destroying the metacarpal. At the assault on Fort Wagner, Corporal Renkins had been wounded when a minié ball passed through his hip and thigh, making it impossible for him to walk one-half mile without pain. Yet, he had returned to duty in November 1863 and had been present at all company musters until December 1864. Renkins was back with his company in time for the company muster completed at the end of April 1865. On June 7, 1865 he received his discharge paper for disability "caused by wounds received in Battle of Fort Wagner."[59]

Andrew Deforest and Henry F. Stewart, both corporals in company E, were among the wounded on November 30. Corporal Deforest, who had received his promotion just six weeks before the battle at Honey Hill, was not a stranger to warfare, having been wounded at Fort Wagner in July 1863 and present at the Battle of Olustee in February, 1864. His wound this time was more severe and he was admitted to the Regimental Hospital in Beaufort, South Carolina. Deforest was nineteen years old when he enlisted at Syracuse, New York on March 29, 1863. The son of Henry and Rosina Deforest, young Andrew had followed his father's profession, working as a waiter at the time of his enlistment. He was not the last in his family to enlist. His younger brother William joined the 14th Rhode Island Heavy Artillery (11th USCHA) in January, 1864.[60]

Corporal Henry F. Stewart enrolled at Horseheads, New York as a nineteen-year-old recruit on March 29, 1863, giving his occupation as barber, and was promptly promoted to the rank of corporal. After a brief hospital stay, Corporal Stewart was returned to his company by January, 1865. On March 3, 1865 he was promoted to the rank of Sergeant. Stewart ran into major trouble in August 1865 when he was accused of larceny for having entered the store of Mrs. H. S. Gargle in Charleston and stealing several articles. Mrs. Gargle was the only witness and she claimed that Sgt. Stewart had pushed her "off the walk into the street and ran off." His military records indicate that a general court martial was called for on August 11, but do not include a record the verdict. It appears that his punishment may have been a reduction to the ranks, dated to five days before the alleged larceny.[61]

Private George Reynolds, Company G, had been lucky up until the encounter at Honey Hill on November 30, 1864. His first experiences in battle had been at James Island on July 16, 1863 and at Fort Wagner two days later. He had also escaped major injury at the Battle of Olustee on February 20, 1864. At Honey Hill a musket ball broke the metacarpal bone of his left index finger and, according to the regiment's surgeon, Dr. Charles E. Briggs, the finger "united so irregularly as to weaken the palm of the hand and make it so tender that he cannot perform the manual of arms or heavy fatigue duty." Discharged by reason of his disability on June 3, 1865, the twenty-two-year-old returned to his hometown of Corning, New York.

George Alexander enlisted in Syracuse, New York on April 21, 1863, giving his age as eighteen years, birthplace as Charleston, South Carolina and occupation as farmer. The young private had traveled full circle before he was wounded at Honey Hill. The wounds ended his military career, sending him first to the hospital in Beaufort, then to the hospital at David's Island in New York City's harbor, and lastly to the U.S. Hospital at Worcester, Massachusetts. After treatment of a gunshot wound that resulted in the loss of motion of his left hand, he was discharged from the service on June 29, 1865. Upon leaving the hospital he gave his address as Sycamore, DeKalb Co., Illinois. Private Alexander applied for a pension on November 15, 1865, but never received one, indicating he may have died before a certificate could be issued.[62]

Among those wounded at Honey Hill were John Shorter and Lorenzo T. Lewis, enlistees from Hillsdale and Dearborn, Michigan respectively. Interestingly both gave their birthplaces as Seneca County, New York and both the Lewis and Shorter families moved from Seneca County to Michigan about the same time, yet it is unknown if the families were acquainted with each other. John Shorter, son of Charles and Mariah Shorter, was one of the youngest of the recruits, being just shy of his sixteenth birthday when he enlisted on April 9, 1863. His wounds at Honey Hill resulted in his receiving a disability discharge on June 3, 1865 at St. Andrews Parrish, South Carolina. Lorenzo Lewis, nineteen-year-old son of Robert and Jane (Key) Lewis, gave his birthplace as Fayette, Seneca County, New York and occupation as woodsman. His family had moved to Michigan about 1848 and over the next few years moved for brief periods to Wisconsin and Canada, before settling permanently in Michigan.[63]

After the encounter at Honey Hill, the 54th and 55th Massachusetts remained in the area, hoping for a second opportunity to fulfill the orders of General Sherman in cutting the railroad link between Savannah and Charleston. On December 21, 1864, the city of Savannah, Georgia surrendered to Sherman's army and the Confederate forces moved into the countryside to try to engage the Union troops. Charleston, South Carolina capitulated on February 18, 1865 and Companies B and F, of the 54th Massachusetts, were among the first troops to march into the city. The end of the war seemed to be finally within sight. On April 9th, General Robert E. Lee surrendered his army to General Ulysses S. Grant at Appomattox Court House in Virginia – a date often identified as the official end of the Civil War. Yet, there were still battles to be won. On April 18th the 54th Massachusetts engaged the enemy in one last fight at Boykin's Mills, South Carolina.

Two men from Elmira, New York and one man from Owego, New York were included in the casualties at Boykin's Mills – all were members of Company F. Killed that day was Corporal James P. Johnson, a twenty-two-year old barber, who enlisted at Owego, New York. He was appointed corporal on November 19, 1863 at Morris Island, South Carolina, filling the position previously held by Charles R. Douglass, who had not been able to join the company because of ill health. Forty-year-old Corporal Andrew Miller, of Elmira died two days after receiving a gunshot wound to the head. Twenty-year-old Private James Postley was wounded severely in the leg and was transported to the General Hospital at Beaufort, South Carolina. In late August he was mustered at DeCamp General Hospital on David's Island in New York Harbor and on September 2nd moved to the U.S. Hospital at Worcester, Massachusetts. Postley was deemed well enough to be discharged from the service on October 12, 1865, but his disability was considered "total at the present." A severe wound of the thigh had healed "with atrophy of limb" and a "contusion of left ankle by an accidental blow from a comrade while in bed in Hospital" had resulted in "entire loss of use of foot."[64]

With the war, for all intents and purposes, at an end, the final months in service would prove to be challenging in different ways for the soldiers of the 54th and 55th Massachusetts Volunteers. Maintaining discipline and morale between the end of April and the muster out dates of August 20 and August 29, 1865 was not an easy task. There were two more desertions by men from western New York from the 54th Massachusetts. John R. O'Neal, of Company D, enlisted on March 17, 1863 at Buffalo, New York. His service records provide more questions than answers. Sometime before the end of June 1863 he had lost through "carelessness" a rifle and full set of equipments – for which he owed the government $21.50. In February 1864, he did not accompany his regiment to Florida, but was left at Hilton Head, South Carolina on detached service.

Beginning on October 22, 1864, Private O'Neal was "detailed on special duty at Head Quarters" on Morris Island, South Carolina. Exactly what his special duty was is unknown, but it could be related to his occupation prior to enlistment as a cook. On April 25, 1865, O'Neal was listed as a deserter with the notation "Probably to be found with contrabands at Wackamaw [Waccamaw] Island. Has in his possession gun and equipments." The private now owed the government a total of $42.50, according to Muster Out Roll for his company. From all accounts, it would appear O'Neal had little to complain about regarding his time in service, having spent most of it at Head Quarters and not in the field of battle.[65]

The last "desertions' took place on August 5, 1865, just twenty days before the regiment was mustered out. Private Benjamin Franklin Boyer, called Frank by his fellow soldiers, was only nineteen-years old when he enlisted in Company F on April 8, 1863. The son of Jacob and Rebecca Boyer, the young soldier was born in Danville, Pennsylvania, but by 1860 he and his family were living in Elmira, New York, neighbors to two other soldiers of the 54th Massachusetts – Levi Carter and Wesley R. Armstrong. From November 1863 until February 1865, Private Boyer was on daily duty in the Regimental Drum Corps. On July 16, 1865, Private Boyer was admitted to the Post Hospital at Charleston, South Carolina. He received a pass from the hospital on August 3rd. Having failed to return, he was reported a deserter on the morning of August 5, 1865 and was still on the list of deserters as of August 31st. His muster-out roll, dated August 20th, makes no mention of a desertion and indicates that he purchased his gun and equipment for $6.00. The regimental history by Luis F. Emilio makes no mention of a desertion by Private Boyer but does indicate that he had died since the war. It may be that Boyer did not return to the hospital after his pass expired, but simply returned to the regiment in time to be mustered out with his comrades.[66]

Thirty-one-year-old James F. Price enlisted at Buffalo, New York in late April of 1863 and climbed quickly in the ranks, being appointed Corporal at his mustering into Company H on May 13th and to Sergeant on July 21st, two days after the assault on Fort Wagner. Sergeant Price was one of the fortunate few that were given furloughs in the fall of 1864, when he traveled to Buffalo to see family. On July 9, 1865 Sergeant Price's fortunes took a downward turn. He was reduced to the ranks for "Disobedience of Orders" and absence without leave. The order was signed by Maj. George Pope and 1st Lieut. Stephen Swails. One can only wonder if the waiting had become too much for the sergeant and the rules and regulations began to seem onerous, unnecessary or even moot. It is likely that there was a general lowering of expectations concerning military discipline in these final months of service.

The end of service for the 54th Massachusetts started with the Muster-Out on August 20, 1865 at Charleston. The men, able to travel, left Charleston in three stages on August 21st, 22nd and 28th – all disembarking at Gallop's Island in Boston Harbor, where they remained until September 2nd, while final payment was made and discharges given out. On September 2nd the 54th Massachusetts was transported to Boston's Commercial Wharf, where they were greeted by a large contingent, including many dignitaries. As they marched through the streets, the crowds enthusiastically welcomed home the "conquering heroes."[67] The 55th Regiment's Muster-Out was completed on August 29, 1865 in Charleston and the men boarded ships for the return to Boston on September 6th and 14th, with all having arrived at Gallop's Island by September 20th. On Saturday, September 23rd, the troops received final payments and were officially discharged from service. Two days later, they marched through the streets of Boston for final ceremonies.[68]

The men of these two Massachusetts regiments returned home imbued with the lessons learned in battle and in their political fight for equal pay and equal treatment. It is doubtful that many held any illusions that achieving equality on the home front would be easy, but they had confidence in their ability to affect change. The confidence would be sorely tested, especially as the South emerged from the Reconstruction Era, which had promised so much to the newly freed slaves and by extension African Americans throughout the United States. The next assault on equality came in the form of the Jim Crow Laws, which had their roots in the onerous Black Laws that had defined and restricted life for free persons of color throughout the country before the Civil War. For many in the deep South, it heralded a return to life during slavery, with the use of euphemisms to obscure the real intent.

"The Fifty-Fifth Massachusetts Colored Regiment
Singing John Brown's March in the Streets of Charleston,
February 22, 1865."
This illustration appeared in the Harper's Weekly on
March 18, 1865.
Library of Congress.

Massachusetts' Third Regiment Takes to the Field

The 5th Massachusetts Cavalry, the third black regiment raised in Massachusetts, followed a different trajectory than that of its more famous "brother" units. Permission from the War Department was finally issued on November 23, 1863 and recruitment efforts went into operation. For the first time, New Yorkers had more choices when it came to selecting where they wanted to serve. Rhode Island, Connecticut and New York were all competing to attract African American soldiers to their newly formed regiments, but the allure of serving in a cavalry unit was an added bonus for Massachusetts. When enlistments began, the equal pay issue had yet to be resolved, but Governor Andrew devised an innovative plan which allowed the men to get their bounty of $325 either at the end of their time in service or in $20 monthly installments.[69] This arrangement eased the fear of recruits that their families would endure hardships after their enlistments.

As with the 54th and 55th Massachusetts regiments, the 5th Massachusetts Cavalry was made up of men who hailed from many states and before their enlistment had not set foot in the Commonwealth of Massachusetts. The recruits began to arrive at Camp Meigs in late December 1863 and by January 9, 1864, there were enough present to form Company A, which included eight men who had either indicated they were born in Western New York or were residents of the state prior to their enlistment. James W. Collins, age 24, gave his birthplace as Ithaca, New York and occupation as barber, when he signed up on December 22, 1863 in Newton, Massachusetts. The *Company Descriptive Book* stated that he was five feet, six inches tall with light complexion, dark eyes and hair. On February 1, 1864, Collins was promoted to rank of Quarter Master Sergeant, a rank he held through the end of his service in October 1865. Sergeant Collins appears to have been an exemplary soldier yet records from his life after the war indicate that he may not have been fully truthful on his enlistment papers.

In July 1873, twenty-nine-year old James W. Collins, now using the name Juan DeColaines, married Anna Dwyer in Montpelier, Vermont, giving his birthplace as Green Bay, Wisconsin and parents as Juan and Lucilla DeColaines. In the 1880 census, DeColaines, identified as mulatto and working as a barber, gave his birthplace as Wisconsin and that of his father and mother as Jamaica and Mexico, respectively. His wife and children are all identified as white. Ten years later he told the census taker that his father was born in Spain and mother in Mexico and all in the family are identified as white. No census record for anyone with name of James Collins or Juan DeColaines has been located prior to 1880, so it is hard to determine the full story for this person. What is known, that at some point between 1865 and 1873 he created a new persona or took back his original name, which must frustrate his descendants trying to trace their roots. The one "fact" that remains consistent after 1865 is his place of birth as Wisconsin. There is a draft registration in Rochester, New York, made in July 1863, for a John Gamut, age 26, black, born in Wisconsin. Is this perhaps another clue?[70]

Thirty-eight-year-old Solomon Peterson and thirty-five-year-old John S. Peterson (may be brothers-in-law) enlisted on December 26, 1863, leaving behind their wives and a total of eight children, ages one to eleven years old. The two men had registered for the draft in Olean, Cattaraugus County, New York, but because of age most likely could have received an exemption, if drafted. The Peterson men traveled to Boston in company with Alfred W. Butler, age thirty-eight, Irenas J. Palmer, age twenty-two, George H. Johnson, age twenty years, all of Olean, New York and John Nelson, age eighteen years, of Batavia, New York. They were joined by William Elebeck, of

Buffalo. All seven men were mustered into Company A on January 9, 1864. Several weeks later, twenty-four-year-old Ephraim Johnson, of Olean, New York arrived at Camp Meigs and was mustered into Company D.

John Nelson's time in the 5th Massachusetts was cut short when he was "retained by Civil Authority" in late January 1864. The company muster roll, dated February 29, 1864, stated that he was turned over to the Deputy U.S. Marshal on January 28, 1864. The 1865 March/April Company Muster Roll noted that Nelson was "dropped from rolls as deserter" as of March 27, 1865. Exactly where Private Nelson had been between January 28, 1864 and March 27, 1865 is unclear.[71]

On the other hand, Irenas J. Palmer, described as being six feet tall, with light complexion and dark hair and eyes, was appointed First Sergeant of Company A on February 1, 1864, a position he would hold until the regiment was mustered out in October 1865. The young man, born on February 20, 1842 in Hindsdale, Cattaraugus County, New York to Hannibal and Anna Palmer, maintained an unblemished record with the 5th Massachusetts Cavalry, having never been away from his command during his service, except for a brief furlough granted him while at Point Lookout, Maryland in February 1865. Left fatherless while still a young boy, he built a reputation as a hard worker, taking on jobs as a farm laborer, chopping wood and rafting on the river between Olean, New York and Warren, Pennsylvania before his enlistment. After the war, he worked as a carpenter and architect.[72]

Training as a cavalry unit required learning to ride and maneuver horses in squads and regimental formations, as well as learning to fire and care for weapons, all based on the standard tactics used by all army cavalry regiments. As recruits continued to arrive in camp, additional companies were formed and training began anew. A total of seventeen men with ties to

61

Western New York would eventually sign up with the 5th Massachusetts Cavalry. One of the last to arrive in camp was Charles R. Douglass, son of Frederick Douglass. He had originally enlisted in the 54th Massachusetts in March 1863, but was transferred into Co. I of the 5th Massachusetts Cavalry on March 26, 1864. Douglass was promoted to rank of 1st Sergeant on May 18th, but his time in service was short-lived as he received an honorable discharge on September 10, 1864, due to continued bad health.[73]

As additional companies were formed, the training continued until the first week of May, 1864, when it was reported in the abolitionist newspaper, *The Liberator*, that the 5th Massachusetts Cavalry was 'mounted, armed, equipped, and ready for service' with a force of one thousand one hundred men.[74] The 1st Battalion, consisting of companies A, B, C, and D, moved to Washington, D.C. and from there to nearby Camp Casey. Within the next few days, the 2nd and 3rd Battalion were also sent to Camp Casey, where all companies were dismounted and in effect turned into an infantry regiment, a situation which continued through most of the war. Being dismounted must have been a blow to the morale of the men of the 5th Massachusetts Cavalry. It also meant that all their training had not prepared them for the role of an infantryman.

From Camp Casey the regiment was ordered to Fort Monroe, Virginia, and then on to City Point, located on the James River, south of Richmond. The 5th Massachusetts Cavalry (dismounted) was assigned to the 18th Corps and over the next few weeks performed picket and guard duty, while more forces arrived as part of a planned advance on Richmond. It was a difficult time of adjustment for the men, who found themselves shifted from one camp to another, wondering if they would ever again be a mounted unit and when they would get to fight. On June 15, 1864 the men of the 5th Massachusetts Cavalry went into battle at Baylor's Farm, on the road to

Petersburg. The exact details of the battle remain contradictory, but the effects of the fight were devastating to the raw recruits who bravely tried to follow confusing directions from their officers. The official report of General Edward W. Hinks, commander of the 18th Corps, described the unit's ability to maneuver on the line as "awkward", due to their lack of training as infantry. Yet the General also made note of its gallantry in the face of the enemy.[75]

Two weeks later, the 5th Massachusetts Cavalry was reassigned to Point Lookout, Maryland. For the next seven months the regiment's main duty was to guard Confederate prisoners of war, housed in Camp Hoffman at Point Lookout, which by all accounts was a tedious, contentious and thankless duty. The move was seen to many as "punishment" for their performance at Baylor's Farm.

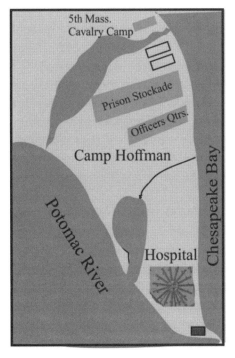

Point Lookout was situated on a remote stretch of land, located at the southern tip of a peninsula, bordered on the west by the Potomac River, on the east and south by Chesapeake Bay. Prior to the Civil War, the area had become a popular summer resort escape, with scattered cottages, a wharf and lighthouse. In 1862 the Federal government leased the land and built a hospital. In early 1863, Camp Hoffman was established, on land adjacent to the hospital, to house a small group of Confederate prisoners. When the 5th Massachusetts Cavalry arrived in August 1864 the number of prisoners had swelled to over 15,000, in a space designed to handle half that number. The prison was a way-station for many prisoners, who were transferred to other northern prisons, and it is estimated that as many as 50,000 prisoners passed through the camp. Some reports compare the prison conditions at Camp Hoffman to those at the infamous Andersonville prison. The official death toll among prisoners has been set at 3,384 men, but some researchers place the number much higher. The physical location of Point Lookout proved deadly for prisoners and guards alike. Undrained marshes, contaminated water supplies, icy winds of winter, hot sun of summer, poor quality of food, and overcrowded conditions all contributed to the unhealthy conditions.

There were two deaths among the soldiers from Western New York while the regiment was at Point Lookout. Musician John S. Peterson, of Wirt, Allegany County, New York, died at the Point Lookout Hospital on August 3, 1864, less than a month after his arrival at Point Lookout. The cause of death was chronic diarrhea. From February through July, the Company Muster Rolls indicated Peterson was "on daily duty with Regt. Band" and gave no indication of his illness. He was survived by his wife Harriet and four children, William, age nine years, Mary Catherine, age six years, Henry, age four years and John, age two years. The Peterson family was part of a large extended family group that moved frequently between northern Pennsylvania and the southern tier counties of New York State.

John S. Peterson, 1828-1864
Used with permission of Dr. Stanton F. Biddle

Harriet and John S. Peterson, children of Richard and Mary Peterson and William B. and Catherine Peterson, respectively, married in 1851 and settled down in the town of Wirt, Allegany County, New York, living in close proximity to Harriet's parents and other relatives. The final resting place of John S. Peterson is bit uncertain. United States Burial Registers indicate he was buried first at Point Lookout Cemetery and then moved to Arlington National Cemetery. Yet there is a monument with his name in the Maple Grove Cemetery in Friendship, Allegany Co., New York.[76] It is unlikely that the family removed his body from Arlington, but they did erect an impressive marker for him and his widow, Harriet, who died in 1876. Harriet remarried in 1870 to Moses Ray and had two more sons – Clarence, born in 1870 and Walter, born in 1874.

The three grown sons of John S. Peterson carried on the musical tradition of their father. Left to right: Henry, William, and John. Used with permission of Dr. Stanton F. Biddle.

The second death was of Private William Brown, a member of Company C. Brown listed his birthplace as Rochester, New York, but it does not appear that he was a resident of the city at the time of his enlistment in Swansea, Massachusetts on January 12, 1864. The twenty-one-year old sailor was described as being five feet, four inches tall, with a colored complexion and black eyes and hair. Private Brown died at the Point Lookout Hospital of diarrhea on November 12, 1864. There were also two discharges due to disability among the western New York men during their time a Point Lookout.

Alfred W. Butler was among the older recruits, being thirty-eight years old at the time of his enlistment, and this may have contributed to his early discharge for disability. According to military records, Private Butler "ruptured himself on or about the 28th day of July 1864 ... in the performance of his duty on a fatigue party." His discharge was official on October 19, 1864.[77] Charles R. Douglass, son of Frederick Douglass and Sergeant in Company I, was given an honorable discharge on September 15, 1864. The military record does not give a reason for the discharge, but he may have continued to suffer from ill health, that had prevented him from serving in the 54th Massachusetts, alongside his brother.[78]

Disease and death were not the only challenges facing the soldiers of the 5th Massachusetts Cavalry during their time at Point Lookout. Having black soldiers guarding white prisoners was fraught with potential conflict as both sides were distrustful of each other. John Jacob Omenhausser, of the 46th Virginia Infantry, expressed his dislike for the black troops, as guards, through several drawings, created while he was imprisoned at Camp Lookout. One of his drawing depicts a sentry warning a prisoner to get away from the fence or be shot and taunting him by saying that the "bottom rails on top now." A second drawing shows a prisoner carrying a black soldier on his back. The soldier tells the prisoner "Double-quick" or he'll "pop a cap." The soldier also threatens to kill the prisoner, if he should to tell the major about the incident.[79] Regardless of the racial stereotyping by Omenhausser, his collection of drawings provides a valuable snapshot into the everyday life at Camp Hoffman and Point Lookout for both the guards and the prisoners.

Having been banished to Point Lookout, the officers and men of the 5th Massachusetts Cavalry never gave up hope that they would be returned to the battle front as a cavalry unit. The arrival of Lt. Col. Charles Francis Adams, Jr., son of the United States Ambassador to Britain and grandson and great grandson of two presidents, in September 1864 moved the goal forward, by securing a supply of horses. The regiment returned to training as a cavalry unit, while still acting as guards. Word finally came from Washington, D.C. in late March 1865, informing the regiment that they were to proceed with haste to City Point, Virginia.

On March 28, 1865, the 5th Massachusetts Cavalry (mounted) joined the Twenty-Fifth Army Corps, under the command of Major General Godfrey Weitzel, at the Bermuda Hundred, the same area as its first encounter with the enemy in July 1864. On April 2, 1865, Confederate General Robert E. Lee, wrote to Jefferson Davis that it was "absolutely necessary that we should abandon our position" at Petersburg and Richmond. The Confederate Army evacuated Petersburg on that very same day and began its evacuation of Richmond. On April 3rd, the 5th Massachusetts Cavalry regiment, as part of the Twenty-Fifth Corps, moved toward Richmond. Meeting no resistance from the enemy, the regiment had reached the outskirts of Richmond by mid-morning.

There is some debate about which Union regiments reached the capital of the Confederacy first, but it is usually accepted that the 5th Massachusetts was the first black cavalry regiment to enter the burning city on April 3, 1865. On the morning of April 4th, President Abraham Lincoln arrived in Richmond and was escorted around the city with a squad of men from the 5th Massachusetts Cavalry.[80] For a regiment that had been side-lined for so long, this was indeed a welcomed honor.

On April 6th, the regiment moved from Richmond back to the Petersburg area, where they remained until early June. In late May the regiment received orders to join an expedition designed to end Confederate resistance still active in Texas and parts of Louisiana, and to secure the territory against Mexican aggression. The entire Twenty-Fifth Corps, a force of about 20,000 black troops, was scheduled to leave Virginia in early June. The 5th Massachusetts Cavalry arrived at Fort Monroe, Virginia in preparation for embarkation to Texas on June 13, 1865. Rumors and fears took hold among many of the black soldiers who were being sent to Texas. One of the most pervasive rumors was that the white officers had conspired to take the troops to Cuba to sell into slavery. Regardless of the unrest and uncertainty of the next phase of duty, the men of the 5th Massachusetts Cavalry boarded the steamers on June 23rd and disembarked at Brazos de Santiago, Texas on July 3rd for their new assignment.

Not on board when the regiment shipped out for Texas was Private William Elebeck, of Company A, who was listed as "sick at Fort Monroe beginning May 21, 1865. Although he had claimed to be twenty years old at the time of his enlistment, the census records place him closer to sixteen years old. The son of Junius H. and Mary A. Elebeck, William was born and raised in Buffalo, New York, where his father worked as a barber and was a civil rights activist. Standing at barely five feet two inches tall, it is surprising that the recruiter did not challenge his purported age. Private Elebeck was discharged, by reason of disability, on June 21, 1865 at Fort Monroe. He returned to Buffalo, where he was enumerated in the 1865 census, living with his widowed mother.[81]

Private Elebeck's pension file provides additional information about the nature of his disability, indicating that he had suffered an injury to his left leg, while felling a tree at Point Lookout, Maryland. In addition, he had contracted a severe cold, which resulted in a general decline of his health. Elebeck initiated his pension application on April 9, 1888, but he died two months later, before the process was completed. His mother, Mary Elebeck, made her own application as a dependent mother and was granted a pension. Her son was buried in the Civil War section of Forest Lawn Cemetery in Buffalo.[82]

Once in Texas, the 5th Massachusetts was stationed at Clarksville, located at the mouth of the Rio Grande River. Their duty consisted mainly of heavy labor, unloading transport ships and building up fortifications to fend off possible attacks originating from Mexico and Confederate forces which still held out hope of a different outcome to the war. Fortunately, their stay in Texas came to an end with a formal mustering out on October 31, 1865. Of the seventeen recruits with ties to western New York, nine were with the regiment when it left Texas. They were: Solomon Peterson, Irenas J. Palmer, George H. Johnson, and Ephraim Johnson, all of Olean; Joseph Lee of Oswego; James A. Mason and James W. Collins (alias Juan DeColaines), of Rochester; George C. Warren, of Syracuse; and William Jackson of Buffalo. There had been two deaths, one rejection prior to muster-in, two desertions and three early discharges for disabilities among the western New Yorkers.

The regiment returned to Massachusetts for final ceremonies and the men began the hard work of returning to civilian life. Solomon Peterson was welcomed home to Olean, New York by his wife Sophia and children, Olean Sophia, age thirteen; Jefferson, age eleven; Mary, age nine; and Americus, age two. Over the next few years Peterson appears to have prospered and become an active participant in the life of the African American community of Olean. In 1865 his real estate was valued at $100 and 10 years later, the value of his property was recorded as $1,000. In 1879 he was appointed to the board of trustees of the newly formed African Methodist Episcopal Church.

In 1880 Mr. Peterson's health had begun to fail and he applied for an invalid's pension, based on his Civil War service, highlighting illnesses he suffered while a soldier. From June through early September 1864 he had been hospitalized, first at Fort Monroe and then at Portsmouth, Virginia. Poor health again removed him from his company from April through June of 1865. Having recovered sufficiently by early June, he traveled with the regiment to Texas.[83] Solomon and Sophia Peterson were mainstays in the African American community until their deaths. Mrs. Peterson died in March, 1896 and her funeral was held from the African Methodist Episcopal church, that she and her husband had been instrumental in establishing. Solomon Peterson died on January 6, 1904. The couple were buried in Mount View Cemetery in Olean.[84]

Posters with a similar message would have been distributed throughout New York State regarding the upcoming draft.

The 8ᵗʰ USCT and the Draft of 1863 in Western New York

In early 1863 two events intersected that changed the landscape of the Civil War. The first was the issuing of the Emancipation Proclamation by President Abraham Lincoln on January 1ˢᵗ. The final version of this landmark document contained a single sentence that made it official government policy that African Americans "will be received into the armed service of the United States." The second was the passage on March 3ʳᵈ of the Civil War Military Draft Act. The specter of "military necessity" was the backdrop that made these two acts possible.

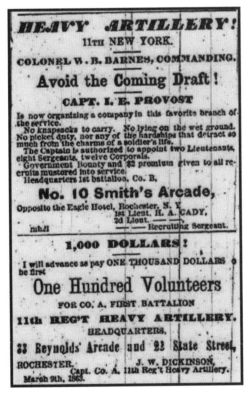

As soon as the Draft Act became law, the recruitment machine went into high gear. Enlistment offices for 11ᵗʰ New York Heavy Artillery were set up in Rochester. Headlines of "Avoid the Coming Draft!" and "1000 Dollars" were designed to pull in potential recruits. Promises of "No knapsacks to carry. No lying on the wet ground, No picket duty, nor any of the hardships that detract so much from the charms of a soldier's life" sealed the deal."[85]

What the advertisement left unsaid, was that only white recruits were invited to enroll. African Americans of New York, who wished to enlist at that time and secure that handsome bounty, were not welcome in any regiment being formed in the state prior to the draft. Yet, the Draft Act made no exception for race, calling for the enrollment of all male citizens and immigrants, who had declared an intention to become citizens, between the ages of 20 and 45 years old. New York, with 31 Congressional Districts, was divided into three administrative divisions - Southern, Eastern/Central; and Western. The Southern Division was comprised of Congressional districts one through ten (New York City area, Long Island and Westchester County) with headquarters in New York City. Congressional Districts eleven through twenty were included in the Eastern/Central Division, with its headquarters located in Albany. The remaining eleven districts made up the Western Division, which spanned east to west from Utica to Buffalo and north to south from Lake Ontario to the Pennsylvania State line. The city of Elmira in Chemung County was the headquarters of the Western Division.

The enrollment process was a daunting task. Not only did it need to be done quickly and hopefully accurately, but it had to be done in an atmosphere that was in many cases very hostile. In the rural areas the census was conducted often by town assessors, who were familiar with the residents. The process in urban areas was more challenging due to the transient nature of its citizens. Information collected on each person included name, age, race, marital status, occupation and any other comments that might influence the person's ability to perform as a soldier. The resulting rolls were filled with inaccurate and incomplete information, creating confusion for draft committees throughout the state.

In June 1863 the Secretary of War notified the states of the number of men required for them to meet their quota or portion of the total number of troops needed for the current call up of troops. The actual number to be drawn in the draft from each district was 50 percent greater than the quota for each district, to ensure that after all the exemptions had been granted, there were still sufficient numbers to meet the established quota. The exemptions were very liberal. The biggest loopholes were that the draftee could secure a substitute or pay a $300 fee to the government, which exempted him from service for that round of the draft.

The draft in New York State began in mid-July 1863 and was dealt a serious set back by the events in New York City between July 13th and 16th. What started as a protest to the draft shifted to anger against African Americans and Republicans. Four days of mob violence ruled ending with in over one hundred deaths and destruction of millions of dollars of property.

Drafts in the Western Division of New York State got underway on July 17th in Owego, Tioga County, headquarters for the 26th Congressional District. Next on the schedule was the 24th Congressional District, beginning on July 23rd in Auburn, the hometown of Secretary of State William H. Seward. Seward's wife wrote her husband that agitators might cause problems and she feared that the "colored people" would have no one to protect them.[86] In an attempt to insure a quiet day on the 23rd, Auburn's Mayor Jonas White requested that inn keepers of the city "refrain from selling alcohol" for 36 hours beginning on the 22nd at 9 p.m.[87]

The Provost Marshal of the 24th Congressional District began his work at 10 a.m. at the Court House in Auburn for 2,062 men from the counties of Cayuga, Seneca and Wayne. The draft process spanned three days and was completed without incident. The draft in New York's 25th Congressional District began a week later in Canandaigua and men from Ontario, Yates and Livingston counties were added to the list. During the month of August and into early September the scene was repeated across western New York. Draftees assembled in cities of the various districts to be examined by a surgeon to determine fitness, to apply for an exemption, provide proof of enlistment in one of the volunteer regiments being organized, make arrangements for a substitute or pay the commutation fee.

A total of 45,385 names were pulled from the lottery boxes within the Western Division of New York State, but only 1,732 actually made it onto the final list of draftees. 22,500 received exemptions, 7,562 paid the commutation fee of $300, and 3,292 furnished substitutes. The total on the final draft list for the entire state of New York was a mere 3,216, of which the Western Division accounted for 55 percent.[88] The draft in New York State did not generate many bodies for the depleted ranks of the armies of the North.

There were instances where almost all of the men drafted in a district were found to qualify for exemptions. The town of Arcadia in Wayne County drew the names of 140 men, but only eight men were not exempted.[89] It was reported that of the 650 men from the 25th Congressional District, which included counties of Ontario, Livingston and Yates, examined by the surgeon at the Court House in Canandaigua, only 150 were accepted. The *Geneva Gazette* writer lamented that "we are becoming a nation of invalids."[90] The Town Clerk of LeRoy, Genesee County, New York commented on the rolls of soldiers compiled in 1865 that only two men from those conscripted in the town served in the war. The two men were George Fountain and Lloyd McKenzie, both African Americans.[91] The unfairness of the draft was exposed in that the less well-off or well-connected often found that having their name pulled from the lottery drum meant that they would be entering the army.

The draft registration records contained duplications, omissions and errors so it is difficult to determine an accurate number of African Americans on the rolls of the Western Division, but it is unlikely that there were more than 1,400 black men on the draft registration rolls. An estimate for the 24th Congressional District (Cayuga, Seneca and Wayne counties) put the number at 146 men. Another 159 men appear to be on the draft lists of the 25th Congressional District (Ontario, Livingston and Yates counties).[92] There is also no total count of African Americans whose names were drawn during the initial days of the draft procedure in the Western Division during the summer of 1863, but there are pieces of information. The *Binghamton Standard* said the "eight colored men were gobbled up" in the draft in that city.[93] The Geneva newspaper reported that thirteen of those drafted in its village were African American.[94] Auburn's newspaper put the number of African Americans drafted in that city at seven.[95]

Records for Wayne County listed the names of at least eight black men among the drafted. Of the eight, Saliby Hardy of Galen and William Stone of Huron were found to be physically unfit for military service. Hardy could have been exempt on several levels. He was 36 years old and married with four young children. William Stone apparently had little use of one arm. Dexter Taylor of Huron paid his brother-in-law Bradley Gregor to go in his stead and in the end, four served in the Army.[96] William A. Copey of Auburn and James Bias of Seneca Falls, both from the 24th Congressional District were able to secure the services of a substitute.[97] With no New York units being raised to accept black soldiers, those drafted black men of the Western Division were in most cases assigned to the 8th United States Colored Troops (USCT), being organized at Camp William Penn in Philadelphia.

Camp William Penn and the 8th USCT

If the Lincoln Administration had thought raising black troops in the North would be a relatively simple task, it would have been sorely disappointed. It became apparent that a centralized policy was required if black troops were to play an effective role in the war effort. On May 22, 1863, the War Department issued orders which established a Bureau that would oversee the organization of regiments of black soldiers, with the designation of United States Colored Troops. The Bureau would also standardize recruitment of officers and create recruiting stations and depots "as circumstances shall require, and officers will be detailed to muster and inspect the troops."[98]

The largest of these depots in the North was set up northwest of Philadelphia. Camp William Penn opened its doors in late June of 1863 and began receiving recruits for the 3rd USCT on the 4th of July. By mid-September two full regiments of the United States Colored Troops had been organized at Camp William Penn – the 3rd and the 6th. On September 25th forty-seven draftees and substitutes from Western New York were mustered into Co. B of the 8th USCT, the third regiment to be organized at Camp William Penn. On November 3rd, the second contingent of thirty-nine men from the same area were mustered into Company G of the same regiment. Who were these soldiers from Western New York State and what was their war experience?

The eighty-six men identified from Western New York that served in the 8th USCT ranged in age from 19 to 44 years old, with an average age of 26 years. The group included 31 laborers, 26 farmers, 13 barbers, four boatmen, and an assortment of other occupations. Sixty-seven of them were draftees and the remaining thirteen were serving as substitutes for drafted men – both black and white. Almost one-third came from just two Congressional Districts - the 24th and 25th - which included the counties of Cayuga, Seneca, Wayne, Ontario, Livingston and Yates. The soldiers from these two districts also suffered the greatest losses, accounting for 60% of the deaths within the Western New York contingent.

There were three sets of brothers among the recruits. Bradley and Elijah Gregor from Wayne County, New York served in Company B. Bradley was serving as a substitute for his brother-in-law Dexter Taylor. Richard and Gerrit S. Russell from Madison County also served in Company B. Brothers Amos and George Van Schaick of Cayuga County were assigned to Company G. There was also a father and son team from Cayuga County in Company G – James and Stephen Butler. The Russell family is the only one that emerged from the war intact. Bradley Gregor and James Butler died from wounds suffered in battle; Elijah Gregor and George Van Schaik died from illness.

Within the two companies were many family and friendship ties that must have eased the pain of separation from home. Five of the men in Company B were from a small African American community located on the outskirts of Sodus Point, New York. Another four soldiers in the same company were from Geneva, New York. Interestingly, the African American families of Sodus Point and Geneva, were also linked by relationships formed during their time in slavery. That sense of being connected may also have heightened their feelings of loss when one of their own died. It is very likely that Sergeant Charles H. Cooper, of Sodus Point, would have been the one to write to Molly Lee and Madeline Dorsey regarding the death of grandson and brother, William T. Dorsey, who died from illness on the eve of Christmas Day 1863 at Camp William Penn, outside of Philadelphia.[99]

Twenty-one-year old William Dorsey, the son of Charles Dorsey, was the "breadwinner" for his younger sister and elderly grandmother and his death must have been a severe blow to the two women, although hardship was nothing new to this family. Molly Lee, her parents, Abraham and Ven Bradington, and her siblings were once enslaved by Peregrine Fitzhugh, who moved his family and human property from Frederick County, Maryland to Sodus Point, New York about 1803.

William's father was also a former slave, who started his journey of self-emancipation in 1836 from Frederick County, Maryland, the former residence of Mr. Fitzhugh, along with three brothers – Basil, William, and Thomas. The four young men reached Philadelphia and were assisted by Robert Purvis, an African American, who found work for them. When slave hunters came looking for the Dorsey brothers in 1837, Mr. Purvis once again came to their aid. He was able to gain the release of Basil Dorsey from jail and quickly send him on to New York City. Thomas Dorsey was captured and taken to Baltimore, before being rescued by friends, who purchased him to secure his freedom. Brothers William and Charles Dorsey, having eluded the slave hunters, were sent to Canada.

If Charles Dorsey reached Canada, his stay there was brief, as by 1842 he and his wife, a daughter of Molly Lee, welcomed the birth of their son, William Thomas Dorsey, in Sodus Point, New York. Two years late a daughter joined the family. William's mother died between 1844 and 1850 and his father, most likely, died between 1850 and 1860.[100] It was the sale of small parcel of land, located on the outskirts of Sodus Point that unlocked the story of the Charles Dorsey's escape from slavery and his subsequent life in Sodus Point.[101]

Once the recruits arrived in Camp William Penn, the job of molding them into soldiers began in earnest. Camp life must have seemed chaotic at times, with a constant flux of incoming and outgoing troops, so establishing a daily routine was essential to good order. Each day started with reveille and roll call at 6 a.m., followed by surgeon's call and breakfast. Drilling began at 8 a.m. and continued until dinner was served at noon. There was additional drilling in the afternoon with an evening dress parade scheduled for 5:30 p.m. Taps were sounded at 9 p.m.[102] What appears on the surface to be a full day of training proved to be inadequate for what faced the men of the 8th USCT once they took to the field of battle in February 1864.

Camp William Penn, view of hospital and officer's quarters. Photo from collection of Historical Society of Pennsylvania; https://hsp.org.life-camp-william-penn.

The organization of the regiment's command structure took hold during November and December. Colonel Charles W. Fribley, formerly a captain with the 84th Pennsylvania, was appointed Colonel. In Company B the top rank was filled by Captain Romanzo C. Bailey. James E. Griffin and Jacob Scheiffelin were the 1st and 2nd Lieutenants respectively within the same company. Captain Electus A. Pratt, 1st Lieut. Thomas Young, 2nd Lieut. William H. Brooks and 2nd Lieut. J. Francis

Jenness were the officers of Company G. The appointments of 1st Sergeant, Sergeants and Corporals were also made during this time period.

There was a certain amount of trial and error in these appointments. Levi A. Preston, a substitute from Canandaigua, New York, was listed with rank of Sergeant in Company B at muster-in on September 25th, but on November 17th a Court Martial after being "absent without leave for three days" resulted in a guilty sentence. Preston was reduced in rank to private and fined one month's pay. Preston had a relatively rocky military career. He climbed his way up the ranks again by December 31, 1863 when he was promoted to Corporal. Then on the 1st of March 1864 he was made 3rd Sergeant, only to be reduced to the ranks six weeks later where he remained until the close of his term in the military.[103] Theodore Duffin, a barber from Geneva, New York, was a corporal for all of two days. He received his promotion on October 5, 1863 and was reduced to the ranks on the 7th. He was found to have stolen tobacco from a fellow soldier.[104] There were also some soldiers that preferred to remain privates. William P. Woodlin requested that he be relieved of his duty as a Corporal on January 15, 1864, in order to join the regimental band.[105]

Not all appointments from the ranks were unsuccessful. Edgar Fryman, from Oswego, New York, was made a sergeant at the time of muster-in of Company G and was promoted to 1st Sergeant in that same company in May 1864.[106] Charles H. Cooper replaced Levi A. Preston as sergeant on December 1, 1863 in Company B. The twenty-four-year-old farmer from Wayne County, remained in that position until the regiment was mustered out in November 1865.[107] Cooper shared duties with Sgt. Robert T. Mann of Bath, New York who served in that capacity from January 1, 1864 until he was promoted to 1st Sergeant in July 1865.[108]

Edwin H. Brown was a twenty-seven-year-old barber in Rochester, New York when he was drafted in the summer of 1863. He was mustered into Company G on November 3rd and appointed to the position of 1st Sergeant in the company two weeks later. He must have exhibited exceptional qualities as on November 18[th,] he was appointed Regimental Quarter Master Sergeant and transferred to the Field Staff. By December 14, 1864 he was promoted to the rank of Sergeant Major.[109]

Initially the troops were housed in tents, but with the winter months approaching camp officials began to build wooden barracks. On December 8th, the newly minted soldiers moved into their improved quarters.[110] They had little time to get comfortable as they began preparing to leave camp for active duty in South Carolina. Private William P. Woodlin of Co. G, wrote in his diary of the regiment's departure from Camp William Penn and debarkation from New York City:

> *January 16th   We rec'd orders to pack up this morning at roll call to be ready to move at a moments warning. Fell in at 10 A.M. and the start was put off until ½ past 1 P.M. When the whole Reg was formed in lane, and march out in review before the 22nd [USCT]. Band playing Yankee Doodle. Paraded through Front & across Walnut Strs and took the carr [cars] for New York where we arrived at about 9 A.M.*
>
> *17[th]   Paraded through Cort [Court] & Broadway down Canall [Canal] Strs to the wharf where we shipped at night on board the City of Bath and the Promet[h]ius.[111]*

Private Woodlin, a resident of Onondaga County at the time of his being drafted, was born in Louisiana about 1841. He was among a group of about twenty slaves freed and brought north by the Rev. John Gorham Palfrey, a Unitarian minister in Boston, after the death of his father in 1843. In 1850, Woodlin was listed under the name of William Palfry, age nine, living in the home of David and Edna Thomas in Cayuga County, New York.[112] Five years later he assumed the name of William P. Woodlin and was again listed with the Thomas family.[113] His diary provides researchers with one of the few first-hand accounts of the African American soldiers during the Civil War.

UNITED STATES SOLDIERS AT CAMP "WILLIAM PENN" PHILADELPHIA, PA.

This recruitment poster is thought to have been created from photograph of soldiers taken at Camp William Penn in winter of 1863-1864. The 8th USCT left the training center in January 1864, so it is possible some of these soldiers were from this regiment.
Source: https://militaryimages.atavist.com/photo-sleuth-autumn-2015

The 8th USCT Faces the Enemy in Battle of Olustee

The 8th USCT arrived in Hilton Head, South Carolina on January 24, 1864 where it joined Howell's Brigade of Seymour's Division, in the Department of the South. In less than two weeks the regiment was on the move again. A force of about seven thousand soldiers left Hilton Head for Florida on the 5th of February, under the command of General Truman Seymour. Two weeks more and the soldiers of the 8th USCT met the enemy in battle and the results were devastating.

A great deal has been written about the Battle of Olustee which took place in north central Florida on February 20, 1864. It is judged to have been the second bloodiest battle of the Civil War with a total of 203 killed, 1,152 wounded and 506 missing – from a total force of about 5,500 Union soldiers. Blame for the defeat and subsequent retreat of the Union forces could be spread over a wide swath of the commanders in the field and behind the scenes.

Pvt. William Woodlin, as an unarmed band member, described the events of the day in an entry dated February 20th as follows:

> We rec'd our rations last evening and got underway about ½ past 6 A.M. at a quick step on the left of the division, passed Sanders Station about 11 A.M. ... we had a very rapid as well as fatiguing march; ... After this halt we were ordered forward, soon could hear the roar of Canon & the rattle of Musketry ahead of us, we were hurried up to the line of battle at double quick and our Reg was place[d] in the center and rec'd the hottest fire that was given; The Col. fell the Major was wounded Capt & several lieutenants. The band and Drum Core [sic] went up to the front ahead of the Cavalry and were exposed to very hot fire; for a while

when we fell back to the R.R. until we were in danger of being taken by a flank movement of the Rebs; we got away however and had another station for a while; when we were again moved a mile farther from the battlefield, which was in the front of Lake City. We built some fires there, & were halted by the Division Dr. for a while after which we moved on untill [sic] we reached the station. We left in the morning ... below the scene of action nearly worn out with fatigue & cold. We reached there about 1 a.m. that night and stayed until daylight. [114]

A month later, twenty-year-old Private George Van Schaick of Company G wrote to his mother the following account:

We had a battle about 80 miles from here on the 20th of febuary at a plase called Lustee   we lost about 1500 men and the rebels lost more than we did   our regiment lost about 300 and we Lost or [our] colonel and magor. The Enemy were entrenched and We was on the open field and they out numbered us and after fighting for 3 and ¼ hours we had to retreat   we came back to Jacksonville ...[115]

The 8th USCT, not fully trained and totally untested, suffered the second most casualties of any unit that participated in the battle.   Captain Romanzo C. Bailey of Company B wrote a report dated February 24th summarizing the Battle of Olustee from his vantage point:

After leaving the railroad along which we had been advancing until within about 1,000 yards of the enemy, Colonel Fribley received orders to 'put his regiment in,' when we were ordered to change direction to the left, moving now in double-quick time by the right flank on a line nearly parallel with the railroad and about 300 yards to its right. We were soon under fire of the enemy, when our line of battle was formed under a terrific fire of musketry at short range ...Col. Fribley now ordered the regiment to fall back slowly, which we did, firing as we retired, being unable to withstand so disastrous a fire. The order reached me...when the colonel fell mortally wounded. The command now devolved on major Burritt, who soon received two wounds and retired from the field, the regiment at this time engaging the enemy with steadiness, and holding the ground for some time near Hamilton's battery, which we were trying to save. We here lost 3 color-sergeants and 5 of the color guard while attempting to save one gun, but we were driven back, leaving the gun and, as afterward learned, the color beside it during the excitement.[116]

Letters written by Lt. Oliver W. Norton, of Company K, to family members confirm that the 8th USCT was ill prepared for battle on February 20th.

We have had very little practice in firing, and though they could stand and be killed, they could not kill a concealed enemy fast enough to satisfy my feelings." In a letter to his father Norton stated that "No new regiment ever went into their first fight in more unfavorable circumstances. ... no braver men ever faced an enemy. ... Our regiment has been drilled too much for dress parade and too little for the field. They can march well, but they cannot shoot rapidly or with effect.[117]

The 8th USCT went into battle with about 550 men and official reports dated February 25, 1864 put the number of casualties for the regiment at 310, with 49 killed, 188 wounded and 73 missing. The numbers would be revised many times during the next few months, but inaccuracies still remained. William Woodlin wrote in his diary on July 5, 1864 that "This Reg lost 320 men killed, wounded & missing. 29 killed, 76 taken prisoners and the rest wounded."[118] The men of Western New York were not spared in the battle. Close to one third of their total number of eighty-five were among the casualties - four killed, fifteen wounded and at least another five wounded and taken prisoner.

All four of those killed were members of Company B. George Alexander at twenty years old was the youngest. Initially listed among the "missing and supposed to be killed", his status was not changed until the end of the war. According to his military records he was five feet, five inches tall and earned his living as a laborer in Steuben County, New York. The 1855 census places George, age 11, living in Bath, New York with his parents Benjamin and Betsey Alexander and six siblings, aged one month to fourteen years. The census enumerator indicated that Benjamin was a farmer and that all members of the family had been born in Steuben County.[119] No wife, mother or father applied for a Civil War Pension in the name of George Alexander.

The Elisha Charles family of Madison County, New York said good-bye to two sons in the summer of 1863. The first was son, Henry, who at the age of eighteen traveled to Readville, Massachusetts where he enlisted on June 3rd in the 55th Massachusetts and was assigned to Company F. On August 31st, Henry's older brother, William, was drafted and four weeks later he was a soldier in Company B of the 8th USCT. Only one son returned. William S. Charles died on the field at Olustee, Florida.[120] Private Charles was survived by his wife Dianna and a child Flora, born 25 January 1862. His widow began the process of applying for a pension within a month of his death.

The death of Bradley Gregor of Wayne County, New York at Olustee was only the first loss that his family would suffer during the war. His brother Elijah, also a soldier in Company B, was wounded in the battle, but recovered and was able to serve until his death from disease in September 1865. Private Gregor was survived by his wife, Almira Taylor, who he had married in 1859 and was the parent of one daughter, Phoebe, born in 1861. While Almira Gregor waited until 1908 to file an application for a pension based on her husband's service, her in-laws, James and Almira Gregor did apply for and receive payment of a $100 bounty and arrears of pay to include February 20, 1864, based on the claim that their son left "no widow, nor minor child or children, and was never married." Imagine Almira's surprise that her in-laws did not acknowledge her marriage to Bradley.[121]

The fourth death on the battlefield at Olustee was that of Henry Thompson, a farmer from Cayuga County, New York. He was identified on the draft registration records as only twenty-three years old, unmarried, born in New Jersey and a farmer, while on his *Company Descriptive Book* his age was given as thirty-three-years old, which was more likely closer to the case. The 1860 census for the town of Mentz in Cayuga County included a listing for Henry, age twenty-eight, Maria, age twenty-seven and Hellen M., age eleven months.[122]

Any retreat from the field of battle has to be chaotic and hurried, but with so many officers dead and wounded there was a feeling of panic that accompanied the aftermath of the Battle at Olustee. Dr. A. P. Heichhold, Surgeon with the 8th USCT wrote:

> *I saw at an early stage of the fight that we would be whipped and went round among the wounded and told them, as many as could get away, to start for Barber [Station] and then started the ambulance crowded full.*

The day and the field being lost to us we started on the retreat ... I had but one ambulance to a regiment and the railroad was useless, because we had no locomotive. However, we got some horse cars to within 18 miles of the field, which aided us greatly...[123]

It was against great odds that the retreating forces were able to bring 860 wounded soldiers back to Jacksonville, arriving there on February 22nd. Over 200 of the most seriously wounded were loaded onto the transport *Cosmopolitan* and taken to hospitals in Beaufort and Hilton Head, arriving there on the evening of February 23.

One of those wounded at Olustee who would eventually succumb to his wounds was James Fayette, a twenty-five-year old barber, who was drafted from the town of Starkey, Yates County in August of 1863. Two months later he was mustered into Company G with the rank of sergeant, followed by promotion to 1st Sergeant on December 28, 1863. In battle, he suffered a gunshot wound to the left side and was taken from Jacksonville by transport to the General Hospital at Beaufort, South Carolina, where he remained until he was transferred to General Hospital at Willetts Point in New York City Harbor. When Fayette died on March 13, 1865, the cause was attributed to "gun shot wounds and Diarrhea." He was survived by his wife Martha and a three-year-old son, James L. Fayette. The marriage of James Fayette to Martha Jones took place in Elmira, New York on September 15, 1863, while James awaited transfer to Camp William Penn. Since young James was born on December 9, 1862, prior to the marriage of his parents, he was not entitled to status as a surviving minor child by the Pension Office. However, Martha Jones Fayette was able to secure a pension for herself.[124]

Daniel Prue of Geneva, New York suffered a gunshot wound to his left arm at Olustee and for all intents and purposes his active duty days had come to an end. For the next year he was shifted from hospital to hospital until he was discharged on April 23, 1865 on a Surgeon's Certificate of Disability having lost the use of his arm. Private Prue had a very interesting past.

In November 1857, Daniel Prue along with another young man from Geneva, New York, John Hite, were enticed to travel with a white man named Napoleon VanTuyl to Columbus, Ohio with the promise of a job in the hotel of VanTuyl's uncle. Prue became suspicious of VanTuyl when he overheard him telling a fellow passenger that he was traveling to Cincinnati, not Columbus. Prue acted quickly and exited the train at the next stop, only to be accosted by VanTuyl and another man about an hour later, claiming to bystanders that Prue was his slave. Since he had no proof of ownership, Prue was released and quickly left on foot for Columbus. From Columbus Prue wrote his father, John Prue, explaining what had happened and that he thought that Hite had been taken to Kentucky.

Calvin Walker and Robert Lay, white citizens of Geneva, set out for Ohio to recover Prue and to search for John Hite. They found that VanTuyl had indeed sold Hite to a Benton W. Jenkins, who had in turn sold the young man to a Judge Graves for about $800. Walker and Lay rescued John Hite from a slave pen in Louisville, Kentucky. After the war, Daniel Prue returned to Geneva, New York and continued to live in the family home until his death in 1895.[125]

A third soldier that saw very little duty, if any, after his being wounded at Olustee was Thomas Lloyd of Wayne County, New York. Lloyd had entered the service as a substitute for William A. Copey at Auburn and was listed as "in hospital" at Beaufort from February 20, 1864 through June. Muster Rolls show him as present in July and August 1864, but from that point on the record listed him again as "sick in Hospital." On October 18, 1864 he was admitted to Summit House General Hospital in Philadelphia, due to his being wounded at Olustee by a minié ball. A notation on the hospital record indicated he needed no treatment as the wound was healed. Another note stated that Lloyd was "Transferred to Guard" on November 2nd and that he deserted on December 27th. What happened to him next is a puzzle. No record of a Civil War pension application by Thomas Lloyd or William Thomas Lloyd has been located. Had he simply decided to go home?[126]

There was great fear among the ranks of the United States Colored Troops that if taken prisoner they would be shot or forced into slavery and not afforded the status of a prisoner of war. Surgeon A. P. Heichhold for the 8th USCT wrote a letter to *The Christian Recorder* that appeared in the issue of March 12th under the title *"How Our Colored Troops Fought in Florida."* Heichhold wrote:

> *We were compelled to leave a few of our men behind, and they fell into the hands of the enemy. It could not be helped ... How the rebels have disposed of the colored men who fell into their hands we have not heard yet; but we hope that the fear of retaliation, if not the dictates of humanity, will cause them to reconsider their threat of outlawry.*[127]

The fear was not unfounded. A Confederate soldier wrote home after the Battle of Olustee that the "negroes were badly cut up and killed   Our men killed some of them after they fell in our hands wounded." Another soldier reported to his wife:

> *The Yankees ... pitched three negro regiments against us, and all acknowledged that they fought well. We walked over many a wooly heads as we drove them*

back ... took about 400 prisoners and killed about the
same number. How our boys did walk into the niggers,
they beg and pray but it did them no good...[128]

Yet not all black soldiers left behind were murdered. The Confederate Commander, Brig. Gen. Joseph Finegan wrote to his superiors on February 23rd indicating that he had forwarded 150 unwounded prisoners to Maj. Gen. Gilmer. This group included three black soldiers. He asked "What shall I do with the large number of the enemy's wounded in my hands? Many of these are negroes."[129]   In early April, General Patton Anderson, Commander of the Confederate Army in Florida, provided the Federal forces with a list of 315 prisoners of war from the Battle of Olustee.[130]

Many of the prisoners (black and white) were sent to the newly opened prison at Andersonville, Georgia, located about 140 miles north of Tallahassee, Florida. Records for the prison contain the names of close to 300 soldiers taken prisoner at Olustee on February 20th. There were three black regiments in the field at Olustee that day – the 8th USCT, 54th Massachusetts, and 1st North Carolina Volunteers (later named the 35th USCT). Records identify only forty-three soldiers captured at Olustee as belonging to those units, including one white officer from the 1st North Carolina. At least thirty of those were from the 8th USCT, of which sixteen died at Andersonville.[131]

Conditions at Andersonville were horrific. Of the 45,000 men said to have been imprisoned there between February 1864 and March 1865, almost 13,000 died from disease, exposure, and starvation. There were five men from Western New York among the captured soldiers of the 8th USCT sent to Andersonville - Private John Thompson, Corporal William T. Lewis, Sergeant Richard Chancellor, and Private Joseph Ford, all of Company B, and Private Paul Blackman of Company G.

Corporal William T. Lewis from Company B was originally listed as "killed in action," but his name was included in a list of prisoners provided by General Patton Anderson, Commanding Officer of Confederate forces on 7 April 1864.[132] William, son of Peter and Emeline Lewis, was born in Schuyler County, New York about 1839 and was working on a farm in the town of Ulysses, Tompkins County when he was drafted. The twenty-five-year-old soldier died of scurvy at Andersonville on November 12, 1864, but his family was still unaware of his death as late as July 1865.[133]

The other captives from Western New York all lived to be included in a major prisoner exchange that took place at North East Ferry, North Carolina, near Wilmington, on March 4, 1865. From there they were sent to Camp Parole, located at Annapolis, Maryland. Unfortunately, this did not guarantee they would live long lives. Private John Thompson was admitted to the McKim's Mansion Hospital in Baltimore where he died from inflammation of the bladder three weeks later. Private Thompson, born in Oswego, New York, went into the service as a substitute, and was one of three brothers who joined the army in 1863. Brothers Jeremiah and Henry served in the 14th Rhode Island Heavy Artillery Regiment, also known as the 11th USCHA. The young men were the children of Charles and Mary (Peterson) Thompson who moved to Oswego from New Jersey about 1837.[134]

Private Paul Blackman had been living in Camillus, Onondaga County prior to his entering the army, working as a farm laborer for Sylvester Whedon. According to a deposition by Ezra Whedon made in 1883, Blackman, a former slave, had been brought north by a white officer. Mr. Whedon described him as being an "active, smart, able bodied man" who "could turn handstands easily" prior to his enlistment. Wounded in the right foot during the Battle of Olustee, Blackman came home with a severe limp and a wound that had never completely healed. On March 18th Blackman was issued a thirty-day furlough and records indicate that he traveled to Syracuse, New York, located just a few miles east of Camillus.

He returned to Maryland on April 18 and within the month transferred to the U. S. A. General Hospital at Fort Monroe where he was confined at the time his regiment was mustered out in November. In 1866 a doctor recommended that the former private receive a pension based on a three-quarter disability. In September of that year the Reverend Mr. Jermain Loguen of Syracuse presided at the marriage of Paul Blackman and Harriet A. Myers, widow of James A. Myers, another Civil War soldier. Mr. Blackman's health continued to deteriorate and he died in March of 1870. [135]

Sgt. Richard Chancellor was a blacksmith in the town of Hector, located in Schuyler County when he was drafted in July 1863. Blacksmithing was a job requiring strength and great stamina. Chancellor was described in the military records as being thirty-four years old, born in Virginia, 5' 8 ½' tall, with black complexion, hair and eyes. Initially listed as "killed in action" on February 20, 1864, he was in fact, wounded and captured on the field of action. According to his pension application, Chancellor was treated for a gun-shot wound of his right leg at the Confederate Hospital at Tallahassee, Florida and then transferred to prison in Andersonville, Georgia.

After arriving at Camp Parole in March 1865, he was granted a thirty-day furlough and traveled home to Schuyler County. Upon his return to Maryland, he was to be mustered out as of May 3rd, but his poor health required that he be admitted to the hospital at Fort Monroe, which delayed the date of his discharge until June 7th. The pension file for Sergeant

Chancellor clearly shows that he never recovered his health, suffering from chronic diarrhea, which eventually resulted in his death in December of 1882.[136]

Virginia native Joseph Ford made his way north to Sheridan, Cattaraugus County, New York where he was employed as a railroad laborer in the summer of 1863. At thirty-five-years old when drafted, Ford would have been considered an "old timer" in the ranks of the 8th, yet he lived the longest of the five prisoners taken at Olustee. In February 1866 Ford began the application process for an invalid pension based on wounds to the left leg and foot that he had sustained in the Battle of Olustee. It was not until June 1871 that he received his pension awarding him $14 per month based on one-half disability, commencing June 30, 1865. By that time, he had moved to Washington, D.C. where he lived until his death in September 1901.[137]

In Florida After Olustee

The 8th USCT remained in and around Jacksonville, Florida until early August 1864. The initial concern after the Battle at Olustee was the activities of the Rebel forces. Would they press forward and attack Jacksonville? Lt. Oliver Norton of Company K provided an officer's view of the situation of the 8th USCT when he wrote to his father on March 9, 1864 that:

> the whole force is hard at work nearly all the time, either on the fortifications or on picket. ...Ever since the battle the men have slept with their shoes and equipments on, and they fall in every hour before light and stand in the line till sunrise.[138]

The time also offered an opportunity for the regiment to train and hopefully to become better prepared for new challenges of the war. Lt. Norton wrote to his mother from Jacksonville on

April 14th that "The Regiment, so far as I can judge by observation is improving rapidly. I think another fight will give them a different story to tell."[139]

During its time in Florida the 8th USCT was charged with helping to secure the St. John's River above and below Jacksonville. In mid-April the regiment was moved to Yellow Bluff located about seven miles from the mouth of the river. Daily life seems to have been dominated by patrolling the river to guard against the enemy's planting torpedoes and picket duty. Lt. Norton provides a running commentary of what he perceived as the ineptitude of different commanders in his letters home, but he also gives us glimpses into the life of the ordinary soldier. On April 23rd he wrote from Yellow Bluffs to his sister:

> *About all the duty I have is to patrol the river one night in three. The steamers Maple Leaf and General Hunter have been blown up by torpedoes, and our business is to prevent the rebels from putting down any more of them between here and St. Johns Bluff, six miles below. We have four boat's crews beside the guard in the two companies [Companies B and K]... I will give you an outline of the night's work. About dark I shall leave the wharf with a crew of seven men and run down the river among the islands and past the mouths of creeks and bayous to St. Johns Bluff, keeping a bright lookout for any strange boat. I shall get out on shore, build up a fire and wait an hour for my oarsmen to rest, then come back again, reaching camp about midnight. Then I shall take a new crew and do the same thing over again, getting back at sunrise.[140]*

Of course, the Lieutenant placed himself in the center of the story, but it was the men doing the hard work. Beginning in June the 8th took part in several excursions into the

97

countryside in which they occasionally engaged the enemy, but for the most part appear to have been mostly to assess the strength of the Confederate forces.

For the men of the 8th USCT a major bone of contention was payment for their work. Sergeant Major Rufus Sibb Jones wrote to *The Christian Recorder* on April 16, 1864:

It seems the farther South the 8th advances, the farther 'pay-day' gets away from it. Just think of the colored troops not receiving any pay for nine months! Every vessel which lands at Jacksonville, from the North, is expected to bring the Paymaster; but I have begun to think none has been sent; and that the privilege of fighting and getting killed, is the only pay given.[141]

Interestingly the very day this letter appeared in *The Christian Recorder*, the paymaster finally caught up with the 8th USCT in Jacksonville, but there was controversy over the amount to be paid the soldiers. Private Woodlin wrote in his diary on May 6th that "excitement was quite high … in reference to the smallness of the $7 pay per month."[142] The Federal government had not yet rectified the inequity in pay for the black troops versus that of white troops. White privates were paid $13 per month, while black privates were to be paid only $10 per month with $3 being deducted each month for clothing allowance. Private George Van Schaick, of Company G wrote home to his mother in Brutus, New York on May 18th:

The Pay Master was here and offered to pay us off at 7 dollars a month   he sayed it had not passed the house what Coloured soldiers was to get and if it was over that that when he came around again which will be next month he would make it up to us   some company took it and others did not   only 8 of our company [Co. G] took it   since then We have heard that the Bill has

passed   that we are to get 13 dollars a month from the
first of January and only 7 for what time we were in
before that up to the first of January.   When we get
paid shall send it home if i can find any safe way of
doing."[143]

Lt. Oliver Norton also commented on the pay issue in a letter dated May 10th:

The paymaster came on Saturday with his $7 per
month. Not half the men would sign the rolls or take
their pay, and those who did, did so under protest. It
is too bad. Seven dollars a month for the heroes of
Olustee! I received two month's pay, deducting the tax,
$213.49. Some difference between that and $26.[144]

On May 21st Private Woodlin wrote that he had "read the law today giving the colored men their pay as white men."[145] That was only partially true. Equal pay was to be retroactive to January 1, 1864 for those soldiers who had been free prior to the start of the war. The Company Muster Rolls for the black soldiers made note of the status of the men beginning on July and August 1864 records with the statement "Free on or before April 19th /61." It was not until the fall of 1865 that the pay became equal for all black soldiers.

The less seriously wounded of the Western New York soldiers of Companies B and G straggled back into camp between March and July, helping to bolster the numbers of men available for duty. Unfortunately, there were other forces at work that made the men susceptible to illness during the stay in Florida. William Woodlin reported that on July 24th that "We buried 7 men ... Making 11 men up to this date died of acclimation."[146]

George Van Schaick of Brutus, Cayuga County, New York and James W. Clark of Canandaigua, Ontario County, New York, both of Company G, were among those who died of disease while stationed in Florida. George Van Schaick and his brother Amos (sometimes referred to as Enos) had been drafted in July of 1863, leaving at home parents Richard and Orrealia, as well as several siblings. On March 23rd, 1864 George wrote to his mother from Jacksonville and told of his state of health:

My Dear Mother

I now take my pen in hand to write a few lines to you to let you now that i am not very well at the present and i hope that this may find you all engaging Better health than it leaves me in at present i have got a bad cold Enos is well and sends his love to you all ...[147]

On May 18th George Van Schaick again wrote to his mother, this time from Yellow Bluffs, Florida telling her that "I am quite well at present And hope this may find you all at home enjoying The same great blessing." In the same letter, he added:

the wether is the warmest I ever saw we cant hardly get along We don't drill much now the snakes and Alligators and Mosquitoes and Gnats are very Bothersome Nights when we are on picket duty which is ever[y] other night

Private Van Schaick's health did not hold up and he died at Yellow Bluffs on June 10th of typhoid fever. After the death of his father in March 1868, George's mother applied for a pension stating that her son had helped to support her and the family prior to his time in the army and had indicated he would continue to do so as supported in his letters home. Two of the letters were included along with her pension application.[148]

March 23

Jacksonville Florida 1864

My Dear Mother

I now take my pen in hand
To write a few lines to you
To let you know that i am not
very well at present and i hope
That this may find you all enjoying
Better health than it leaves
me in at present i have got a bad
cold Enos is well and send his love
To you all i received your letter
And Postage stamps and am
much obliged to you for them
for we cant get any here, we had
a battle about 50 mils from here on
The 20th of febuary at a plase called
Lustee we lost about 1500 men and
the rebels lost more than we did
our regment lost about 300 and we
Lost our colinel and magar

Portion of letter from George Van Schaick, dated March 23, 1864.

On July 25th Corporal Stephen W. Clark, succumbed to remittent fever, which could have been malaria or typhoid fever, as the symptoms are similar. News of Stephen's death reached his wife, Mary Elizabeth, in Canandaigua, New York quickly as by the middle of September she had begun the process of applying for a widow's pension. The soldier was survived by his wife and two sons, Stephen Alexander and George Francis, ages two years and two months, respectively.[149] The widow and her children were surrounded by a closely-knit family and community that insured their support during this difficult time. Ten days after the death of Private Clark, the 8th USCT was leaving Florida to join the Army of the Potomac.

From the Bermuda Hundred to Appomattox

On August 4, 1864 Private Woodlin wrote in his diary "...orders to Evacuate ... and report to Jacksonville enroute for Fortress Monroe and the Army of the Potomac." The regiment left Jacksonville the next day and arrived at Fortress Monroe on the 11th after a brief stopover at Hilton Head. From there the 8th traveled up the James River to City Point, disembarking at Bermuda Hundred on the 12th of August. That night Private William Woodlin wrote in his diary "we took up the line of march for Gen [Benjamin Franklin] Butler's Hed Qur's about 7 miles distant through Virginia dust, which is terrible indeed...the evening was enlivened by the bombardment of Petersburg."[150] According to Woodlin, the men of the 8th had barely arrived in camp, removed their knapsacks and grabbed a few hours of sleep before the war became very real to them once more:

The morning was ushered in by the Monitors shelling the woods. Things very uncertain about our future destiny. The Guns soon opened on us and some 8 or 9 shells were thrown in on our camp before we could get out of the way our Srgt. Major [Rufus Sibb Jones] was wounded and several in the 7th U.S.C.T. ... Sunrise was ushered in by sharp skirmishing.[151]

The 8th USCT was attached to the 10th Corps, Army of the James, under the command of Gen. Benjamin F. Butler and over the next few months was engaged in a number of crucial battles of the Civil War. Within a few days of its arrival in Virginia, the regiment was at Strawberry Plain where Private Woodlin reported that "Our Regt stood their ground loosing but 3 men wounded." On August 29th he commented that "the Sharp Shooters are very bad here throwing a saucy good ball & at long range too ... there was one man shot through the head during the day."

Thomas Morris Chester, an African American war correspondent for the *Philadelphia Press*, wrote of the dangers on the picket line in a dispatch with dateline of Deep Bottom, Va., Sept. 13, 1864:

One of the most dreaded features about here is the certain shooting of any of our men who exhibits the least part of his head where the enemy may see it. With a view of trying the expertness of his sharpshooters, caps are frequently raised on a ramrod just above the breastworks, when immediately a ball passes through, to the amusement of the troops. Many of those persons who are shot in the trenches by muskets may attribute their misfortunes to carelessness or a foolish display of courage.[152]

The dispatch included a list of soldiers wounded and killed by sharp shooters during the previous week. Among the list was that of Calvin Vonhazel [sic], Company B, 8th USCT, one of the Western New York men. On September 3, 1864, Calvin Van Hazen (alias Calvin Hazel) was shot while on picket before

103

Petersburg. Private Van Hazen enlisted at Auburn, New York as a substitute for James Bias of Seneca Falls, New York.[153] He claimed to be twenty-one years old, but he was more likely only sixteen years old at the time, which may account for the slight alteration of his name to hide his real identity. Calvin was relatively tall at five feet, nine inches which may have helped to fool the enlisting officer.

The son of Sampson and Caroline (Smith) Hazel, Calvin was one of four brothers who joined the army during the Civil War. His was the second death that year for the Hazel family as his brother Allen died of disease in Louisiana in May where he was serving with the 14th Rhode Island (also known as 11th USCHA).[154] The alteration in his name and confusion over his regiment may have prevented his mother from being successful in her application for a pension as a dependent parent. Her application identified her son as Calvin Hazel and his regiment as the 8th USCHA, which had been designation for the 14th Rhode Island, son Allen's regiment, for a brief period of time.[155]

The second Western New York soldier to be killed by a sharpshooter on the front of Petersburg that month was Joseph R. Smith (Company B) of Ithaca, New York. On September 24, 1864, Private Smith was part of a fatigue detail digging trenches before Petersburg when he was shot. Smith must have been a striking figure at slightly over six feet tall, making him an easy target for the sharpshooter. He left behind a wife, the former Helen Whitaker, who resided in Ithaca, New York and no children. Mrs. Smith started her application for a widow's pension very quickly. Five days after her husband's death she appeared before the Deputy Clerk of the Supreme Court of Tompkins County, New York to fill out paper work establishing her status as the widow of Joseph R. Smith.[156]

From the end of September through the end of October the 8th USCT would be in several major fights. A series of engagements over three days at the end of September, referred to as the Battle at Chapin's Farm (sometimes called Chaffin's Farm) took a toll on the black regiments in the Army of the James, yet it also proved to the doubters once and for all that the black soldiers could fight, and fight well. Fourteen black soldiers would receive the prestigious Medal of Honor for their bravery during this battle. Private Woodlin recorded in his diary with the date of September 28th a synopsis of the battle from his viewpoint with the 8th USCT:

> *...went to Deep Bottom ... we continued to advance until 3 P.M. when we came to the 4th line on the New Market road where our brigade made a charge one at a time but they were repulsed. Our Regt losing 65 men in all ... We held our position that night but the Johnnies made a furious attack on the 30th three times but were repulsed with great loss ... there was a tremendous fire of shells, grape & canister and the like loss about 10 wounded in our Regt...*[157]

During the three days of the battle six men from Western New York were wounded in action. One of those most seriously wounded was Milton Frank, a private in Company G, from Utica, New York. Frank's military records indicated he was twenty-one years old at the time of enrollment, stood five feet, seven inches tall, was born in Oneida County, New York and made his living as a farmer. In November Frank was sent to the Lovell Hospital in Portsmouth Grove, Rhode Island where he died from his wounds on January 30, 1865.[158] His was the second death in the Frank family in less than a year. His father, Robert Frank, had enlisted in the army on January 1, 1864 at the age of fifty-two and "while he was in the service in the line of his duty, March 16, 1864, performing duty as a Sentinel on

Guard, at Rikers' Island, N.Y. he fell from the warf [sic] into the East River and before aid could be obtained he was drowned."[159]

Richard Burke (Company G) of Ridgeway, Orleans County, New York suffered the amputation of his right hand at the wrist from a "solid shot … received in the line of duty at Deep Bottom, Va., Sept. 29th 1864." His disability was described as "total" and he was discharged from General Hospital Central Park, New York City on June 5th 1865.[160] Private Burke returned to Orleans County and in the 1865 census was listed as a boarder in the household headed by Richard Hawkins, a saloon keeper. Burke married Alice J., a daughter of Richard and Caroline Hawkins about 1866 and they had two daughters Carrie L. and Alice Jane.[161] The Hawkins family was very familiar to the toll the war inflicted on soldiers, having four sons serve in the army. Alice's brother, Isaac, was taken prisoner at the Battle Olustee, while serving with the 54th Massachusetts Regiment.

Samuel Dennis, of Company G, enlisted on August 5, 1863 in Rochester, New York after agreeing to serve as a substitute for William Johnson, a resident of that city. Private Dennis was wounded slightly in the Battle of Olustee but would not be so fortunate at the Battle of Chapin's Farm. A "gunshot wound of left side, penetrating the left lung, received in action at Petersburg Sep 30, 1864" resulted in his discharge from the army on January 7, 1865 with a disability assessed at "three-fourths."[162]

Private William Brooks, of Company B, was also a substitute, serving in place of Daniel Dorsey. William was only nineteen years old at the time of his enlistment on September 8, 1863 and required the permission of a parent or guardian. Francis J. Bailey, a barber living in Elmira, New York signed the document stating that as guardian he gave his "full consent

106

that he may enlist as a substitute in the army of the United States for the term of three years." According the Company Muster Roll, Brooks was still in the hospital at Fort Monroe, Virginia when the regiment was mustered out on November 10, 1865. There is no record that he ever applied for or received a pension. In 1901 his mother Hannah Lodine made an application for a pension but did not receive a certificate.

Another young man from Elmira was also among those wounded at Chapin's Farm. James Marshall, a twenty-two-year-old laborer, was drafted on July 20, 1863 and was mustered into Company G on November 3rd. Private Marshall did not leave Camp William Penn with the regiment, being sick in the hospital. He was able to rejoin his fellow soldiers by May. He was back in the hospital due to wounds received on September 29th and was still in the hospital more than a year later when the regiment was mustered out in November 1865.

Forty-five-year-old James Butler (Company G) of Throop, Cayuga County, New York had returned to duty after a month in the hospital, only four days before the start of the Battle of Chapin's Farm. Butler was wounded on September 30th, but apparently only slightly as he was not listed as absent on the muster roll of September and October 1864. However, he was charged with "straggling" and found guilty at a court martial conducted on October 8, 1864. His punishment was the forfeiture of one month's pay. One can only wonder if his straggling resulted from his being ill or was he just reluctant to put himself in harm's way, since he had also been wounded at Olustee. On December 29, 1864 James Butler died in quarters of illness so it is obvious that his health had been sorely compromised during his time in the army. His widow, Mary, applied for and received a pension in 1865.[163]

The action around Petersburg and Richmond did not slow-down in October 1864. On the 7th William Woodlin wrote that "The Rebs made an attack on the right but were repulsed at every point ... the signals are established along the entire line from right to left. Everything is working favorable to us..." [164] During the following week both armies waited in anticipation of another confrontation. It finally came on October 13th. Thomas Morris Chester wrote to his newspaper the next day:

The quiet of the past few days was broken yesterday morning by an advance of the 10th Corps, under General Terry ... It was a grand reconnaissance in force to develop the enemy's new line of works between the Charles City and New Market roads.[165]

William P. Woodlin wrote in his diary that:

we had hot work as stretcher-bearers the Regt lost 29 men in killed & wounded among them four officers. We fell back just before night ... the whole thing was only a faint [sic] to keep the Rebs from reinforcing near Petersburg, where the firing was heavy ..."[166]

The engagement, known as the Battle of Darbytown Road, meant death for one of the men from Western New York. Corporal Dwight Jupiter (Company B) of Geneva, New York was "killed in action October 13, 1864." [167] The son of Moses and Mary Jane (Jupiter) Ray, Dwight had been raised by his maternal grandparents after the death of his mother about 1852, adopting the Jupiter surname as his own. His Aunt Harriet (Jupiter) Foster would name her only son George Harvey Dwight to honor her brother Harvey Jupiter who died in New Orleans on May 2, 1864 while a soldier in the 20th USCT and her nephew Dwight who died just four months later.[168] This was indeed a cruel war for the families left behind.

There was one more troop movement facing the 8th USCT in October at Fair Oaks, Virginia – an attempt to hold the Confederates in position north of the James River while other Union troops were advancing on the South Side Railroad. The ranks of the Western New York men were fortunate in that there were none killed or wounded during this engagement. On December 3, 1864, the 8th USCT was assigned to the Second Brigade of the Second Division in the newly created Twenty-Fifth Army Corps, commanded by Major General Godfrey Weitzel. The Twenty-Fifth was made up of all black troops, included 32 regiments of infantry, one regiment of cavalry and artillery of 56 guns with a total strength of over 13,500 men. The 8th remained in place as part of the Army of the James and continued to take part in the siege of Petersburg and Richmond, bottling up the Army of Northern Virginia.

The soldiers on each side of the conflict were forced to wait and hope that the war would end soon. General Ulysses S. Grant wrote in his memoirs about his fears during March 1865:

One of the most anxious periods of my experience during the rebellion was the last few weeks before Petersburg. I felt that the situation of the Confederate army was such that they would try to make an escape at the earliest practicable moment, and I was afraid, every morning, that I would awake from my sleep to hear that Lee had gone, and that nothing was left but a picket line. ...I was led to this fear by the fact that I could not see how it was possible for the Confederates to hold out much longer where they were. ... I was naturally very impatient for the time to come when I could commence the spring campaign, which I thoroughly believed would close the war.[169]

On March 28, 1865 the spring campaign began in earnest. The 8th USCT participated in the engagement at Hatcher's Run, designed to put the Federal forces in position to take control of the South Side and Danville Railroads. With the fall of Petersburg on April 2nd, the regiment was among the first to enter that city. From Petersburg the unit joined in pursuit of the Army of Northern Virginia culminating in the surrender of General Robert E. Lee to General Ulysses S. Grant on April 9th at Appomattox Court House. Returning to Petersburg from Appomattox on April 11th, the 8th was part of the occupying army through the end of May.

Even with the momentous end of the war at hand, some members of the 8th USCT were contemplating the next phase of the struggle for the African Americans. In the midst of the final push from Petersburg to Appomattox, William P. Woodlin orchestrated the collection of funds from his fellow comrades for the support of Wilberforce University. In a letter dated April 28, 1865, Private Woodlin wrote to the Rev. James A. Shorter, a member of the Trustees of Wilberforce University the following:

> *The appeal of the Trustees of the Wilberforce University for aid, in the columns of the Recorder, suggested the idea to a friend of our race, of the following collection; and I, as the agent, am happy to state that the men of the regiment, representing at least ten different States, have responded to my solicitations with the alacrity, and I am enabled to present you, as the result of my labors, the sum of $241, which, it too late for a redemption fund, we desire it to be placed in the endowment. The great changes which are now so rapidly moulding [sic] the public mind, have brought us to realize the necessity of intellectual improvement to a much greater degree than ever before. We wish, therefore, to show our interest practically now, so that in days to come posterity may enjoy it. It may be of some interest to you to know that this money was*

collected on the march after General Lee, from Petersburg to Appomattox Court-house, and some of it the day after his surrender...[170]

Forty-four soldiers signed their names to the petition which stated that as representatives of the 8th USCT they wished to "show our appreciation of the great opening now presented for forwarding the educational interests of our race" and identifying the cause as "a fitting object for our support, and one that will yield returns long after the things of to-day have passed away."[171] Twelve of the donors were men from Western New York. In addition to a $5.00 donation by William Woodlin were donations from Gerrit S. Russell and Thomas Skank, Co. B.; Glenalvin Brown, James H. Smith, John Waller, John Coy, William W. Smith, John Thomas, Thomas Bonner, Henry Murray, and George Butler, all of Company G.

As early as May the great army amassed to fight the Confederacy was being disbanded, but the fate of the 8th USCT and other African American regiments was still under consideration by the government. Oliver W. Norton wrote to his sister on May 7, 1865 what was being bandied about camp concerning the troops:

There are rumors already looking to the final disposition of the colored troops that I expected to be made. They will not be discharged till Congress has made some provision to incorporate a portion of them into the regular army. The men are to be re-enlisted, those who choose to do so... There are to be no more "U.S.C.T." but "U.S.A."[172]

The men of the 8th USCT would be no different than other soldiers in hoping that they would soon return home to their families now that the war was over, but within that month the Twenty-Fifth Army Corps, including the 8th USCT, was ordered to garrison duty in southern Texas. The regiment left City

Point, Va. on May 24, 1865 and traveled to Hampton Roads before boarding larger vessels. After a brief stopover at Mobile, the troops sailed across the Gulf of Mexico to Brazos de Santiago, Texas, arriving on Tuesday June 13th. The disembarkation of the regiment proved to be very dangerous as reported by Oliver W. Norton in letters to his father dated June 15, 1865:

> *Our trip across the Gulf had nothing of interest till on Tuesday morning we sighted land, the Isla dell Padre, and at 9 o'clock anchored off Brazos. There are only nine feet of water on the bar, and as our ship draws nineteen, we could not get over and it has been too rough to transfer the men to a lighter till to-day, when we got them off on a schooner, though it was a perilous job. I expected to see at least one or two drowned, but they all got off in safety.*[173]

On June 27th Norton provided additional details of the arrival in Brazos in a letter to his sister:

> *At the mouth of the strait is a bar and a very dangerous one too. There is only about seven feet of water and the breakers roar and tumble over it so that at most times a small boat could not live ten minutes. The ships anchor outside and are unloaded by littler sloops called lighters ... our regiment was ship-wrecked when they came ashore...*[174]

The 8th USCT remained in Texas almost five months and was mustered out in Brownsville, Texas on November 10, 1865. The regiment traveled from Texas to New Orleans, arriving in Philadelphia on December 3, 1865 where the final muster-out ceremony took place on December 12th. There were at least two more deaths and a probable third among the men from Western New York while the regiment was stationed in Texas.

Corporal Thomas Brown of Company B enlisted in the army and may have been a substitute. Born in Maryland about 1838, Corporal Brown was living in Conquest, Cayuga County at the time of his enlistment. The Company Muster-out Roll indicated that Brown had been "absent sick in Genl Hosp., at Mobile, Ala., since June 30/65." After that the army appears to have lost track of him. In 1867 the Adjutant General's Office wrote that he had "Died either at Mobile, Ala., or in Gen'l Hospt'l New Orleans."

The Surgeon General's Office had identified two men with the name of Thomas Brown who died the summer of 1865. One was Corporal Thomas Brown, Co. C, 20th USCT died in New Orleans, La, on July 13th, 1865. The information on this soldier appears fairly conclusive that he was not Thomas Brown of the 8th USCT. The other soldier was identified as Private Thomas Brown, Co. C, 100th USCT, who died on September 7, 1865 in Mobile, Alabama. Cause of death was "exhaustion from Sepperation [sic] of Knee Joint." A check of records for the 100th USCT do not include any soldier named Thomas Brown. It seems likely that the Thomas Brown who died in Mobile on September 7th was really Thomas Brown of the 8th USCT.[175]

The records of the Post Hospital, located at Ringgold Barracks, Texas, include the death from typhoid fever on September 10, 1865 of a man they identified as Levi Dennis, Co. G., 8th USCT. There was no Levi Dennis in the 8th USCT, but there was a Dennis Low in Co. G. who did die on September 10, 1865 at that same place. Record keeping seems to have gotten a bit lax after the end of the war. Dennis Low was survived by his wife, Susan, who lived in Elmira, Chemung County, New York. The couple was married on October 28, 1862 in Elmira and had no children at the time of the soldier's death. Dennis Low had made it through all the battles faced by the 8th USCT with no injuries, but he could not defeat the disease that took his life.[176]

The Company Muster-Out roll for Elijah Gregor of Company B stated that he was "sick in Genl Hosp., at New Orleans, La." on November 10, 1865 and that no discharge was furnished. Private Gregor, who had been serving on detached duty as a sharpshooter with the second division of the Twenty-Fifth Army Corps beginning in February 1864, appeared on the Detachment Muster Roll for July and August 1865 with a notation that he had been sent to the General Hospital at Brazos Santiago on July 11, 1865. Waiting at home for him was his wife, Harriet, and a son, Myron, who was only six weeks old when the soldier left for Camp William Penn in September 1863.

On December 2, 1865 Harriet Gregor started the process of applying for a widow's pension, stating that her husband died in New Orleans on or about September 1, 1865 of disease. Three years went by and Mrs. Gregor received no pension and attempted once again to put forth her claim as the widow of a deceased soldier. On August 3, 1869, the Surgeon General's Office wrote that Elijah Gregory [sic] was admitted to the hospital in New Orleans on August 5, 1865, suffering from scurvy and that he had "deserted Sept. 16.65." Further remarks state that "the death records of this office furnish no evidence in this case." Harriet Gregor tried again in 1874 to secure a pension, but once again was rebuffed. Did Elijah Gregor desert while a patient at the hospital or did he die as Harriet must have been told "on or about September 1, 1865?" What seems strange is that the file contains no indication that any attempt was made to contact fellow soldiers of Company B. Sergeant Charles H. Cooper, of Sodus, New York was from the same hometown as Elijah Gregor and he may have been the source of the approximate death date for Private Gregor. Perhaps the answer lies in his status as "on detached duty" and a report of his death simply failed to reach the right people.[177]

When the final muster-out occurred there had been a total of 19 deaths within the ranks of the soldiers from Western New York that served in the 8th USCT. Four fell at the Battle of Olustee; three died before Petersburg; three died of wounds received; and nine died of disease. What happened to those that survived is also part of the story that should to be told.

Coming Home

Among those from Western New York were four who served together as musicians in the 8th USCT. Members of a regimental band played important roles in the life of the soldier. The men awoke to the blare of a bugle and the beat of drums ended each day. Buglers, drummers and fifers set the beat for marching and assisted in military communications during battle. The band, performing during dress parades and inspections, was a source of pride for the entire regiment. Entertaining at serenades and evening events the band members brought together men to sing and enjoy a moment of rest and relaxation.

Colonel Charles W. Fribley, commander of the 8th USCT, recognized the value of a regimental band and shortly after his appointment to lead the regiment he set out to locate potential musicians and raise funds to purchase instruments for the band. On December 10, 1863, William Woodlin, wrote in his diary that "the Brass Instruments having come I was taken in for one of them." The next day Woodlin and his fellow band members "went over the the school room and practiced on our instruments." By December 28th, the musicians "played Yankee Doodle for the first time ... it went off well. We practiced for 6 hours on nothin else all day." The band made its first appearance at a dress parade on January 8, 1864 and played both "Yankee Doodle" and "John Brown" and according to Woodlin, "It went off well."[178] Over the next few months,

Woodlin's diary chronicles the growing repertoire of songs the band had learned and how the band members also served as ambulance drivers and stretcher bearers.

In a letter written by Sgt. Rufus Sibb Jones to the*The Christian Recorder*, dated April 16, 1864, he commented about the band:

> *Captain Anderson (instructor of the band), of Philadelphia is with the regiment, and gives his undivided attention having already taught it some twenty pieces of music. The band is highly prized being the only one belonging to a colored regiment, except the 55th Mass. in the department*[179]

In addition to Willam P. Woodlin, the regimental band included Orange C. Thompson and Gerrit Smith Russell of Madison County; and Glenalvin Brown of Geneva, New York – all members of Company B. Thompson would have been considered the "old-timer" of the group at twenty-seven-years old and married with two children. The other three musicians were single and between twenty and twenty-two years old. All but Thompson were either born into slavery or their parents were former slaves.

Twenty-two-year old William P. Woodlin was born a slave on the Forlorn Hope Plantation, located in St. Martin's Parish, Louisiana. John Palfrey, owner of the plantation, died in 1843 leaving an estate which included extensive land holdings and over forty slaves. His son, John Gorham Palfrey, a Unitarian clergyman in Boston, insisted his share would be made up from the slaves, whom he intended to grant "unconditional emancipation." In different accounts the actual number of slaves freed by Mr. Palfrey varies from sixteen to forty. What is not in dispute is that the Rev. Palfrey arranged for passage of a number of former slaves to Massachusetts and found homes and employment for them in the North. In 1850, four children named Woodlin, born in Louisiana and aged between nine and seventeen years, were living separately in Quaker households, located in Ledyard Cayuga County, Farmington, Ontario County and Macedon, Wayne County, New York.[180]

The full story of Mr. Woodlin's life after he left the army is still incomplete, but it is known that he married Emeline J. Freeman, of New York State, about 1866. The couple was living in Michigan when their daughter Alice was born in 1867. There were at least four more children born to the couple before 1880, when they were living in Battle Creek, Michigan. In September 1889, William P. Woodlin placed an advertisement in the *Advent Review and Sabbath Herald*, a Seventh Day Adventist publication, looking for a position as a teacher in a school, located in the southwestern states, explaining that he was a "middle-aged man, competent to teach the grammar grades" and that he had some teaching experience in Tennessee.[181] He directed correspondence to his home address in Battle Creek, Michigan. There is no indication that he secured a job as a teacher, but the 1900 census finds Mr. Woodlin in Bowling Green, Kentucky, widowed, working as Missionary and boarding with Leonidas Webb. A year later, Brother Woodlin was described as a "self-supporting missionary" within the Tennessee River Conference of the Seventh Day Adventists.[182]

On August 31, 1863 Orange C. Thompson and Gerrit S. Russell, both residents of Madison County, New York, enlisted at Oswego, New York. Within a month the two men were mustered into Company B of the 8th USCT. Orange C. Thompson, son of Thomas and Mary (Charles) Thompson, was born in Peterboro, Madison County about 1836. He married Catherine J. Vanderpool about 1859 and the couple, along with their infant daughter Mary O'Della, was living in Madison County in 1860. By the time Private Thompson was drafted into the army, a second child, George, had joined the family. It is not stated what instrument Thompson played, but in a letter dated March 14, 1865 that appeared in the *Weekly Anglo-African*, the writer described a grand review of the Twenty-Fifth Army Corps, pointing out that "the music (brass bands) was furnished from the heroes of Olustee, the 8th U.S. Colored Troops, Orange C. Thompson, leader ..." In June 1865 he was elevated to rank of Principal Musician, holding that position until September 16th, when he plead guilty of "disorderly conduct to the prejudice of good order". His punishment was reduction in rank to private and forfeiture of ten dollars of his monthly pay.[183]

The life of Orange Thompson after the war took a very different track from any of his fellow musicians. He did not return north, but instead settled in Louisiana. He stated in his pension file that he began living in New Orleans in November 1866 and between then and 1902 lived in Baton Rouge, Plaquemine, Assumption, Iberia and St. May, before settling in in St. Martin's Parish, the same area where William P. Woodlin was born in 1841. He worked as a swamper, farm laborer and cook during those years. He left out the fact that he had served five years in the Louisiana State Penitentiary between 1867 and 1871. In 1889 he married Emma Carlin. The 1900 Census recorded Orange Thompson as head of household in Ward 1, Saint Martin Parish, Louisiana, putting his birth as November 1831.

Two years later Mr. Thompson was dead, shot twice by Frank Hidalgo on Ruth Plantation in St. Martin's Parish, on June 12, 1902. Mr. Hidalgo, overseer of the plantation, was charged with the death and released on a bond of $3,000. Hidalgo was able to hire six lawyers for the trial held in September and the outcome was very predictable. He was found "Not Guilty" by a jury of his peers. In 1907 Emma Carlin Thompson, began the pension application process, which was rejected. A poignant letter in the pension file, dated March 22, 1906, addressed to the Pension Office reads: "Is Orange Charles Thompson on the Rolls. If so whear is he living. If Dead whear did he Die." The letter was signed by Miss Mary O'Della Thompson, of Norwich, Chenango County, New York.[184]

The noted abolitionist Gerrit Smith of Peterboro, New York played a major role in the life of our next musician, Gerrit S. Russell. In 1841 Mr. Smith negotiated the purchase of Samuel and Harriet Russell, along with their children, then living in Kentucky. Harriet Russell had once been enslaved by the family of Ann Fitzhugh Smith, wife of Gerrit Smith. At the urging of Mrs. Smith, her husband secured the freedom of the Russell family and relocated them to Peterboro, Madison County, New York. In 1842 the Russell family welcomed their first child, born outside of slavery. Mr. Smith suggested the name of "Freeborn" for the son, but his parents named him, Gerrit Smith Russell, to honor their benefactor.

Gerrit S. Russell was mustered into Company B as Corporal on September 25, 1863. On joining the band, he was reduced in rank to a private. Russell was elevated to Principal Musician and Fife Major on May 1, 1865, joining the regiment's non-commissioned staff. According to his obituary, Mr. Russell "was a fifer of well-known ability and his services were in frequent demand." After the war Russell married and settled in Clinton, Oneida County, where he was employed for many years by Hamilton College professor Oren Root, father of Elihu Root, Secretary of State under President Theodore Roosevelt. Gerrit S. Russell died in November 1906 and members of the G.A.R. Hinckly Post, 227, attended the funeral as a body. He was buried at his old home in Peterboro.[185]

The fourth band member from Western New York was Glenalvin "Glen" Brown, son of William T. and Frances S. Brown. The twenty-one-year-old was born in Maryland and came north to Geneva, New York with his family about 1850. His father had purchased his own freedom in the early 1830s, married and started a family before leaving Hagerstown, Maryland. The move may have been prompted by the passage of the Fugitive Slave Law of 1850. Although he, his wife and children were all free at the time, there was the fear that there was no protection from unscrupulous "slave catchers" who were known to kidnap persons of color and claim them as runaway slaves.[186]

In the early fall of 1863, Glen Brown traveled to Camp William Penn to join the 8th USCT. Private Brown was described as a small person, being under five feet, three inches tall, with a dark complexion. His occupation was given as teamster, which meant he most likely worked for his father, who was listed in census records as a hackman. Brown's overall military record was mostly spotless, but there is a notation regarding absence of "Drummer Brown" without leave between December 30, 1863 through January 2, 1864. He apparently returned to duty as no further action was taken by authorities.[187]

After he left the army, Glen Brown resided with his parents on Castle Street in the village of Geneva, where he continued to work with his father. With the death of his father in 1874, Brown became the main breadwinner for his mother and sister, Louise, who still lived at home. According to his pension application, his ability to care for his family was compromised as a result of illness contracted while in the service. He claimed to have had a severe cold and fever while at Camp William Penn and again when his unit was in Florida. The July and August 1864 Company Muster Roll indicated he was "absent" and had been "sent to the rear sick August 13/64." According Dr. M. H. Picot, who treated him before and after the war, his patient suffered from catarrh which "has affected his general constitution very severely, and he is totally disabled for manual labor and only able to do light errands." Other depositions recall his coughing fits and difficulty breathing at times. Glen Brown died on May 30, 1892 in Geneva, New York. His obituary reported that on the day of his death he was at the rail station when he was taken with an "epileptic fit" and taken to his home on Castle street, where he died shortly after noon.[188]

No photo has been located of the 8th USCT Regimental Band. Above is segment of a photo of the 107th USCT, taken in 1865. Library of Congress.

Advertisement promoting enlistment in the 14th Rhode Island Regiment, Heavy Artillery, appeared in the *New-York Daily Reformer*, Watertown, New York on September 19, 1863. David H. Ray, Sr. is identified as "General Enrolling Officer," assisted by Sergt. H. I. (Henry Isaac) Lee.

Rhode Island Recruits in Western New York

Rhode Island's Governor William Sprague had received permission to raise a regiment of black soldiers in January 1863, but it was not until mid-June of 1863 that the Rhode Island Adjutant-General's Office issued orders to raise a company of heavy artillery. The response was good enough that permission to raise a second company was granted on August 14th and finally a call for a full regiment was issued on September 9th to be called the 14th Rhode Island Heavy Artillery.* Statistics from the 1860 United States census records put the total black male population of Rhode Island between the ages of 15 and 40 at less than 800 persons.[189] It is therefore obvious that, as in the case of Massachusetts, recruitment efforts would need to reach well beyond the borders of Rhode Island.

When Massachusetts had recruited for the 54th and 55th Massachusetts, they had relied heavily on black leaders as far away as Ohio to encourage enlistment. This was also partly the case in recruitment for the 14th Rhode Island Heavy Artillery. David H. Ray, Sr. of Palmyra, New York was one of those recruiters who played a significant role in upstate New York. Yet there was a difference in the manner Rhode Island handled its recruitment which set it apart and brought approbation upon the head recruiter, Major James C. Engley. Most of the recruits for the 14th Rhode Island regiment were funneled through one office in Providence, headed by Major Engley. An unusual series of orders issued by Rhode Island's Governor James Y. Smith allowed Engley to take control of all

---

* *The 14th Rhode Island Regiment Heavy Artillery underwent several name changes. In July 1864, the regiment became the 8th United States Colored Artillery (Heavy); on August 28, 1864, it was renamed the 11th United States Colored Artillery (Heavy). For purposes of this book it will be referred to as the 14th Rhode Island Regiment of Heavy Artillery.*

recruitment efforts for the 14th Rhode Island. An elaborate (and confusing) system of agents and sub-agents, both black and white, quickly developed and spread into New York, Ohio, New Jersey, Pennsylvania, and beyond. The state government authorized a bounty of $300 for each soldier that was enlisted and mustered into the service. Recruiters were to receive a "head fee" of $10 to $12 for each soldier brought into the regiment.

In August of 1863, Hugh B. Brown of Orange, New Jersey secured from Major Engley recruitment "rights" to Central New York, a region that stretched from Utica west to the Rochester area. David H. Ray, Sr., a black barber from Palmyra, New York, became the head-agent for Mr. Brown and began recruiting aggressively for the 14th Rhode Island Regiment of Heavy Artillery.[190] Ray is said to have received the rank of 1st Lieutenant in Co. C, but there is no record of his actual enlistment or of his ever having served in any capacity as a soldier.[191] Since only white men could be "officers" in black units, it is unlikely that his rank was official, yet would very likely prove to be a good recruiting tool.

David H. Ray, Sr. was well-prepared for his role as recruiting officer in central and western New York. While there were larger black populations in some of the upstate cities of Albany, Syracuse and Rochester, much of the population was dispersed in smaller groupings located in villages, small cities and rural areas. It was his knowledge of and connections to the African American communities in the smaller urban centers that would be an important element in his success as recruiter.

Mr. Ray had lived what might be described as a nomadic life for over 30 years, plying his trade as a master barber throughout upstate New York. He grew up in the vicinity of the village of Geneva, New York, located on the north shore of Seneca Lake. He appears to have spent a few years in

Schenectady, New York in the early 1830s, but by April 1835 he was back in Geneva, operating a barber shop located "just two doors down from the post office."[192] Two years later, he moved his business to Canandaigua, another small community, located about 20 miles to the west of Geneva.[193] Both Geneva and Canandaigua had small black communities, which included many former slaves brought to the area by some of the early white settlers. By 1843 Ray had relocated his family and business to the fast-growing city of Rochester, New York. In 1850 David Ray moved once again. This time he traveled to Watertown, New York, a manufacturing center with about 7,000 residents located about 70 miles north of Syracuse. Between 1855 and 1859 he pulled up stakes for Gouverneur, New York, a village in the foothills of the Adirondacks midway between Watertown and Ogdensburg, a major crossing point into Canada for the Underground Railroad. Sometime in May of 1863 Ray moved his family for the last time.[194] He returned closer to his roots and settled in Palmyra, New York, a small village on the banks of the Erie Canal about 15 miles north of Canandaigua and 25 miles east of Rochester.

Wherever Ray lived he became an integral part of the African American community. In addition, he built a network of contacts in the larger community of black activists through participation a myriad of meetings and conventions aimed at improving the condition of the black residents of New York State. Yet it was probably the brotherhood of the black barbers that would prove to be Ray's biggest asset as he began the job of recruiting for the 14th Rhode Island Regiment.

African Americans held a prominent place in the barber trade in New York during the mid-1800s. Many villages and cities in Western New York supported at least one black barber and their clientele was not fellow black residents, but the white community. There was no official trade association for black barbers, but there was connectivity among these independent business men and their families that produced strong affiliations that linked generations both socially and economically. Children of barbers married children of barbers. In addition to training their own sons, barbers trained their nephews, cousins, sons of friends and of other barbers. The journeyman barber carried his tools and trekked the highways in search of temporary work with other barbers. Since barbers often held positions of leadership in the black communities, they would have been an invaluable conduit for David H. Ray to spread the word and solicit recruits.

From his headquarters in Palmyra, New York, Ray began the work of reaching into his extensive network of friends and associates. Flyers provided by Hugh B. Brown were distributed throughout central and western New York, promoting the fact that each recruit would receive a bounty of $250.[195] On September 19th an advertisement with the headline of "COLORED MEN, TO ARMS: Your Opportunity has at length Come" appeared in the *New-York Daily Reformer*, a newspaper in Watertown, New York. David H. Ray, Sr. was identified as a General Enrolling Officer for the Rhode Island Brigade with an assistant, Sergt. H. I. Lee. The ad assured the potential recruits that "the Government is pledged that the Pay, Bounty and Protection of the Colored Soldiers shall be the same as that now given to the white troops."[196] Those interested could find more information at the Enrolling Office in Palmyra.

On October 3rd, the Watertown newspaper reported that "Lieut. Ray left this place last evening with 10 men recruited in this section, to join the Brigade of colored troops in Rhode Island."[197] On the October 6th and 8th, six men from the Watertown area enlisted in the 14th Rhode Island. They included two barbers, a laborer, a farmer, a boatman and a maltster, aged 18 to 31 years old. Later that month an additional three men from Watertown were in Providence for enlistment ceremonies.

Mr. Ray traveled to Providence with recruits on at least two more occasions. In December of 1865, David H. Ray, Sr. provided a deposition in support of the pension application of Lydia Bogart, mother of George Washington Bogart, who had died on July 7, 1864 at Camp Parapet, Louisiana. Ray stated that he "was First Lieut. Co. C. 14th Rhode Island Heavy Artillery Vol. in the year 1863 and recruiting officer" and that he enlisted George Washington, son of Lydia Bogart, at Palmyra, Wayne County, New York and "took said George Washington to Providence, Rhode Island."[198] Bogart enlisted in Providence on December 9, 1863. Bogart may have been part of a larger group being escorted to Providence by Mr. Ray. On Saturday, December 5th fourteen enlistments were recorded for men from Western New York – five from Geneva, three from Schroeppel in Oswego County, one each from Auburn, Oswego, Waterloo, Corning, Vernon in Oneida County, and Sullivan in Madison County. Ray was also in Providence just before Christmas when three men from Wayne County, two from Genesee County and one from Orleans County enlisted.[199]

Between early September and late January more than 125 men made the trip from Western New York to Providence to enlist in the 14th Rhode Island Regiment. There is only one enlistment record found that included the name of D. H. Ray as recruiting officer. Henry Fields of Albion, New York, enlisted on December 23, 1863 with "D. H. Ray Sen" identified as witness to Field's signature in the Declaration of Recruit. In addition, the name "D. H. Ray" appears next to the title of Recruiting Officer.[200] It is likely that a large number of recruits from Western New York passed through the hands of David H. Ray, Sr., but since in the vast majority of enlistment records Major J. C. Engley was identified as the enlisting officer, it is difficult to determine the exact number of men who were first enrolled by Mr. Ray or were taken to Providence by him. What can be established is that forty of the enlistees were residents of villages that had been home to David H. Ray at some time between 1835 and 1863. Another seventeen men were from communities within the counties where these villages were located. And an additional seven soldiers were barbers by occupation, living in villages located on the Erie Canal.

The regiment was almost at full strength by the end of December 1863, although there were a few more men from Western New York who arrived in January and into early February of 1864. With recruitment winding down, officials in Rhode Island were beginning to become aware of serious allegations surrounding the practices of Major J. C. Engley, the chief recruiter of the 14th. The legislature of the State of Rhode Island had authorized the payment of a $300 bounty for each recruit and agreed to pay a recruiter between $10 and $12 for each man enlisted. What would seem to be a fairly straightforward contract between the State and the recruit and its recruiting agents became anything but straightforward.

The payment system for the recruitment in Rhode Island was seriously flawed and it is therefore impossible to determine what was paid to recruiters such as Mr. Ray for their efforts. Again, the official recruiter was identified as Major Engley and he was also the conduit for all money paid out by the Paymaster General, Colonel J. N. Francis. Since Mr. Ray was a sub-agent of Engley's agent, it seems likely that his share was minimal at best.

It is also difficult to sort out which recruits received all or any part of the promised bounties. Initially the recruits were promised a bounty of $300. In September Governor Smith authorized payment to Engley of $50 from each bounty. The ad placed by David Ray, Sr. in the Watertown newspaper reflected the reduction in bounty from $300 to $250. In the same order Engley was authorized to receive an amount of up to $25 "upon orders of the recruits." This appears to be part of a scheme developed by Engley to sell such things a watches and gloves to the recruits and then have the recruits sign off the cost to be paid to Engley from their bounty. It was reported that the goods sold were of shoddy quality and the prices very inflated. Many recruits claimed to have not purchased anything, yet their bounties had been reduced to reflect their having done so.

In October, the Governor issued an order authorizing the Paymaster General to pay Engley an additional $25 from the bounty of each recruit without any order from the recruits. Orders in November and December continued to whittle away the bounties for the recruits of the 14th Rhode Island. To add injury to insult, recruits considered to be "contrabands" (former slaves who had escaped to Union lines) were only to be paid $50 bounty and the remaining $250 was to be paid to Engley. In fact, when all the orders were assembled, it was possible that the entire amount of the bounty could be paid to Engley, with nothing going to a recruit.

The recruitment and financial practices of Engley were under investigation as early as January 1864 and came to a head in January of 1865 with completion of a report by the Finance Committee of the House of Representatives. Investigators assembled voluminous documentation, but no legal action was taken nor was any restitution made to recruits who had not received the promised bounty. The committee did conclude that:

Taking into consideration the treatment of these men by the State officials as that treatment is disclosed in the evidence before the committee, and how the men who were about to hazard their lives in defence [sic] of the State of the country, were wronged in proportion as they were without the means of asserting their rights; and how poor ignorant contraband, who had

just broken the bonds of slavery to enlist in the army
of the Union, in defence [sic] of his new-born liberty,
should be taken by the sanction of any citizen of the
State, to gratify the propensities on any recruiting
officer, present a state of things which is a source of
regret to your Committee, and should be to every
person who has any regard for the honor of the State.[201]

The committee took particular exception to paying recruits identified as contrabands only one sixth of the bounty and allowing the recruiting officer to the remaining five-sixths of the bounty. The report stated that this "policy indicates a disposition to oppress a class of citizens in proportion as they are without the means of resisting oppression."[202]

The shady dealings of Major Engley do not detract from the important role that David H. Ray, Sr. appears to have played in the recruitment of men for the 14th Rhode Island Regiment of Heavy Artillery. Nor do they reflect on the men who served in the regiment. Yet they are an important piece of the history of the 14th Rhode Island Regiment. What follows is a closer look at the men from Western New York who served in the 14th and participated in what for many soldiers was the defining event of their lives.

Who Were the Recruits?

More than 130 men from Western New York have been identified as members of the 14th Rhode Island Heavy Artillery Regiment, ranging in age from 15 to 55 years old. The official records place the average age at 24 years, but it appears that there were several instances where the ages on the enlistment records were either inflated or deflated to conform to minimum age of eighteen and maximum age of forty-five.

Two of the youngest recruits were brothers Richard and George H. Champlin of Brownsville, Jefferson County, New York, who both claimed to be 18 years old on their enlistment papers. In reality Richard had celebrated his 16th birthday less than three months before enlistment and George would not be 15 years old for another four months. George joined on October 30, 1863 and his brother followed him into the service on November 16th. The boys were the children of Richard and Eliza Champlin and were both born in Jefferson County, New York.[203] A third youngster was 15-year-old James Fowler Henry from Bath, New York. He joined on the 8th of December, one month after his 43-year-old father, Richard "Theodore" Henry, had enlisted. Unfortunately, James did not return home to live out his life. He died from diarrhea on August 7, 1864 at the Corps D'Afrique General Hospital in New Orleans.[204]

The four oldest recruits from Western New York were Jacob W. Redder (also Reader) of Bath, Steuben County, New York, Prime Cortright, of Huron, Wayne County, New York, Thomas A. Wycoff, of Norwich, Chenango County, New York, and Roderick S. Fletcher of Canandaigua, Ontario County, New York. Jacob W. Redder claimed to be only 39 years old at enlistment, but he was just two months shy of his 56th birthday in November 1863. Cortright and Wycoff were both closer to the age of 55 years old, while their papers gave their ages as 45 and 42 respectively.

Private Cortright joined with two of his sons, John Wesley and George Whitfield, in being mustered into Company M. Private Wycoff was married with at least six minor children at home in Norwich. Roderick S. Fletcher shaved only five years off his age when he listed his age as forty-three with the recruiting officer. The 48-year-old soldier joined Company L on February 4, 1863. While Prime Cortright survived his time in the army, Redder, Wycoff and Fletcher all died of disease. Redder contracted small pox and died at the Corps D'Afrique

Hospital in New Orleans on 30 April 1864.[205] Private Fletcher died July 1, 1864 while at Camp Parapet in Louisiana - after only four months in the army.[206] Thomas Wycoff died of consumption at Plaquemine on November 12, 1864.[207]

Prime Cortright was given an early discharge on January 18, 1865, as he was deemed "unfit for duty on account of lameness caused by the kick of a mule while in the discharge of his duty as a teamster (in June 1864)."[208] Dr. Benoni Carpenter, Regimental Surgeon, examined Cortright and judged that the soldier was incapable of performing his duties because of "permanent lameness in right nee [knee] joint produced by inflammation of the joint ... This man is fifty (50) years old ... has done no active service for several months past nor is there any probability of his doing duty in future. Can earn ½ his living." Prime Cortright did not stop with fudging the truth when he apparently gave an "inflated" account of his injury as shown by the records of the Huron Town Clerk which stated Cortright "was badly wounded in a skirmish and was discharged from the army."[209] In 1879 Mr. Cortright began the process of applying for an invalid pension which was granted, giving him a pension of $2.00 per month retroactive to February 1865.[210] Prime lived 25 years after his discharge, dying in February 1890 at Sodus Point, New York.[211]

The occupations of the men from Western New York included laborers (42%), farmers (35%), and tradesmen (29%). The farmers in most cases were not landowners, but more likely rented land or worked as farm laborers. The head recruiting officer for the Western New York region, David H. Ray, Sr.., had lived in many of the communities from which these men came. In many cases, he knew their parents. His children may have been friends with many of the younger enlistees. He may have worked with some of the men who identified themselves as barbers on their enlistment papers. In fact, at least eighteen of the men from Western New York were fellow barbers.

William Lloyd Garrison Freeman, of Phelps, Ontario County, New York, was one of the barbers. Freeman, aged thirty-seven years, enlisted on October 4, 1863 and was mustered into Company G on November 4th. In August 1864 Private Freeman was promoted to the rank of Corporal, which he maintained until he was mustered out with the regiment October 2, 1865. There was nothing in his military record of note, except that he appears to have escaped many of the ills that plagued his fellow soldiers, being present for all muster rolls. After his return from the war he settled in Seneca Falls, New York where he worked as a waiter, janitor and barber at various times. He died in that city on June 20, 1894 and his obituary described him as "well known about town ... very quiet, industrious and honorable man and enjoyed the respect of all." Freeman maintained his connections to his military service by becoming an active member of Cross Post G.A.R.[212]

There were many reasons these men would enlist. The promise of a $250 bounty and a monthly wage of $13.00 per month were definitely incentives for men who were fortunate to earn $300 a year. Unfortunately, the reality for the soldiers was very different from the promise. Not only was the bounty in many cases absorbed by unscrupulous agents, but the United States government was only paying black soldiers a paltry $10 per month, with $3 of that withheld for clothing. Others may have thought of their enlistment as an adventure or even their duty. It is doubtful that most of these men could envision the hardships that they and their families would suffer over the next two years.

William Lloyd Garrison Freeman was born in Bath, Steuben County, New York about 1826. Pictured here wearing a G.A.R. badge. Photograph from collection of the Seneca County Historical Society.

14th Rhode Island Regiment Heavy Artillery Organizes

The men of the 14th Rhode Island Heavy Artillery Regiment began to arrive at Dexter Training Grounds in Providence in mid-summer of 1863. Beginning in early September they were moved gradually to Dutch Island, located at the western entrance to Narragansett Bay, to be trained and to work on construction of a fort designed to protect the Providence from possible harassment by Confederate naval ships. By the end of September, companies A, B, C, and D, designated as the First Battalion, had all been assembled on Dutch Island. As other companies were formed, they too were transported to the island in preparation for final assignments to the regular armed forces. In late December, the regiment consisted of twelve companies, divided into three battalions with a total strength of about 1,600 men.

The First Battalion received its orders to join the command of General Nathaniel P. Banks in the Department of the Gulf in late November and was ready to leave Dutch Island on December 7 for a brief stay at Dexter Training Ground. On December 19, the four companies left Providence for New Orleans, arriving there on December 30th. From there they were sent to Fort Esperanza on Matagorda Island, located about 100 miles from Galveston, Texas. Only three of the men of the First Battalion have been identified as being from Western New York – James Castles and George H. Green, both born in Rochester; and Amos A. Lunn of Palmyra.

On January 21, 1864, the Second Battalion sailed for New Orleans. The contingent included forty-four soldiers from Western New York, with one-half assigned to Company G. After a rough trip the transport arrived at its destination on February 3rd, only to be faced with quarantine because of several cases of mumps and measles among the troops. The Battalion was moved to a place about fifteen miles down-river from New

Orleans called English Turn where they remained until mid-March. The move was made to prevent the spread of illnesses but the selection of the site had the opposite effect on the troops of the Second Battalion. Nine men died during the six weeks the Battalion was encamped at English Turn. The first death of a man from Western New York occurred within Company G. Private Philip Lenison from Syracuse died on February 9, 1864 of "Putrid Sore Throat." He had joined the regiment on October 29, 1863, giving his age as 21 and birthplace as Syracuse, New York.[213] Capt. Joshua M. Addeman spoke of the conditions that the Second Battalion experienced at English Turn in his "Reminiscences of Two Years with the Colored Troops."

> *The place was decidedly unhealthy. Our men were dropping off rapidly from a species of putrid sore throat which was very prevalent. The soil was so full of moisture that we had to use the levee for a burial ground. Elsewhere a grave dug two feet deep would rapidly fill with water, and to cover a coffin decently, it was necessary that two men should stand on it, while the extemporized sextons completed their task.*[214]

Finally, in mid-March companies E, F, G and H transferred to Plaquemine, Louisiana to garrison a fort situated on the west bank of the Mississippi River, north of New Orleans.

Departure of the Third Battalion from Dutch Island was scheduled for late February, but an outbreak of small pox delayed the movement of troops. It was not until April 3rd that the men of companies I, K, L and M boarded the *America* for New Orleans. Eighty-three men from Western New York were in the battalion, but only seventy-nine were deployed. David H. Ray, Jr., son of the lead recruiter in Central New York, had deserted from Dutch Island just three days before the battalion set sail.[215] Charles F. Taylor, of Rochester, New York was assigned to Company L, but on February 23rd he deserted from Dutch Island, taking with him one Austrian rifle.[216] Benjamin Jones of Clyde, New York and George Carpenter of Schroeppel, New York were in the hospital at Portsmouth when the battalion shipped out. Jones was discharged on a surgeon's certificate of disability on April 11th and Carpenter was discharged a month later.[217]

The first death in the third Battalion was recorded while on route to New Orleans. Private Stephen L. Watkins of Canandaigua "died of apoplexy on the 12th instant [April], and was buried with military honors on the 14th, the purser reading the Church Burial Service. We committed his body to the deep, a new and solemn sight to the most of us..."[218] Private Watkins was one of the last to be mustered into Company M, having joined the company on January 25, 1864, and the first to die. He was also one of the older recruits, giving his age at the time of enlistment as forty years and his occupation as blacksmith.[219] He left behind a wife, Elizabeth, and five minor children ages five to fifteen – William H., Eliza J., Frances, Stephen Jr., and Sarah J. There is no record that Elizabeth Watkins ever applied for a widow's pension for herself or on behalf of any minor children. She moved to Rochester, New York by 1866 and remarried about 1869 to George E. Chase.[220]

Upon arrival in New Orleans, the Third Battalion was ordered to Camp Parapet at Carrolton, located about eight miles above New Orleans and part of the defense of the city. There they took up quarters on the site of a former Confederate fortification which was constructed to protect the city of New Orleans from Union troops moving south on the Mississippi. The Third Battalion remained at this place until the regiment was mustered out in October 1865. The Second Battalion was also in place at Plaquemine for the majority of its deployment in Louisiana, moving only a few miles downriver to Donaldsonville in June 1865 before joining the rest of the regiment at Camp Parapet in September of that year.

The First Battalion experienced more moves than the other battalions during its war service. In January 1864, it had been assigned to Matagorda Island in Texas. In May 1864, it was recalled and joined the Third Battalion at Camp Parapet. Its stay was brief as in July the Battalion was ordered to duty at Fort Jackson, located south of New Orleans, where it would remain until April 1865, when it was moved to Brashear City, Louisiana. In September, it rejoined the regiment at Camp Parapet in preparation for it being mustered out.

The reuniting of the three battalions and the anticipated mustering out caused much joy, yet there was a melancholy which was expressed by an officer in a letter to the *Providence Journal* dated September 16, 1865. He wrote:

No news could have been more grateful to the officers and men of this command, and it was as unexpected as it was welcome. The war is over, and there is an almost universal desire to return to the peaceful pursuits of civil life...
If spared to reach the State of which we have reason to be proud, and which we are all anxious to see, we shall have the largest regiment which has ever been seen together in Rhode Island. But even in that case it will be with decimated ranks. We have probably lost five hundred men by death and discharge. We leave many a brave comrade to moulder away in the soil of Louisiana. Some have fallen by the bullets of the enemy, but the greater portion by the terrible diseases of the climate ... Many have already returned to their homes, with constitutions shattered in the service of their country...[221]

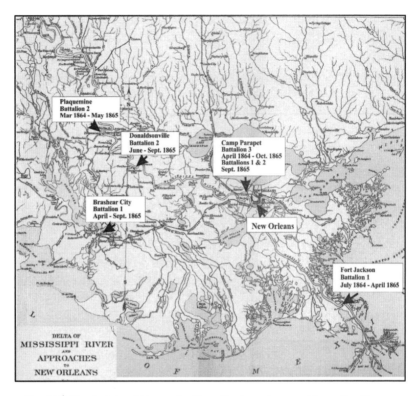

The 14th Rhode Island Heavy Artillery Regiment served its entire time in the army in the Mississippi River Delta. The above map illustrates the movements of the battalions between March 1864 and September 1865.

These men had not engaged in any of the major battles of the Civil War yet had played a vital role in maintaining federal control of the Mississippi River between Plaquemine, located south of Baton Rouge, and Fort Jackson, located where the mighty river empties into the Gulf of Mexico. Their daily life must have been monotonous (even tedious), yet they faced constant threats from regulars of the Confederate Army and guerillas supported by a population that was sympathetic to the Confederate cause.

139

This danger became reality on August 6, 1864 when pickets manned by members of Company G at Plaquemine were overrun by a band of mounted men thought to have been irregulars from Texas. Three soldiers were captured and later murdered by the rebels. It was a harsh reminder that black soldiers and their officers often faced different "rules of war" when confronted with possible capture. Twenty-two of the soldiers of Company G were from Western New York, but none were among the dead.

Camp life for the men of the 14th Rhode Island was similar to that experienced by all soldiers. There was the usual grumbling from the ranks about officers and rules. There were men who would overtly and covertly disregard the rules and regulations. Leisure time was filled with activities such as card games, gambling, drinking, and a search for women. Some would seek and receive permission to visit New Orleans on leave. Others were not so lucky but took "leave" anyway.

As pointed out in the letter to the *Providence Journal*, disease was the enemy that was the cause of the vast majority of the deaths suffered by the 14th Rhode Island Heavy Artillery. Lieutenant-Colonel Nelson Viall, commander of the 3rd Battalion, noted that on February 16th, 1865 "our entire regiment numbers 1,452, over three hundred men having died of disease. The daily sound of the dead march by the drum corps became so frequent and depressing that an order was issued to discontinue music at funerals."[222] The final death toll from illness was close to 350 men. Twenty-six of those who died were from Western New York.

On October 2, 1865, the soldiers of the 14th Rhode Island Regiment of Heavy Artillery were mustered out in New Orleans. The regiment left for New York aboard the aptly named *North Star* on October 7th for the first leg of the long journey home.

Nine days later, the troops disembarked at New York City and marched to Castle Garden where they stayed the night. The next day *The New York Times* reported:

> *No more imposing spectacle has been presented to the citizens of New York since the commencement of the return of our soldiers than was witnessed this afternoon in the march of the 11th United States (colored) heavy artillery up Broadway, preceded by a brass band of some thirty pieces and a drum corps of equal number, all colored... In overcoats, knapsacks and white gloves marched in solid column with a steadiness and regularity that drew the most enthusiastic plaudits from thousands of spectators that line each side of the street.*[223]

From New York, the regiment was taken by steamer to Portsmouth Grove, a facility used as a hospital during the war, where they were paid and disbanded. On the 21st of October, the regiment made its final appearance in the city of Providence. The men lined up for a dress parade and marched before Governor James Y. Smith and staff and hundreds of spectators. It must have been a joyous occasion, but one tempered by knowing the uncertainty of what lay ahead. The men returning to Western New York were now veterans of the war that saved the Union and ended slavery yet left their place in society uncertain.

Portsmouth Grove, Rhode Island. Library of Congress

Death and Disease

As in life, there was inequality in death for the black soldiers. In the year ending December 31, 1864 there had been only two deaths among the officers, while it was reported that 269 deaths had occurred among the enlisted men.[224] The final tally would be close to 350 enlisted men dead. One in four of African American men from Western New York, who were deployed to Louisiana with the 14th Rhode Island Heavy Artillery Regiment, did not survive the war - all but one died from disease.

The circumstances surrounding the death of Hezekiah Dixon, Jr. of Rochester, New York were very different from any others that occurred among the men from Western New York. Hezekiah was just eighteen years old when he signed his enlistment papers in Providence on December 3, 1863. He was mustered into Company M on January 25, 1864. Three months later this young man was dead. By all indicators, Hezekiah had not adjusted well to military life. About two weeks after being mustered into his company, he was charged with breaking the door to the magazine while in confinement there. It is not clear as to why he was under arrest, but the fact that almost two months elapsed between enlistment and muster may indicate that Hezekiah had been "absent without leave" and considered a deserter who had been returned to Providence and confined in the Guard House.

His unruliness did not end with the breaking of the magazine door. Records state that he owed the government for one ball and chain "thrown overboard in embarking upon transport *America*" on April 1, 1864. We can only assume that he was not attached to the ball and chain at time of the event. His military record for March and April 1864 state he was "present" and confined to "guard house." It was in the Guard

House in Camp Parapet that Hezekiah Dixon died on April 30, 1864. His death was attributed to a "blow at the hands of Officer of Guard" which he had suffered on the day before his death.

A Court of Inquiry was convened to examine "the circumstances attendant upon the death of Private Hezikiah [sic] Dixon late of Company M. 14th R. I. Heavy Artillery (colored)." Captain Ira Berry of the 14th New Hampshire Volunteers, Captain George W. Spinks of the 14th Rhode Island Heavy Artillery, and 1st Lieut. H. B. Walton of the 12th Maine Volunteers were appointed as the court and began to hear evidence on May 3rd. Witnesses included Dr. Benoni Carpenter, Lieut. Albert W. Delanah, Captain Henry Southwick, Lieut. Frank Frost, and Corporal Peter Miller.

According to the testimony, Dixon had been confined to the Guard House since the beginning of March for striking Lieut. Frost, prior to the Battalion leaving Rhode Island. Frost testified that Dixon had refused to pay a bill he owed to the laundress on Dutch Island and that words were exchanged "where upon he struck me under the left ear with his fist." Captain Southwick was called to explain the events that had occurred on the morning of Friday, April 29th. He stated that in his capacity as Field Officer of the Day, he had observed that the prisoners were "enjoying themselves in the shade" which was contrary to the orders of Lt. Col. Viall, who had directed that "prisoners must be worked, and if possible to some useful purpose in the Fort" and that "the Guard House must be made a hard place to be in."

Southwick informed Lieut. Martin D. Smith, Officer of the Guard of his displeasure, and ordered the guard to "set them [prisoners] to marching in a circle in the sun." Hezekiah Dixon did not respond to the orders in an appropriate manner according to Southwick. He kept "stepping his heels together

143

and tossing his head in a very insulting manner ... I then ordered him out of the circle and to take a ball & chain and to carry it. He paid not the slightest attention but kept on marching, knocking his heels together and making gestures." Capt. Southwick pulled Hezekiah out of the circle and the soldier appeared ready to fight at which point Southwick struck him with his fist.

Davis did pick up the ball and chain, but when ordered to take his place in the ranks of prisoners he did not respond. Southwick then drew his sword and struck him over the shoulders. Hezekiah pulled away and held the chain and shackle in a manner that appeared to threaten the captain. Southwick used his sword again, striking Hezekiah on the arm, but not cutting him. Hezekiah returned to the circle but continued to disobey Southwick's orders. Hezekiah held the ball in his left hand and shackle end of the chain in his right hand and witnesses testified that they perceived that Dixon was about to attack Capt. Southwick. Lieut. Smith quickly stepped forward, taking a musket from a sentinel and struck Dixon over the head.

Private Davis staggered, walked a few steps before collapsing onto the ground, bleeding. Captain Southwick indicated that he ordered a corporal to take the prisoner to the hospital and to return him to the Guard House after his being treated. Corporal Peter Miller testified that he did take the prisoner to the hospital and that the wound was dressed by a steward as the doctor was not available. He then took the prisoner back to jail. Davis was taken back to see the Regimental Surgeon, Dr. Benoni Carpenter, later that day and once again returned to the Guard House, after the surgeon determined that he was not seriously injured.

Dixon languished in the Guard House until he died sometime late Saturday night or early Sunday morning. Dr. Carpenter testified at the court of Inquiry that he performed a post mortem examination of the soldier and reported that the skull had been penetrated by some small instrument and "pierced completly [sic] through and the wound reached the brain." Carpenter went on to say that death was "evidently caused by pressure on the brain from the blow and the man died in all probability under a condition similar to that of apoplexy." The Court determined that the Lieut. Smith "was acting strictly within the limits of his duty" and was exonerated from any fault for the death of Hezekiah Dixon.[225]

Although it is obvious that Hezekiah Dixon had not adjusted to army life, it is sad to think that this healthy, young man should die after only three months in the army. Perhaps even sadder is it appears that his family in Rochester, New York was not informed of his death by any official as of June 1865 – over two years after his death. The census enumerator for the New York State 1865 census for the third ward of Rochester recorded the names of the household of Hezekiah Dixon, Sr. on 26 June 1865 and it included a listing for Hezekiah Dixon, age 22, mulatto, child of Hezekiah, Sr.[226] As someone in the family must have provided the census taker with the information, it can be assumed that the family believed that Hezekiah was still alive.

In 1880 Hezekiah Dixon, Sr. applied for a pension based on his son's service in the Civil War stating that his son had died from a "concussion of the brain." Hezekiah, Sr. had made his living as a whitewasher in Rochester at the time his son enlisted, but, according to his pension application, was partially dependent upon his son's wages to help support his family. Two years later his application was "rejected for the reason that the injury, which resulted in soldier's death, was not received while in the line of duty." The widow of Hezekiah Dixon, Sr. also applied for a "mother's pension", but she too was denied since she was a step-mother, not "his natural mother.[227] One can only wonder if the parents of Hezekiah Dixon, Jr. were informed fully of the circumstances surrounding their son's death.

As the summer of 1864 arrived in Louisiana, illness struck with deadly results for the men of the 14th Rhode Island Heavy Artillery. Twelve men from Western New York died between late May and early September. Eight of the men were members of the third battalion stationed at Camp Parapet, located just above New Orleans. The first of the summer deaths occurred on May 20, 1864. John Sullivan joined the ranks on October 30, 1863, traveling to Providence from Peterboro, Madison County, New York. A Frances Sullivan of Homer, New York applied for a widow's pension, providing statements that she had married Mr. Sullivan in March of 1863.[228] Eight days later, twenty-year-old Allen Hazel of Camden, Oneida County, New York died. He had enlisted on November 18, 1863, giving his occupation as farmer. He must have been a frugal man for at the time of his death he had in his possession thirty-three dollars and five cents ($33.05). Records show that he had been paid through the end of April.[229]

David R. Fletcher's death on June 5th was attributed to consumption in his military records, which would indicate that his condition must have been overlooked by the attending physician at the time of his enlistment four months earlier on February 4th. Yet there are documents in the pension application file of his widow claiming that he had not had any symptoms of consumption prior to his enlistment and a document signed by the Regimental Surgeon, Dr. Benoni Carpenter stating that the soldier had died of dysentery.[230]

When Private Fletcher left his Canandaigua, New York home in early February 1864 he had a wife, Mary E. and a two-year-old daughter Emily. Nine days before his death, Mary E. Fletcher gave birth to a second daughter she named Mahasca Fletcher. Mrs. Fletcher must have had a premonition about the death of her husband because in January she insisted that they needed to be remarried to ensure that she had proof of their union. They had originally tied the knot on July 4th of 1860 at the house of David Blake in Canandaigua. The officiating minister was the Rev. Mr. Beebe who had neglected to issue a certificate to the couple. This time the Rev. David Blake, a Minister of the Gospel, performed the ceremony at his house in Canandaigua and gave Mary and David a certificate of marriage that would prove theirs was a legal union. The only problem was that to the pension office that made Emily "illegitimate," thus the need to prove that there had been an earlier ceremony prior to Emily's birth.[231]

David Fletcher's story is particularly poignant. Not only did he not get to see his youngest child, or perhaps even know of her birth, but two younger brothers – Martin Van Buren Fletcher and Charles Morris Fletcher – also would perish from disease a few months later at Beaufort, South Carolina, while serving with the 26th USCT. The three young men were the sons of Archelaus Fletcher, Jr. and Matilda (Reeder) Fletcher and grandsons of Archelaus Fletcher, Sr., a Revolutionary war soldier.

Franklin Fisher (Co. K) of Ithaca, New York made his living as a boatman before he enlisted on November 28, 1863. The doctor identified "Congestion of the brain" as the cause of death of the twenty-year-old on June 21, 1864. According the pension application of his mother, Ellen Fisher, the soldier had been her main support for the past six years, which would have meant that he was only thirteen when he assumed that responsibility.[232]

147

On July 1st Roderick S. Fletcher, private in Company L, died of consumption in the Regimental Hospital at Camp Parapet. Roderick had arrived in Providence at the same time as David R. Fletcher, who was fourteen years his junior. There is no doubt that Roderick and David Fletcher were related, but whether they were half-brothers, first cousins or even second cousins have not been determined. Roderick Fletcher was 48 years old when he enlisted but gave his age as only 43 to the enlisting officer. The inventory of his effects included a great coat, a uniform coat, a blouse, pair of trousers, two pairs of socks, a pair of boots, a blanket, a haversack, a knapsack, a canteen, and a rubber blanket. The clothes were judged to be "worn and worthless", yet at auction brought $2.75, with the woolen blanket bringing the most - $.60.[233]

In August, there were six deaths in the ranks of the third battalion of the men from Western New York. Sergeant William H. Mann of Steuben County, New York died at the Regimental Hospital at Camp Parapet on August 1st. The cause of death was Intermittent Fever, a condition often used to describe malaria. His mother, Susan Mann, began the process of applying for a mother's pension on August 23, 1864.[234]

George Washington Bogart, age twenty-four, of Palmyra, New York and James F. Henry, age sixteen years, of Bath, New York both succumbed to diarrhea on August 7th. Bogart's mother had a difficult time acquiring a mother's pension because her son had been enlisted under the name of George Washington and not with his surname of Bogart.[235] George was the son of Lafayette and Lydia (Sutphin) Bogart and had a brother named Benjamin Franklin Bogart – attesting to the patriotic sentiments of this family.

George left home for Providence in company of David H. Ray, Sr., the chief recruiter in Western New York, in late December 1864. On December 13, 1865, within days of what would have been the second anniversary of George's enlistment, Mr. Ray signed a statement stating that he had enlisted the soldier at Palmyra, Wayne County, New York and that he "took said George Washington to Providence Rhode Island." Lydia Bogart had been partially dependent on her son for her support for a number of years and he had written to her two or three times telling her he "would send her money as soon as he was paid, but that she did not receive any money from him."

Corporal John E. Brown of Auburn, New York contracted malaria during the latter part of the summer of 1864, dying on the 31st of August. Born in Rochester, New York about 1838 it is very likely that his parents had crossed paths with David H. Ray, who had lived in Rochester between 1838 and 1850. Brown's occupation as barber would also have provided a link to Ray. In December 1864, Sarah Brown started the sad process of applying for a widow's pension, stating that the couple had married in Auburn on December 5, 1859. They had no children.

The last of the summer deaths occurred on September 5th. Hannibal F. Davis of Company G, part of the Second Battalion, was stationed at Plaquemine, Louisiana just below Baton Rouge at the time of his death. This twenty-five-year-old barber enlisted on October 30, 1863.[236] His father, David, and brother, Gabriel, were also members of the Brotherhood of Barbers.[237]

Perhaps it was the cooler weather or that the soldiers were becoming acclimated to their surroundings, but the men of Western New York fared better in September and October 1864 with only two deaths in each of those months. George Moore (Co. M) of Albion, New York enlisted on January 24, 1864, leaving behind a wife Maria and five minor children, the oldest only thirteen years old. Once again "congestion of the brain" was listed as the cause of his death on September 24th at the

Regimental Hospital at Camp Parapet.[238]   Charles H. Moore of
Rochester, New York arrived in Providence on December 30,
1863 for his enlistment, identifying himself as twenty-seven
years old and working as a groomsman.   He was appointed
corporal of Co. M on July 3, but only held that post until his
death on the 12th of October.   Congestive chills were listed as
cause of his death.   It has not been determined if there was a
family connection between George and Charles Moore.

One of the earliest recruits among the men from Western
New York was Amos A. Lunn who was mustered into Co. D on
September 22, 1863.   At the time of his enlistment Amos was
living in Chatham, Columbia County with his young wife Helen
Elizabeth, formerly of Palmyra, New York.[239]   Helen's father
Charles Taylor had moved his family to Palmyra from Columbia
County in the early 1840s, yet it is obvious that there were still
family ties or friendship links between the two communities
that allowed Amos and Helen to meet and fall in love. Three
weeks after his enlistment Helen gave birth to their only child,
Charles, and shortly after his birth, Helen returned to her
father's home in Palmyra.   Private Amos A. Lunn died on
October 21, 1863 at Fort Jackson from "acute diarrhea."[240] It
would seem unlikely that Amos's body was returned to his wife,
yet there is a record of a burial for "Amos Drum" of the 11th
USCHA in the Palmyra Village Cemetery.[241]

The lull in the death march of September and October was
just a memory come November when six men from Western
New York passed away – three each from Second and Third
Battalions. Sergeant John Pell of Company L died on November
1st at the Regimental Hospital at Camp Parapet. The twenty-
seven-year-old was married with two young daughters.   Two
days later forty-two-year-old John Lee of Elmira died in the
hospital at Camp Parapet. In quick succession death struck
George Howland, Co. M, of Syracuse; William T. Cleggett, Co.
M, of Rochester; Thomas A. Wycoff, Co. H, of Norwich; and

Alfred Brewster, Co. I., of Norwich. Alfred Brewster enlisted on November 14, 1863, just four days after his marriage to Fanny L. Jackson in Norwich, Chenango County, New York. One year to the day after his enlistment Alfred was dead from malaria.[242]

The "worst of times" seemed to come to an end by February of 1865. Only four deaths were recorded in December and January. Charles H. Hardy, of Geneva and Aaron Myers of Syracuse died in December. Both men were married and left behind minor children.[243] Forty-year-old Anthony T. White, born in Ontario County, New York, met his death while being treated at Regimental Hospital in Camp Parapet on January 1, 1865, one day after Aaron Myers died.[244] William P. Anderson of Watertown died of consumption on January 28, 1865 at Plaquemine, Louisiana. He had received a Certificate of Disability for Discharge on January 4, 1865, but apparently was too ill to travel. A barber by profession, Virginian-born Anderson was a resident of Watertown at the time of his enlistment. [245]

There were no more deaths among the men until July, when Samuel Fletcher passed away. Being among the last to die is not a distinction that any of the men would have chosen, but there were still two more deaths to record. In September, John W. Cortright, son of Prime Cortright, died at Camp Parapet of malaria.[246] The death of Hugh DePuy occurred on October 3, 1865, just one day after the regiment was mustered out of service at New Orleans. Private DePuy was transported to DeCamp Hospital at David's Island, located in the New York Harbor, arriving there on September 30th.[247]

Private William H. Clark, of Co. M, made it home to Rochester, New York after his discharge on October 2, 1865, but was dead one month later. His mother, Rebecca A. Clark, reached out to two of his friends from Company M for support when she applied for a mother's pension. James Howard and

William Johnson confirmed that they were well acquainted with Private Clark who had suffered from "Swamp Fever" which had afflicted many of the men at Camp Parapet.[248]

The constant fear of death from disease must have weighed heavily on the men of the 14th Rhode Island. The official records of casualties of the 14th Rhode Island for 1864 showed that there had been 260 deaths from disease; five from accidents; three in action and one from sentence of General Court-Martial. The final count of those who died from disease climbed to over 350 by war's end. Many of the dead, buried near the Regimental Hospital at Camp Parapet, were moved to the Chalmette National Cemetery, established in 1864. It is estimated that about 12,000 Civil War troops are buried at Chalmette, with nearly 7,000 whose names are not known, marked by small markers. James R. Henry, Private in Company M, was the only marker located for the men from Western New York who died while serving in the 11th USCHA.

Chalmette National Cemetery, New Orleans and marker for J. R. Henry, U.S.C.T.

Discipline and Desertion

How the white officers saw and described the daily life of the 14th Rhode Island most likely bore little resemblance to the views of the ordinary black soldier. Capt. Joshua M. Addeman of Co. H, 2nd Battalion found that there was "plenty of fun, music, vocal and instrumental." He praised "the mimic talents of our men" which led to "the performance of a variety of entertainments, and in their happy-go-easy dispositions, their troubles set very lightly on them." Addeman also commented on why he thought there were so many deaths in the ranks. "Our men with all their buoyancy of disposition, had not the resolute will of white men, when attacked by sickness, and would succumb with fatal rapidity." [249]

The white officer corps of the United States Colored Troops at the company level had little or no experience in their tasks as Captain, First Lieutenant and Second Lieutenant. In addition to their lack of experience as officers, most had very little prior contact with African Americans in their daily lives, so their biases and prejudices guided much of their dealings with the men they were supposed to lead. The disconnect between the men and their officers brought about unforeseen consequences for both sides.

The case of Private James Castles of Company D, formerly of Rochester, New York, may have been caused by an overreaction to a series of events that put the First Battalion into disarray in March and April of 1864. Interestingly these events were glossed over in the official history of the 14th Rhode Island Regiment of Heavy Artillery, published in 1898. There were only a few oblique mentions of events that must have rocked the First Battalion which was stationed at Fort Esperanza on Matagorda Island.

A misunderstanding about the purpose of roll call inspection called by the captain of Company A on March 17, 1864 set in motion a series of court martial trials that put the men of the First Battalion on edge and in danger of severe punishment. [250] The first trials began on March 23, 1864 and were restricted to men of Company A. The goal of the officers was to make an example of those who had not "followed orders" and to "restore discipline" in the ranks. The basic charge was "conduct prejudicial to discipline." Sentences ranged from one year at hard labor at Fort Jefferson (Dry Tortugas), Florida to three months of hard labor at Matagorda Island. All soldiers lost pay during the term of their sentence and were reduced in rank if sergeants or corporals.

The trials may have been responsible for a true breakdown in discipline, much more serious than the initial event. On the night of March 29, 2nd Lt. Charles Potter of Co. D was serving as Officer of the Guard when he attempted to arrest some soldiers who were said to be drunk and disorderly. The men did not respond to the orders to go to the guardhouse and the fracas drew a crowd of other soldiers. With this, Potter, trying to restore his authority, ordered the men to go back to their tents and even threatened to shoot them if they did not obey.

The rest is a bit of "he said, he said", but the end result was that the word of the black soldier was not accorded any value. Potter claimed that he had called Corporal Charles Cooley, of Company A, to his tent to discuss his charge that Cooley had not obeyed the order to disperse. Potter also claimed that Cooley had attempted to strike him and reached for his revolver, whereupon Potter shot the corporal. There is no doubt that the soldiers of the First Battalion were very riled and words were uttered that appeared to further threaten the authority of the white officers.

These utterances resulted in more men being sentenced to Fort Jefferson in Florida. Private Samuel Douglass was sentenced to ten years at hard labor for allegedly saying that "if we are to be shot by our own officers I am willing to die now."[251] Others received sentences of four months of hard labor at Fort Jefferson. The rash of court martial trials culminated with the trials of Corporal Cooley and Private James Castles. On April 25, Cooley was found guilty of "contempt and disrespect towards a superior officer and conduct prejudicial to good order and military discipline" and sentenced to fifteen years at Fort Jefferson. On the same day, James Castles of Company D, was also sentenced by the court. The charges against Castles were conduct "prejudicial to good order and military discipline", "assault with intent to kill" and "alarming camp by discharge of fire arms." His term of imprisonment was to be ten years with ball and chain at Fort Jefferson.

Private Castles' request for a pardon was met with a response from the Adjutant Generals Office dated June 3, 1864 which read in part that "upon investigation of the case it is ascertained that there are no mitigating circumstances to warrant the granting the request of the prisoner."[252] The request was forwarded to the Commanding Officer of the 14th Rhode Island Heavy Artillery and down through the ranks until it reached Major John J. Comstock, commanding officer of the First Battalion. On July 1, 1864, Major Comstock responded that "James Castles is a hard case he has given me more trouble than any other man in the Regt. He has often threatened to kill his officers and if I had been present when the last act of his occurred, he would never been called upon to appear before a court martial."[253] Private Castles did not get his pardon, but he also did not serve ten years at Fort Jefferson. Orders from the Adjutant General's Office allowed for his release from prison on March 14, 1866. Charles Cooley was released on April 17, 1866 and Samuel Douglass was released five days later.

Did Comstock actually mean that he would have shot and killed Private Castles without a trial? Major Comstock did not hold the black soldiers under his command in very high regard so perhaps it is not difficult to imagine it possible. In a letter he wrote to Governor Smith of Rhode Island providing an overview of the events in March he stated that the one-year sentences were not sufficient as the event amounted to mutiny. As for the shooting by Lt. Potter he stated that the men needed to be taught a lesson and the men knew he would have sustained Potter even if it meant shooting "every man in the Regt." Comstock went on to say that "it is only fear which will keep this class of men in their place and make good soldiers, and the moment an officer is afraid of them, they will over run him and put him down."[254] Substitute the word "slaves" for "men" and "soldiers" and the sentiments of Mr. Comstock would mirror that of the slaveholders of the South. It is possible that the attitude of Major Comstock set a tone within the First Battalion that undermined the trust necessary for the officers and men to form a cohesive unit and would explain why a simple misunderstanding could have ended up causing so much harm to so many.

The harshness of the sentences levied on the men of the First Battalion during March and April 1864 was not duplicated in the other Battalions of the 14th Rhode Island Regiment of Heavy Artillery. Private James C. Thomas (Co. F) of Otsego County, New York faced a Garrison court martial on February 1865 on charges of "contempt and disrespect towards his Commanding officer" and "conduct to the prejudice of good order and military discipline." The charges were similar to those leveled at the men of Company A who had received sentences of one year and loss of all pay. According to testimony Thomas, in speaking to his sergeant, had stated that the sergeant and captain "didn't know anything", lacing his language with some expletives. He was found guilty and his sentence was three months' hard labor with ball and chain in camp and no pay for one month.[255]

There is no doubt that effectively managing young men and molding them into an army was not an easy task. It is also true that not all men who joined the 14th Rhode Island Regiment of Heavy Artillery were going to be good soldiers, or at least good soldiers all the time. John G. Graves of Watertown, New York is listed as having joined the regiment at Providence on October 17, 1863, although his enlistment papers show no signature or "mark" to indicate he had completed the process. He was mustered into Co. G on November 9th. Three days later it was reported that he had deserted. On November 18, 1863, the Rhode Island Provost Marshal's Office notified Col. Nelson Vial, commander of the 14th Rhode Island Regiment, that John G. Graves had been arrested at Woonsocket in "citizens dress en route for Albany and the west and being a clear case of desertion I gave the officer who arrested and returned him a voucher for $30. This amt. you will charge against Graves."[256]

Two weeks later Graves was once again on the move. This time he made it home to Watertown where on January 12, 1864 he was arrested as a deserter. Lockwood R. May of the Watertown Provost Marshal's office wrote on February 9, 1864 to the Commanding Colonel of the 14th Rhode Island Colored Volunteer to inform him that John Graves had been arrested and sent to Fort Columbus, located in New York Harbor and to inquire as to which company Graves had been mustered into. According to May "the fellow either did not know the letter of his company or would not tell us."[257]

Graves rejoined his regiment at Plaquemine, Louisiana on May 18th and returned to duty, without trial. He now owed the government $60.00 for the two arrests. He was quickly detached from duty with his company to become a musician for the regiment – a position he held until January, 1865. John G. Graves appears to have stayed out of trouble until March of 1865 when he was charged with being absent without leave from camp between the hours of three and five in the afternoon on March 11th. His absence was obvious as in his role as Drum Major of the Second Battalion, he had failed to show up for the evening parade. This breech of discipline appears to be just the beginning of Private Graves' downward spiral as a soldier?

First page of enlistment papers of John G. Graves. Note that there is no signature in space following statement that he had "volunteered" to serve a three-year term.

In late April, Lieutenant C. H. Barney preferred charges against John Graves, who was accused of "assault and battery with intent to commit rape." It was stated that in the early hours of April 25, 1865, John Graves had committed a violent assault upon Mrs. John Bull while intoxicated. The serious nature of the charges meant that the trial would be handled by the Judge Advocate at Thibodaux, Louisiana. Private Graves had other plans. On July 9th, he escaped from the Guard House at Battalion headquarters in Donaldson, Louisiana and headed for New Orleans, where he was apprehended two days later. He was supposed to have been returned to Regimental headquarters under guard on July 13, but as of July 20th, he had not arrived and the Judge Advocate was informed that "he no doubt deserted again – he cannot be sent to Thibodaux." A notation in the military file seems to sum up the frustration of the officers of the Second Battalion. "No mercy should be shown this soldier if ever arrested and returned to the command."[258]

It will never be known what the verdict would have been if Private Graves had proceeded to trial, but apparently, he was not willing to take any chances. What is fairly certain is that he did not return to Watertown, New York and his family. His wife Rosella and two children, Catharine and Jeremiah, were listed in the 1865 New York State Census, along with John, but the date of the enumeration was June 9, 1865 which would make it impossible for him to be physically present in the household.[259] It is likely that Rosella was not aware that her husband was in the Guard House awaiting trial when the census taker visited in June. The news might have had to wait until the return to Watertown in October of her brothers George and David Armstrong, who had served with their brother-in-law in the Second Battalion. Was Graves' proclivity to "desertion" tied to a belief that he was not really in the army, as he had not signed the enlistment papers? He left no record of his side of the story.

Apprehending deserters was not always easy. David H. Ray, Jr. absconded from Dutch Island just a few days prior to his battalion being transported south. Ray had enlisted on November 16, 1863, but had not been mustered until three months later and assigned to Company I. In January and February 1864, he was listed on the muster rolls as "detached recruit for second battalion." A letter dated March 31, 1864 from Charles E. Bailey to Lt. Joseph C. Whiting, Jr. stated that "David Ray had his pass extended by His Excellency the Governor until Saturday last and it was supposed that he was now in Camp. He requested a further extension of me on that day but I declined to grant it and directed him to go at once to Camp...I am surprised that money should have been entrusted to him without sufficient security, but it certainly seems to be a private transaction in which we can do nothing but take the man Ray and send him to camp, which will be done if he can be found."[260] When Private Ray had not shown up in camp by the next day he was officially listed as a deserter and remained on the rolls as such for the remainder of the war.

Ray did not suffer any long-term problems from his desertion. In June 1867, he was once again advertising his barber services in Ogdensburg, New York at the same stand he had listed in an ad of August 1863.[261] Had he returned to Ogdensburg from Providence in April 1864 and picked up his life as before his enlistment? Or had he crossed the border into Canada at Ogdensburg and remained there for the duration of the war? By 1870 he was living in Palmyra, New York and doing business with his father.[262]

Winfield B. Van Horn of Company L was also able to elude capture after his desertion on June 15, 1864 from Camp Parapet, Louisiana. His reason for desertion may have been anger or pique. Van Horn, a barber from Rochester, New York, had been appointed 1st Sergeant of his company on December 31, 1863 by Lt. Col. Nelson Viall. The *Compiled Military Records* for Sgt. Van Horn do not provide any background information, but he was reduced in rank from 1st Sergeant to private on orders dated June 9, 1864. Six days later Van Horn is listed as having deserted and nothing in the records indicates he ever returned to duty.[263]

Van Horn returned to Rochester and was reunited with his wife Charlotte and daughter Caroline. In 1866 a second daughter, Blanche, joined the family, followed by Alice in 1869.[264] By 1875, Van Horn, a widower, moved to Saratoga Springs, where he married again and raised a second family, continuing to work as a barber.[265] Mr. Van Horn died in 1920 and there is no record that he ever applied for a civil war pension.

One deserter that did not get away without punishment was twenty-one-year-old Webster Demann of Waterloo, Seneca County, New York. He left his post on June 30th, 1864 and was on the loose for only eight days before he was arrested in New Orleans "dressed as a citizen." The proceedings of a Court Martial held at Camp Parapet found Demann guilty of the charge of desertion and he was sentenced to nine months' hard labor at Fort Jefferson. He arrived at Fort Jefferson in Florida on October 19, 1864 and was released on July 22, 1865 and returned to duty. Although he was listed as present on the muster roll of July and August 1865 it is apparent that he was not well when he arrived for duty. The September and October muster rolls list him as absent.

He was mustered out from the hospital at David's Island in New York City and the records indicate Demann was not furnished a discharge at the time.[266] Had his imprisonment at Fort Jefferson broken his health? There is no pension application for Webster Demann and no census record after the war. There is a record of a marriage of a man with same name who closely matches the age and place of birth of the soldier in Detroit, Michigan on August 26, 1875 to Frances Skellmann. If this is the same person, the occupation of the husband was given as "sailor" and may explain why no other records have been located.[267]

Two of the last desertions recorded involved men from Company K. Thirty-six-year old Thomas Dorsey, of Syracuse, New York, enlisted on November 25, 1863 and was listed as a deserter on June 14, 1865. He listed his occupation as laborer on his enlistment papers and was able to sign his name with apparent ease. There was no indication in the file that he was recovered.[268] William A. Moore, of Elmira, New York, deserted on September 6, 1865 from Camp Parapet. For all intents and purposes the war was over, but it must have seemed an eternity for the men who just wanted to go home. The twenty-year old may have deserted for love, as he married a local girl and remained in New Orleans until his death in 1891.[269]

There is no doubt that there were many infractions of the rules by the men of the 14th Rhode Island Regiment of Heavy Artillery that did not rise to the level requiring a court martial. The Guard House would have been used to confine men found to be drunk, gambling, fighting, missing roll call. Perhaps as the white officers came to know the men under their campaign, the need to "teach them a lesson" or establish who was "boss" through fear lessened, allowing development of common respect which would prove to be enough to manage many of the disputes that had caused so much trouble in the early days for the First Battalion.

Fellowship, Family, and Friends

Much has been written about the bonds that are forged between men serving together in war and this concept of a "band of brothers" is easy to understand. The men of the 14th Rhode Island Heavy Artillery would exhibit the same pattern as they formed alliances with family members, friends and strangers that would provide the support mechanisms needed to survive the war. And many of the alliances would become the basis for life-long friendships.

Joseph P. Bulah, of Jordan, New York, Charles J. Duffin of Geneva, New York and John G. Hill, of Ontario, New York were all acquainted with each other prior to the war, but their lives were definitely more intimately linked thereafter. Joseph Bulah was the first to enlist. The twenty-two-year-old barber had been working in Newark, New York for a couple of years before he entered the service on December 18th and headed to Providence. His young wife of one year, the former Delly Goff, parents James and Mary Bulah and a sister Mary Ann, would anxiously await his safe return. The Bulah family fully understood the dangers Joseph faced as he entered the South - the same place that his parents had escaped from in the mid-1830s.

Snippets of information from various sources help to piece together a portion of the early life of Joseph Bulah. It appears that James Bulah and his wife escaped from slavery in Maryland in the mid-1830s and found their way to Allentown, New Jersey where two children were born – Mary Ann about 1837 and Joseph about 1840. When still a toddler, Joseph's family moved to Albany, New York where Mr. Bulah, a licensed Methodist exhorter, became part of the Anti-Slavery movement, working with local abolitionist Abel Brown and speaking to meetings throughout the region. About 1848 the family relocated to Jordan, New York, a small village on the Erie Canal, located west of Syracuse. With the passage of the Fugitive Slave Law of 1850, Mr. Bulah reported his unease with staying in the United States and elected to take his family into Canada in late 1851. By 1853 the family had returned to Jordan where they put down permanent roots.[270]

The Duffin family's roots in the village of Geneva, New York, reached back into the pioneer days of the community. It is very likely that the grandparents of Charles J. Duffin Jr. – John and Susanna Duffin – were once enslaved by the Nicholas family that settled in the area about 1803, moving from Virginia with about 75 slaves. The two sons of John and Susanna Duffin, James W. and Charles, carved a niche in the area as barbers. James W. Duffin also was well known for his social activism in issues regarding equal rights for the black man. While James remained anchored in Geneva until the 1860s, his younger brother Charles moved frequently, opening shops in Geneva, Auburn, Penn Yan, Newark and Clifton Springs between 1840 and 1865. Yet, Geneva remained the touchstone for the family. Charles J. was the eldest child of Charles and Martha Ann (Stout) Duffin, which eventually included another brother and four sisters. Since the trade of the barber was often passed down from father to son, it is somewhat unusual that Charles J. did not follow in his father's footsteps and pick up the razor as a profession. On the other hand, three of his cousins, the sons of his uncle James W. Duffin, did become barbers.

John G. Hill's background was somewhat different from his friends. Instead of being accustomed to village life, the Hill family were farm laborers. John and his parents, Joseph and Margaret (Robinson) Hill, were all born in the Hudson Valley of eastern New York. Their heritage is not fully documented, but it is very possible that they descended from slaves of the early Dutch settlers that owned large tracts of land between New York City and Albany. Joseph Hill moved his family to rural upstate New York about 1854 from Columbia County, settling first in Avon, Livingston County and then Webster, Monroe County, where he was identified as a farm laborer. In 1863 John was working as a farm laborer in Macedon, Wayne County, New York. Their lives were definitely not any more settled than the Bulah or Duffin families, yet they traveled from farm to farm instead of from village to village in search of jobs and economic security.[271]

The Compiled Military Records of the three men provide only the bare bones of their military experience. John G. Hill was made Sergeant in Company L on December 31, 1863. Joseph P. Bulah received his appointment as Corporal in Company M in early February 1864. Both were demoted in June and July of 1864 to the rank of Private. The military record of Corporal Bulah indicated that his demotion was the result of a sentence of Regimental Court Martial, dated June 19th. Sergeant Hill's record makes no mention for the reason behind the demotion but includes just the notation "Reduced by order of Lt. Col. Nelson Vialle [sic], Command'g Regt."

John G. Hill injured himself while chopping wood in February 1865 and the cut on his left leg, just above the ankle, resulted in his having "no use of his toes." This accident earned him a Certificate of Disability for Discharge on June 3, 1865 at Camp Parapet and he returned to the home of his parents in Ontario, New York. Privates Bulah and Duffin traveled with the regiment from New Orleans to Providence, Rhode Island and participated in the final dress parade.[272]

The pension records for the three men help to fill in a few blanks concerning their time in the army. Joseph Bulah began complaining of a soreness and pain in his left side as well a chronic diarrhea while still stationed at Dutch Island in Rhode Island. Both Joseph G. Hill and Charles J. Duffin corroborated the illness in support of Bulah's pension application. Hill stated that:

165

I knew Joseph P. Bulah very well ... distinctly remember seeing said Bulah sick at Dutchers [sic] at Narragasett [sic] Bay, R.I. in 1863 December. He was then suffering severely from chronic Diarrhea from that time until we were mustered out in 1865 ... It was especially bad at New Orleans – at Camp Parapet ... I know that Doctor Carpenter treated Bulah at Camp Parapet as I reported the sick with the Sergt of Co M and was present at the time and place ...

Duffin confirmed that:

he knew the claimant Joseph P. Bulah while in the service and was his Bunk Mate ... That sometime in the month of February 1862 or 63 [1864?] the applicant ... was wet from nessary [sic] exposier [sic] while in the line of duty and from this time he often complained of severe pain in his side ...

Regimental Hospital Registers show that he sought treatment on at least seven occasions for diarrhea and remittent fever. [273] Regardless of his illnesses, the muster records for Bulah indicated he was always "present" and was fortunate enough to escape being admitted to the hospital for any length of time.

The years following the war found the three men facing unsettling times in which they seem to struggle to find permanency. In May of 1866, John G. Hill married Sophia Matilda Lloyd, half-sister of Delly (Goff) Bulah in Sodus, New York. The couple remained in northern Wayne County for the next ten years where John continued to work as a laborer for a succession of farmers, before making a move to the city of Buffalo, New York about 1874 – their last major move. John, Matilda and their two sons, William and Joseph were listed in the 1875 census, living in the 4th Ward of Buffalo. John transitioned from farm laborer to janitor and, finally, to cook and caterer during his life in Buffalo.[274]

Joseph Bulah and his wife Delly initially set up house in Jordan, New York and even purchased some property near his parents. In search of work the couple moved to Syracuse where he purchased a barber shop on Warren Street, near the Erie Canal Bridge; then to Rochester, New York where he opened a shop in the Lathrop Block; then back to Jordan for a couple of years; and finally, they too moved to Buffalo, arriving there in the summer of 1876. The work life of Bulah in Buffalo was varied, including jobs as a porter for a fire department, a messenger for C.W. Cushman of the Rail Way Car Association, as well as a barber during the next thirty years.[275]

Charles J. Duffin's life after military service was also unsettled. Between 1865 and 1882 he found work in New York City, Geneva, Canandaigua, Newark, Lyons and Buffalo, New York – usually as a servant, waiter or porter. He then moved to Ann Arbor, Michigan, where he lived for about 10 years before returning to Buffalo in the late 1890s, where he rejoined his former comrades and found work as a cook. By then the trio were all struggling with ill health. John G. Hill was the first to die. He died on March 25, 1900 at the age of 56. Joseph Bulah provided a statement with the widow's pension application stating that he

> knew John G. Hill in the army. I had known him before the war but was not much acquainted with him. I was in the same regt. but not the same co. Mrs. Hill was about 18 years old when I first knew her. I married her sister in 1862...[276]

Joseph P. Bulah died February 17, 1909 in Buffalo at the age of 69 years. Delly Bulah reached out to Charles J. Duffin to assist her with the task of applying for a widow's pension. He stated that he

> *has been acquainted and on intimate terms with Delly Bulah (nee Goff) and her late husband Joseph P. Bulah for fifty years or more... that he was present and saw claimant and the soldier united in marriage. The ceremony being performed...on the 24th day of November, 1862..."*[277]

Charles J. Duffin became a boarder and member of the Delly Bulah and Matilda Hill household following the death of his friend and remained with the two sisters until his death in December 1917. All three men were buried in Section 14 of the Forest Lawn Cemetery in Buffalo, New York. Delly Bulah died in 1922 and her sister, Sophia Matilda Hill, died in 1931. They too were buried in Forest Lawn Cemetery.[278]

Black Regiments for New York State
Fighting to Serve

New York State had been a leading contributor to the army of the Union from the very start of the Civil War. The first troops left New York City for Washington on April 19, 1861, just five days after the fall of Fort Sumter and four days after President Lincoln called for 75,000 volunteers. By mid July 1861 over 46,000 men had gone from New York to serve in the Federal Army. On July 25, 1861 New York's Governor Edwin D. Morgan issued a call for another 25,000 men to serve three-year terms. On the very next day representatives of the African American community of the state applied to the Governor for permission to enlist three regiments with the "assurance that their arms, equipments, clothing and pay, while in the service would be provided by the colored population of the State."[279] The offer was not accepted. And it would be over two years before a full court press to attract African American soldiers from New York would get underway, resulting in the formation of three regiments for the United States Colored Troops.

When Abraham Lincoln announced on January 1, 1863 that black men would be allowed to become soldiers in the armed forces of the Federal government there was no groundswell of enthusiasm within the offices of the governors of the northern states. In fact, it was in the areas of the South where the Federal Army was in control where the greatest progress was made. In order to bring order to the recruitment of black soldiers and creation of regiments, the War Department issued an order in May, 1863 that established the Bureau of the United States Colored Troops which was to oversee the process. Yet in the north the responsibility to request permission to raise regiments – black or white – still rested with the Governor.

New York's Governor Horatio Seymour opposed the recruitment of black soldiers and did nothing to facilitate creation of black regiments within the state. That did not deter interest within the African American community of the state. On February 28, 1863 a group of black leaders from the New York area wrote to President Lincoln that "We, the sons of Freedom, take the liberty of addressing you ... We are ready to follow the example of our fathers, and rally to our country's call... We, through our delegate, offer the service of ten thousand of the sable sons, called the Fremont Legion, to be led to the field of battle." The committee also wrote to General Fremont calling on him to be the "Joshua to lead us to the field of battle."[280]

A delegation led by the Rev. Dr. J. N. Gloucester, of the Fleet-Place African Episcopal Church in Brooklyn, from the committee, known as the Association for Promoting Colored Volunteering, took the proposal directly to the President of the United States in mid-March, informing him that 3,000 men had already pledged to enlist under General Fremont. The proposal was accompanied by a resolution signed by thirteen white men in support of the appointment of Fremont as commander of the black troops. Signers included Peter Cooper, Horace Greeley, and William Cullen Bryant.

President Lincoln was said to have listened "with earnestness and indeed solemnity," but expressed the opinion that he could not promise that General Fremont would be assigned such a post. The Committee reported on May 5th before a meeting held at the Church of the Puritans in New York City that they were "pushing the matter with all the energy they could command and were confident that a practical result would soon attest the earnestness with which they had labored."[281] The Association followed up this meeting with a formal application to the governor asking for permission to enlist black soldiers sent on July 9th.

In anticipation of receiving a positive response to the request, a notice was circulated throughout the state announcing that a Convention of Colored Citizens was to be held on July 15th and 16th in Poughkeepsie for the purpose of the "Organization of a large force of Colored Troops, to be commanded by leaders in sympathy with the movement..."[282] The notice called for the appointment of local committees and development of lists of men "capable of bearing arms, who are willing to join the service" in each locality.

Before the meeting could be held General Robert E. Lee brought the war into the North at Gettysburg, Pennsylvania where the battle raged from July 1st to 3rd. Next the draft riots erupted in New York City from July 13th to 16th. The black residents of the city became the target of mob violence causing over one hundred deaths, beatings, rapes and destruction of millions of dollars of property. Surprisingly none of this prevented the holding of the Convention, which opened on Thursday, July 16, 1863 with election of officers and a series of patriotic speeches. Dr. Paschal B. Randolph of Utica presented a *Manifesto of the Colored Citizens of the State of New York* which made no direct mention of the draft riots although some of those attending may have personally experienced the terror as residents of the city. The Manifesto proclaimed that "we the colored citizens of this State, are LOYAL and TRUE to the Government; that our fortunes rise or fall with it; that we are ready, anxious and willing to demonstrate that truth and loyalty on the field of battle."[283]

The Convention attendees passed a series of resolutions. First, they called for the "immediate appointment of trusty and able men of color to canvas the entire State for recruits" and second the formation of State Central Committee to oversee the enrolling and organization of troops. Dr. Paschal B. Randolph, of Utica, was appointed President of the Central Committee with Vice Presidents: John Van Pelt, Glens Falls;

171

Jermain W. Loguen, Syracuse; Nimrod D. Thompson, Buffalo; J. H. Townsend, New York; Charles B. Ray, New York; J. N. Gloucester, Brooklyn; William Crocker, Binghamton; William Rich, Troy; N. Gibbs, Little Falls; and A. Bolin, Poughkeepsie.[284]

The draft of 1863 was completed in New York State by early September and it appears that all the African American draftees were sent to Camp William Penn in Philadelphia and most were attached to the 8th USCT. Some men of military age who were not drafted were traveling directly to Philadelphia and Camp William Penn to enlist. Others were being enticed to join regiments in neighboring states of Rhode Island and Connecticut. Remaining hopeful that the Fremont Legion would find backing, a recruiting office had been established at No. 50 Myrtle Avenue in Brooklyn. It was reported in the August 29th issue of *The Christian Recorder* that "recruiting is still going on both in Brooklyn and New York. No. 50 Myrtle Avenue, Brooklyn receives men for the Fremont Legion while Rhode Island, giving $300 bounty, has the greatest rush..."[285] A week later the same correspondent reported that the recruiting office of the Fremont Legion "has closed, not being able to compete with the other office which gave bounty."[286]

After waiting months for a response to their request from Governor Seymour, the Association for Promoting Colored Volunteering called for a mass meeting in November to plan for the future. A subcommittee wrote to Secretary of War Stanton on November 19th, asking if they could proceed without state approval. Stanton replied that the War Department would consider an application by suitable persons and that the troops raised would be credited to the state.[287] The one thing lacking was the support of Horatio Seymour, New York's governor.

There were other forces at work with the same goals as the Association for Promoting Colored Volunteering. On November 20th, the Union League Club of New York City resolved to become involved in the recruitment of black soldiers as a way to assist the State in raising the quota of volunteers requested by the President. Alexander Van Rensselaer, George Bliss, Jr. and LeGrand B. Cannon, all prominent white New Yorkers, were charged with the task of communicating with Governor Seymour regarding his authorization to recruit a black regiment if the War Department consent was obtained. The Governor responded on November 27th that the "matter rests entirely with the War Department at Washington." Three days later the Union League Club submitted an application to the Secretary of War for authorization "for a regiment of Colored Troops, to be raised in the State of New York, under the auspices of that Club."[288]

Permission was received on December 3rd and the Club Committee followed up with a letter notifying the Governor, dated December 4th, 1863. In the letter to the Governor, George Bliss, Secretary, wrote that it was their hope that "so far as is in your power you will give the movement your aid and countenance." It was also suggested that "steps should be taken to put a stop to the recruiting in this State of men from other States."[289] The Governor made no response to this letter. On December 9th representatives from the Association and the Union League Club met to form a Joint Committee and recruiting began in earnest for the 20th USCT, which was to rendezvous at Riker's Island, New York Harbor, a site that had been used since 1862 as a military training center. In the summer and fall of 1863 it was also used as a depot for draftees – white and black.

Enlistments had been in the works through the Association's efforts to rally behind the Fremont Legion and within a few days the mechanism to direct recruits to the 20th USCT were in place. By December 19th the committee had written to the War Department stating that the "Twentieth Regiment, U. S. Colored Troops is recruited nearly to the maximum" and requested that they be authorized to raise a second regiment. Permission was granted on January 4, 1864 and the new regiment was to be designated the 26th USCT.[290] In less than a month the War Department was informed that the 26th USCT was full and requesting once again for permission to raise another regiment. The authority was quickly granted and the third regiment would have the designation of the 31st USCT.

It is very clear that the African American leaders of New York State, who had so persistently advocated for the enlistment of black soldiers, were correct in their assessment that if allowed to serve, the recruits would respond. With over 1,000 men arriving in the month of December alone, it was quickly apparent that Riker's Island and the army were not prepared for the sudden influx of recruits. The Union League Club's report concluded that

> *for a considerable time the quarters provided for the colored men were insufficient ...Tents were furnished by the Government, but they were so few in number that the men were greatly crowded; they were also without floors or means of warming, causing great suffering from the cold.*[291]

With the crowded conditions came disease and sickness, which put additional strains on the new recruits and their officers. The Union League and the Association worked to address the problems by providing flooring and warming stoves for the tents and advocating for medical attention.

On the surface it would appear that recruitment of black soldiers into the New York State regiments was on the whole a great success story. Yet one has to remember that less than six months had passed since mob violence raged throughout New York City for five days in July. Prejudice against and discrimination of African Americans was part and parcel of life throughout the United States. Perhaps anticipating problems, the Superintendent of Recruiting, Vincent Colyer, circulated guidelines for recruitment that included a statement regarding bounties and pay:

> *Recruits will receive the State bounty of seventy-five dollars, and also the local bounty paid to other volunteers at the place of enlistment. They will not receive any United States bounty. Their pay is at present ten dollars per month, though it is believed that Congress will at once increase the pay of all soldiers, and place the blacks on an equality with the whites in this respect...*[292]

The circular also clearly stated that authorized recruiters were to see that each recruit receive the state and local bounties "into his own hands." Regardless of the well-intentioned rules, it quickly became apparent that "many of the men had been shamefully defrauded in the matter of bounties to which they were entitled and that in some cases there was every reason to suppose that the men had been drugged, had been deceived as to the service expected of them. These cases were confined mostly to the men enlisted at the Headquarters of Gen. Spinola, in Lafayette Hall..."[293]

Oliver Comback, one of the first recruits for the 20th USCT, signed his enlistment papers with a mark on December 9, 1863. He related his experiences at Lafayette Hall to the Regiment's Chaplain, George W. LeVere on the 29th of February 1864:

> *I was taken to the hall by a white man by the name of Henry little ... who told me that i was to get three hundred and twenty five Dollars Bounty   little) told me that he wanted me to go with him   i told him that i would like to enlist for the Rhodisland Regament   he*

then told me that that was the regiment that he belonged to and that it was on rikers island   when he told me this i told him that I would enlist providing i got what was promised ... tried to get me to drink   i refused   i told him that I did not drink but he tried to forse me to drink ... we then left the saloon and went to the Hall   after i got there he told me that they had stoped giving the three hundred and twenty-five dollars down but that i would get fifty dollars thare and the hundred and seventy five Dollars when i got on Rikers Island and that he would be there to see that i got it   he asked me what my name was   i told him that it was Oliver Comback   then the man that was sittin at the table rote my name down   i was examined by the doctor and passed ... i was sworn in and i recived fifty dollars after i recived the money I was placed under guard and stayed a while and was taken down stairs where I stayed until the next morning I was then taken from there to Rikers Island.[294]

This treatment was repeated time and time again by those lining up recruits for Brigadier General Francis B. Spinola, who had obtained his rank in recognition for recruiting and organizing four regiments from the New York City area. He had even gone with his troops into battle, but was deemed by real army generals to be better suited to recruitment and had been assigned duty in New York City where he set up office in Lafayette Hall in the fall of 1863. The fraud was not isolated to the black soldiers, but the official authorization to enlist soldiers for the 20th USCT was certainly fortuitous for those who knew how to work the bounty system to their advantage. The tactics of men like Henry Little ran the gamut of kidnapping, plying men with liquor, false promises of jobs or non-existent bounties. The fact that many of the black enlistees could not read or write made it even easier to perpetrate the fraudulent acts.

By mid-January 1864 the complaints by the recruits could no longer be ignored as just "buyers' remorse" and Spinola was removed from his post. Major General John A. Dix, who had come to New York City in the wake of the draft riots, used the word "plunder" to describe the actions of the brokers working at Lafayette Hall. One of Dix's staff referred to it as "organized pillage."[295] General Spinola was court-martialed, but in the end was allowed to resign in 1865, with no guilt assigned for what had taken place under his watch in Lafayette Hall from November 1863 to January 1864. Some would call it a whitewash and others might say that Spinola was just a scapegoat for a bounty system in which there were too few rules.

When it came time to finalize the organization of the 20th USCT other problems arose. The Union League Club reported that

> *when the rolls were obtained, they were found to be in a most extraordinary condition; men who had been on the island from the first were left off them, and therefore were necessarily put into the third regiment, while others who arrived after there were two full regiments on the Island, were put into the Twentieth. Friends who enlisted together were separated and great trouble and dissatisfaction were caused ...*[296]

A final physical examination of every man in the new regiment, resulted in about eighty men being found physically unfit for duty and needed to be discharged. This resulted in additional shuffling of men from other regiments into the 20th.

By the end of February, the 20th USCT Regiment was finally ready to be activated and plans were made for its departure from New York City. On March 5, 1864 the men arrived in the city and marched to Union Square where the regimental flag was presented and numerous speeches made.

From there the unit marched down Canal Street to board the steamer *Ericcson* to be transported to New Orleans, where it would take up duty on the Mississippi River.

THE TWENTIETH UNITED STATES COLORED TROOPS RECEIVING THEIR COLORS ON UNION SQUARE, MARCH 5, 1864.—[SEE PAGE 187.]

The 20th United States Colored Troops receiving their colors on Union Square, March 5, 1864. Harper's Weekly, March 1864.

The 26th USCT left Riker's Island three weeks later headed for Annapolis, Maryland. Recruitment for the third regiment stalled and when only three companies had been mustered in, they were ordered to join the Army of the Potomac. Eventually the 31st USCT absorbed a contingent of about 300 men raised in Connecticut.

Recruitment of black soldiers from New York State took the efforts of both black and white leaders, but it was the power of the rich white New Yorkers which finally trumped Horatio Seymour's opposition. The motives of the Union League Club had nothing to do with their beliefs that black soldiers had a right to fight for their country but had everything to do with adding numbers and bodies from New York State in order to meet quotas and support a weakened Union army. Regardless the Club's committee appeared to take seriously its responsibilities to the African Americans that enlisted in the New York regiments and worked to ensure that they were treated with dignity and fairness.

Recruits from Western New York

The pool of potential soldiers from Western New York had dwindled significantly before the recruitment of the 20th USCT got under way. When the draft registration was completed in June of 1863 there were less than 1,400 black men between the ages of 20 and 45 on the rolls for the Western Division, which included 26 counties from Oneida on the east to Erie on the west. There is no way to determine exactly how many of these men were actually fit for the military service, but it only stands to reason that many would be exempted for a variety of legitimate reasons. Recruitment for the 54th and 55th Massachusetts; followed by the draft in the summer of 1863; followed by aggressive recruitment for the 14th Rhode Island Heavy Artillery and the 29th Connecticut meant that hundreds of African American New Yorkers were already in the Union army by December 1863. Yet this did not seem to diminish the interest or enthusiasm of those still remaining at home.

The enlistments between December 1863 and March 1864 included a steady stream of men from Western New York who would be assigned to the 20th, 26th and 31st regiments of the United States Colored Troops. On the surface there seems little rhyme or reason to why a soldier would be assigned to one regiment over another. The rush of recruits had interrupted the logical processing of the men. The "luck of the draw" would greatly impact the wartime experiences of the recruits from New York State. The 20th USCT ended up spending most of its service in the Department of the Gulf in defense of New Orleans and the Mississippi River where their fiercest enemy would be disease. The regiment lost over 260 enlisted men to disease and only one death ascribed to contact with the enemy. Its duty was concluded with the mustering out on October 7, 1865 in New Orleans, Louisiana.

The 26th USCT went to Beaufort, South Carolina where it was attached to the Department of the South. The regiment participated in a number of actions between April and December 1864 resulting in the deaths of two officers and twenty-eight enlisted men. The deadliest engagement took place in early July 1864 during the Battle of John's Island as part of the overall Battle of Charleston. Disease took another 112 enlisted men. Its muster out date was August 28, 1865 at Hilton Head, South Carolina.

The 31st USCT was in Virginia where it took part in the siege of Petersburg and suffered its darkest hour at the Battle of the Crater, losing 27 killed, 42 wounded and 66 missing or captured. It was then deployed briefly to Texas after the end of the war for service along the Rio Grande. All told the regiment lost 48 enlisted men killed and mortally wounded. Another 123 enlisted men succumbed to disease. It was the last of the New York regiments to be mustered out. On November 7, 1865 the men of the 31st were mustered out at Brownsville, Texas.

Ontario County proved to be prime recruiting territory. Four men traveled from Geneva, New York to New York City in mid-December. Festus Prince, George Whitney and John Phillips most likely traveled together, having been lured to the City with the promise of a $600 bounty and a ten-day furlough after enlistment and before reporting to duty. Prince and Whitney each told their story to the regimental Chaplain in February 1864 saying that Augustus Jeffries and John Forbes approached Festus Prince and George Whitney on Water Street in Geneva and asked if they might be interested in enlisting in the army. Prince being a boatman and Whitney a farmer and the season being winter, both were unemployed and the offer of such a sizeable bounty was too good to refuse. Before they left Geneva, they were joined by John Phillips. On December 18th the three men were enlisted into the army by Lt. G. Williams, Recruiting Officer, Aide de Camp of General Spinola's Staff.

Prince and Whitney told the chaplain that when they arrived at Lafayette Hall each was given $50 by a white man named Little, who told them that after signing up they would be given a ten day furlough and upon their return to New York City would be given the balance of their bounty of $550. Unfortunately the newly enlisted men were taken directly to the guard room and kept there until they were transferred to Riker's Island the next day.[297] They not only did not get the furlough, but there was no more bounty money coming their way.

The fourth recruit from Geneva enrolled in Brooklyn on December 17th. He was hardly a man, being barely 15 years old, but perhaps fortunately, he too found himself in Company D with his neighbors. Joseph Gillam, born in 1849, enlisted using the alias of Joseph Williams, leaving behind his parents Joseph and Harriet Gillam, two sisters Adalaide and Mary, and a brother Philip. Charles H. Derby writing in support of Gillam's application for a pension many years later, explained the reason for the use of an alias by saying that his cousin Joseph had feared that his father would find him and force him to return home.[298] Since Joseph was underage, the father would most likely have done just that.

Meanwhile recruiting by legitimate agents went forward in Ontario County. Over the next two months at least twenty-four more men from the county enlisted in the army. In addition to the four men that enlisted in New York City, Geneva's contribution included Aaron, William C., Samuel and George Gayton, Nathan Prue, Nelson Reed, Arthur Condol, John Hardy, Harvey and Benjamin Jupiter, Harvey Burns, and William R. Johnson. From Canandaigua were Adam and Isaac Holland, George H. Watts, Augustus Freeland, Alexander Blake, Augustus Smith, Thomas and George W. Clark, and Charles H. Freeman. Brothers Martin V. and Charles M. Fletcher enlisted from Naples. Abram Cook was the lone enlistee from the town of Manchester. Of the twenty-eight recruits from Ontario County, twenty became part of the 26th USCT; three were assigned to the 31st; five joined the 20th USCT; and one was assigned to the 20th USCT, but never left New York State, serving as a teamster in Elmira, New York.

Compared to the African American population of the New York City area and eastern New York, the number of potential recruits in Western New York may have been small, yet the commitment was strong. A letter to the Anglo-African newspaper, dated March 31, 1864 pointed out the contributions of the small African-American community of Geneva, New York once the initial round of enlistments for the New York State regiments was completed. Benjamin F. Cleggett wrote:

> *I think we have the right to claim the honor of being the banner town of the State, for out of a total population of about two hundred, we have sent fifty-nine recruits into the service, which is over one half of our male population ... We deeply feel the loss of so many out of our limited community. We miss them in our churches, schools and quiet firesides ... We are often greeted with pensive look and anxious countenance by some aged parent, loving sister, nephew, cousin, or anxious friend ...[299]*

This same sentiment was repeated throughout all the enclaves of African Americans scattered among the small towns of Western New York in early 1864. Tompkins County, New York sent at least twenty-five men to join the New York regiments, with twenty of them serving in the 26th USCT. Twelve men from Cayuga County and another ten from Yates County were also added to the ranks of the 26th. With each opportunity to enlist the able-bodied (and not so able-bodied) set out for the life of a soldier.

20th USCT and Western New York

When the 20th USCT was ready to parade down Canal Street in New York City on March 5, 1864 there were at least seventeen men from Western New York in the ranks, while by far the majority hailed from New York City and vicinity. Albert Ray had enlisted in Rochester even before the 20th USCT was authorized, most likely thinking he would be going to Camp William Penn to be assigned to a regiment. He signed his name to the enlistment papers on November 30th and two weeks later he was forwarded to Elmira. He waited there until early February before being sent to Riker's Island, where he was assigned to Company G.[300]

Elmira, as headquarters for the Provost Marshal of the Western Division of New York, was an important enlistment center. Recruiting Officer T.C. Cowen brought William Goodman in on December 17. Goodman was soon a soldier in Company H of the 20th USCT. Recruiter Silas Haight delivered John A. Lee on the 18th and on the same day J. A. McWilliams escorted Thomas N. Lush and William Culbert to Elmira for enlistment. Lee, Lush and Culbert were assigned to Company I. Cowen, Haight and McWilliams all received documents identifying themselves as recruiting agents who were eligible to receive a $2.00 finder fee for each man. Harrison Hammit enlisted in Corning, New York on December 26th and was brought that same day to Elmira by agent Silas Haight, who would receive another $2.00 for his efforts. Hammit became a member of Company D. [301]

Harvey Jupiter (also known as Jubiter) of Geneva, New York signed up on December 19th and became a member of Company I.[302] Amasa Carr and Thomas Craig joined the army in Oswego the end of December and were transferred to Riker's Island to be added to the rosters of Company G and A, respectively. George H. Carr enlisted at Oswego on January 4, 1864 and joined his brother Amasa Carr in Company G.[303]

The 20th USCT arrived in New Orleans on March 31, 1864 where it would become part of the army's effort to defend New Orleans and the Mississippi River. Much of their service would be at Plaquemine and Camp Parapet, where parts of the 14th Rhode Island Heavy Artillery (11th USCHA) were also stationed. Disease turned out to be the greatest threat to the men of the regiment. Chaplain George W. Le Vere wrote to the *Anglo-African* in a letter dated May 5, 1864 that as a portion of the regiment was being transferred from Port Hudson, Louisiana to Matagorda Island, Texas it was necessary to leave "about 40 in the General Hospital."[304] The *National Anti-Slavery Standard's* issue of July 23rd, included a piece from the *New York Times* stating that the regiment had lost "about fifty men by disease."[305]

James Clark was among the first of the recruits from Western New York to die. The twenty-four year native of Maryland had enlisted on January 4, 1864 in Scriba, Oswego County, New York. He succumbed to diarrhea on April 22, 1864 at Port Hudson. The next to die was Harvey Jupiter on May 5th at the General Hospital in New Orleans of diarrhea.[306] Nineteen-year-old Amasa Carr was added to the list of dead on August 6th, when he died of disease at Camp Parapet, Louisiana.[307]

By October Lt. Col. A. E. Mather, acting Commanding Officer, seemed hopeful that the worst of the sickness was over. Mather wrote to Vincent Colyer, chairman of the Recruiting Committee of the Union League Club, on October 15, 1864 from Camp Parapet giving an overview of conditions of the regiment:

> *The health of the regiment is improving and I am hoping the cool weather we are now having will greatly diminish the sick list... I am having the tents repaired in anticipation of cold weather, and have been fortunate in securing a quantity of lumber. The stoves given us by the Union League have been invaluable to the regiment. That have not only enabled us to cook rations better than any other regiment here, but have assisted greatly in making with which I intend to purchase others... The walks throughout camp are paved with brick, and each company is now building an oven with the same material.*[308]

Colonel Mather enclosed with his letter to Mr. Colyer extracts from a report of the Carrolton District for months of July and August which described the 20th USC Infantry as being "in the hands of energetic and faithful field officers, who have their regiment unusually well disciplined. Drills are exceedingly creditable to officers and men. Manner of guard duty, soldierly; camp is the finest in the district."[309]

The number of deaths in the first months had reduced the ranks of the regiment to such an extent that Col. Nelson B. Bartram traveled north to undertake a recruitment effort. It was during the late summer and early fall of 1864 that a second wave of recruits from Western New York joined the 20th USCT, mostly promising to serve for only one year. Some of these enlistments may have been driven by the threat of another round of the draft, but regardless the African American men of Western New York once again answered the call.

When the recruiters for the 20th USCT came around in the late summer of 1864 there were even fewer to call upon in the smaller communities of Western New York, yet records indicate that forty-two men enlisted and were assigned to the regiment. When it came time for deployment of the second group to Louisiana the number of recruits from Western New York was reduced by three. Forty-two- year old James Thomas enlisted at Springport, Cayuga County on August 11, 1864, but was identified on the muster roll created in Elmira on December 31, 1864 as a "deserter."[310] Perhaps he had had second thoughts. William Van Horn, aged 38, had enlisted at Avon, New York on September 1st and was listed as "on furlough" on the muster roll dated December 31, 1864 in Elmira, New York. Records show that he was sometimes listed as part of the 26th USCT, but was never assigned to a company and was discharged in April 1865 at Elmira, New York.[311]

Twenty-one-year-old John W. Garthen of West Bloomfield, Ontario County enlisted on September 1, 1864 and was forwarded to Riker's Island from Elmira on December 13th. He was admitted to the Ft. Columbus Hospital in New York Harbor on January 19, 1865 and died there on January 26 of pneumonia. His family physician, Dr. L. F. Wilbur, wrote in an affidavit dated September 13, 1869 that "said John Garthen was physically well and sound when he enlisted."[312] John's eighteen-year-old brother William had enlisted within a few days of his older brother and was assigned to Company D. At home was their widowed mother Sarah Garthen. William survived the war and returned home to his family in Ontario County, New York.

The recruits who made it to Louisiana in the second group faired a bit better in regard to their health than the first enlistees. Of the first seventeen men known to have been from Western New York to arrive in Louisiana, five died from disease. The second wave of recruits numbered about thirty-nine, of which seven would die, mostly from diarrhea or dysentery. There were also three early discharges for disability within the Western New York contingent. Albert Ray had been among the first recruits, having enlisted in Rochester in late November 1863. Sergeant Ray was discharged from the hospital in New Orleans on June 1, 1865. Garret Smith Johnson of Geneva, New York and Peter Washington of Yates County, both included in the second group of enlistees, were discharged in August of 1865 because of illness.

A fourth discharge came too late for the soldier. Martin Wigden of Steuben County, New York was only 20 years old when he enlisted in September 1864. His discharge from the service was dated March 21, 1865, with the Surgeon noting that "This man is unfit for a soldier and in my opinion unless discharged will spend most of the remainder of his term of service in Hospital." Martin only had one more day to "live" in the hospital as he died on March 22nd. Permelia Wigden, claiming to be mother of Martin Wigden (alias Charles M. Holmes), applied for a pension in 1880, but was not successful in her quest.[313] Martin, who was also identified with the surname of Bliss on several census records, was very likely the younger brother or cousin of George Bliss who enlisted on the same day and was also a soldier in Company G of the 20th USCT.[314]

The death of Martin Wigden in March 1865 was followed by the death of George Whitney on April 29th. Private Whitney, one of the men tricked into enlisting in New York City, died just one day short of his second wedding anniversary. He was survived by his wife, the former Charlotte Baker of Geneva,

New York.[315] John Davis, a substitute for A. J. Foland of Sodus, New York, enlisted for a three-year term of service on September 20, 1864 and joined Company C on February 18, 1865. The thirty-five- year old laborer was born in Mississippi and apparently had made his way north before or during the war, only to return South and to his death on May 9, 1865.

Another former slave, Thomas Hart of Springport, Cayuga County, left his wife and five children for the uncertain life of a soldier in October of 1864. At forty-four-year-old Hart was among the oldest of the recruits who joined the 20th USCT that fall. Private Hart had come north from Baltimore, Maryland with his brother James in April 1840 by way of the Underground Railroad. A note written by John Mann of Pennsylvania stating "I have mailed two passengers to thee, in the 'shank's horse diligence' baggage free, and at the risk of the owners" is said to have introduced the Hart brothers to Slocum Howland, a Quaker, of Sherwood's Corners in Cayuga County.[316] Thomas and James did not move on to Canada, but settled in the vicinity of Sherwood's Corners which welcomed many freedom seekers during the years before the Civil War. Leaving his wife of twenty-two years would have been a wrenching experience, but Thomas Hart must have felt strongly in order to make that decision. His death on May 16, 1865 was attributed to "disease."[317]

It was not just the older soldiers who were susceptible to illness. Twenty-seven- year old Harrison Hammit (Company E) of Steuben County was one of the first group of soldiers to join the 20th USCT. He died of Acute Dysentery on May 25, 1865.[318] A month later nineteen-year-old Simon L. Graham, also of Company E, succumbed to what was described as Phthisis Pulmonalis, also known as tuberculosis. The examining physician Dr. A. Bacchus of Rochester, New York stated that at the time of Graham's enlistment in August 1864 "he was physically sound and free from all disease and was passed by me, as fit for the U.S. military service." The doctor went on to say that if the soldier died of Phthisis Pulmonalis, "he must have contracted it after enlistment." Private Graham's mother Lucinda Bennett, applied for a pension based on the fact that she had been dependent on her son for help with paying rent and buying food.[319]

The last deaths of men from Western New York occurred in September 1865. Within a month both men would have been on their way home. Samuel Carpenter could easily have avoided military service as a forty-four-year-old man. His death from dysentery occurred at Milliken's Bend, Louisiana on September 15th.[320] William Alexander was over twenty years younger than Private Carpenter so he was a prime candidate for military service. Alexander was felled by Typhoid Fever on September 23rd.[321] His was the second death for the Alexander family of Steuben County. William's older brother George Alexander had been killed at the Battle of Olustee in February 1864 while serving in the 8th USCT.

For all the deaths and sickness, most of the Western New York men in the 20th USCT were able to return home at the end of the war and pick up their lives as civilians. Three of the four young men who traveled to New York City in December 1863 to enlist in the army returned home. The youngster Joseph Gillam (alias Joseph Williams) learned the trade of a master barber and operated a shop in Geneva, New York for over fifty years. In 1873 Gillam married Mary Douglass of Waterloo, New York, daughter of Henry and Louisa Douglass. The marriage merged two of the Geneva's pioneer African American families. Gillam's great grandfather, Philip Gillam, was brought north as a slave by James Rees about 1801. Mary's grandfather, Henry Douglass and grandmother Phillis Kenny had been enslaved by John Nicholas and were brought to the area about 1803.[322] Joseph and Mary Gillam remained in Geneva until their deaths in 1930 and 1934 respectively.

Festus Prince worked as a boatman on Seneca Lake prior to his enlistment in New York City. After the war he moved about, working in Syracuse as a laborer and in Geneva and Bath, New York as a farm laborer. Prince secured an invalid's pension in 1890 and afterwards would be an "off and on again" resident of the Soldiers and Sailors Home in Bath, New York until his death in 1920. [323] John Phillips was made sergeant of Company D even before the regiment left Riker's Island and maintained the rank throughout his service. After returning to Geneva he took up his old job as a hostler at a hotel in the village where he met his future wife. He married Mariah (Gayton) Proctor in January 1873. It was his first marriage and her second. Phillips died suddenly in October 1891 of a heart attack, leaving his widow and no children. Maria Phillips secured a widow's pension which she received until her death in January 1897.[324]

Benjamin Franklin "Frank" Bogart, Andrew R. Foster and Edwin J. Watkins all enlisted in Palmyra, Wayne County on August 17, 1864, each for a one year term of service. When Frank Bogart came home he was greeted by his wife Mary A. (Cooley) Bogart, a one-year old son Frank Jr., his mother Lydia, and sister Mary. Missing was his younger brother George Washington Bogart who had died in Louisiana just two weeks before Frank signed his enlistment papers, while a soldier in Company L of the 11th USCHA.

It is said that Frank Bogart enlisted as a substitute for Pliny T. Sexton, but nothing in his military record indicates that this was the case. Sexton was the son of Pliny Sexton, a Quaker who was well known for his opposition to slavery and active role in the Underground Railroad. Pliny T. Sexton employed Frank Bogart for many years after the Civil War and perhaps it was this relationship that led some to believe that Sexton was repaying Bogart for taking his place in the war. Regardless of the lack of documentation, the story of Sexton paying Bogart to join the army in his stead is still part of the folklore of the Palmyra community. [325]

Photograph of Benjamin Franklin Bogart and his bride, Mary Cooley in July 1862. From archives of First Presbyterian Church, Palmyra, New York.

Frank Bogart was born in Wayne County about 1832 to Lydia and Lafayette Bogart of the town of Ontario, Wayne County, New York. Frank's wife Mary Cooley was the daughter of Charles and Amanda Cooley, who had moved to Palmyra from Dutchess County, New York about 1836. Both families were well established in the small African American community of Palmyra when the couple married in July of 1862, with the Presbyterian minister, Rev. Mr. Horace Eaton officiating.

Even though Frank Bogart's military service was only one year, he did not escape the debilitating effects of dysentery that he contracted while in Louisiana. His pension application chronicled his condition and the impact it had on his ability to work. His bunkmate, Frederick Bailey of Lewis County, New York backed the claim stating in an affidavit dated April 1, 1891, that he "knew the claimant Frank Boget to be sick with chronic Diarrhea for six or seven months before he was discharged from the service, attended to him during his sickness, dealing out his medicine to him and performing such other service as he required of me..."[326] Frank Bogart died in October 1902 and was buried next to his wife in the Palmyra Village Cemetery.[327]

Palmyra had been home to Andrew R. Foster for about 15 years when he enlisted in the army. Born in Brooklyn, New York, Foster was 16 years old in 1850 and working in the Palmyra Hotel, owned by William P. Nottingham.[328] On Thanksgiving Eve, November 25, 1852 he married seventeen-year-old Angeline Eliza Dewitt, who in 1850 was working for the William F. Aldrich family. Andrew and Angeline were described as "very young and handsome" by the Rev. Horace Eaton, who married them at the Presbyterian Church.[329] During the next twelve years the couple had five children, four of whom were alive when their father joined the 20th USCT in August 1864. Upon his return to Palmyra, Andrew Foster found that his wife was ill and within two years Angeline was dead from tuberculosis.[330] With four children under the age 12, it was only natural that Andrew would remarry and on December 31, 1868 he was joined in marriage to Miranda Nickson at the Western Presbyterian Church in Palmyra. Once again, the Rev. Horace Eaton officiated at the ceremony. Six years later Andrew R. Foster also succumbed to tuberculosis, dying at the age of 42 years.[331]

The town of Manchester, located just to the south of Palmyra, was home to Edwin J. Watkins, the son of Edward and Isabelle (Frost) Watkins. While Bogart and Foster were both mature men in their thirties, Watkins was barely 20 years old at the time of his enlistment. Assigned to Company I, he was promoted to Corporal in March 1865, a rank he held until his discharge on August 23, 1865 at Milliken's Bend, Louisiana.[332] Not long after his return from the war, Watkins married Jane Lloyd of Sodus Point, New York and they set up housekeeping in Manchester, where their daughter Harriet was born in 1867.

The origins of the Watkins and Lloyd families were linked long before the couple married. They were both descendants of slaves brought north by southerners about 1800. Watkins' ancestors were once the slaves of Capt. William Helm, formerly of Virginia, who first settled near Sodus Bay, in what is now Wayne County, New York and later moved to Bath, New York. The roots of the Lloyd family are tied to slaves brought to the Sodus Bay area about the same time by Peregrine Fitzhugh.

Jane Watkins died in October 1867, leaving Edwin to raise his daughter, with the help of his sister Celinda (Watkins) Ross. In April of 1884 Edwin married Josephine (Anderson) Alexander and moved from to Auburn, New York. His new wife had been born in St. Catharines, Ontario, Canada, a famous terminus of the Underground Railroad, and immigrated to Auburn, New York about 1865. Edwin Watkins died in Auburn on April 15, 1921.[333]

Soldiers of the 26th USCT

26th USCT on parade at Riker's Island, March 1864. Photo from National Archives collection. Note: Some online websites identify this photo as being of the 25th USCT leaving Camp William Penn.

The 26th USCT regiment was officially organized at Riker's Island on February 27, 1864 and within a month was ready to be sent to war. Hoping to repeat the fanfare that accompanied the departure of the 20th USCT early in March, the Union League and other benevolent societies prepared festivities to mark the exit of the 26th USCT from Riker's Island and New York City, scheduled for March 26th. Committees organized a program that would include music, orations, presentations of flags and a grand parade by the regiment. Steamers were chartered. Accommodations readied for friends and families of the soldiers. A ferocious storm disrupted all the plans and the regiment instead embarked from Riker's Island on March 27th, foregoing the parade and planned festivities. Before their departure, John Jay of the Union League Club spoke to the troops;

> *On behalf of the ladies of New-York, who have prepared for you a stand of colors, I offer you a cordial greeting and a hearty God speed! They hoped in common with tens of thousands of their fellow-citizens to greet you in person yesterday. This, to their exceeding disappointment, the storm prevented. We therefore, come on this beautiful Easter morning, consecrated to Faith and Hope, to give you, as you depart, our kind farewell...To-day you go forth from home, family and friends ...to do bravely, with God's help your part in the great contest.[334]*

The silk national colors flag included 35 embroidered stars and embroidered designation "26th Regt. U.S. Colored Troops" along the center red stripe. NYS Military Museum Collection.

Colonel William Silliman accepted the colors on behalf of the soldiers stating the banner presented was not only beautiful, but an "emblem of our faith in all of this life which is worth living for. It is to us the symbol of redemption from bondage..."[335]

Even before the regiment left Riker's Island one of the recruits from Ontario County, New York had been lost to death. Augustus Smith of Canandaigua had enlisted on January 12, 1864 and died of complications from measles on February 26 – barely six weeks after he left home. Private Smith was born in Anne Arundel, Maryland about 1838 and by 1863 was living in Canandaigua where he had married an Irish girl, named Mary, becoming the father of three sons, Charles, John and Edward.[336] Mrs. Smith was notified by the Rev. Henry Highland, Honorary Chaplain of Riker's Island in a letter dated February 27, 1864:[337]

My dear Mrs. Smith,

It becomes my painful duty to tell you that your dear husband has gone away from this world of trouble. He died yesterday morning with out a struggle. I did all that I could to soothe his last moments. I loved him very much and he seemed to think much of me. He told me to write to you if it should please God to take him away. I have now fulfilled the sorrowful duty. I trust that God will give you strength to bear your severe [?] affection. Your husband did what he considered to be his duty when he joined the army [illegible]. He loved you, and his dear children as much as a man could – and often did he speak of you while I was sitting on the side of his bed. He had as good attention, and care as any other soldier usually gets – and more. The Lord giveth, and the Lord taketh away – blessed be the name of the Lord. His remains were decently buried in the

"Ever Green" Cemetery where all our soldiers are intered [sic]. He left two or three dollars with Hospital Steward which I will send you, when I get it. I send you the last kind letter which you wrote him – I read it for him, for he was too sick to read it himself.

Now my dear affected friend may God bless you, and your fatherless children – Write to me when you get this letter.

I am your friend
Henry Highland Garnet
Honorary Chaplain of Riker's Island

The Rev. Henry Highland Garnet was most likely familiar with some of the Western New York soldiers who were at Riker's Island that winter, having lived in Geneva, Ontario County, New York between 1849 and 1851. He had also traveled throughout the region, beginning in the 1840s, lecturing and advocating for the abolition of slavery and civil rights for the African American population, before settling in New York City.

The first stop for the regiment after leaving Riker's Island was Annapolis, Maryland where General Ambrose E. Burnside was gathering troops for the 9th Corps. From there the 26th was sent on to Beaufort, South Carolina where it reported to duty on April 13th, becoming part the brigade commanded by General Rufus Saxton in the Department of the South. While in South Carolina, the regiment participated in two major actions. The first took place on John's Island in early July of 1864, as part of a coordinated attack aimed at Confederate strongholds protecting Charleston, South Carolina. The 26th UCST was included in the force that was to cross John's Island in order to launch an attack on James Island. On Saturday, July 2nd the men began a slow and measured march across John's Island, encountering little resistance. The *New York Times* correspondent reported that "nothing of importance transpired with the troops on John's Island ... and today [Wednesday, July 6] they are bivouacked within easy distance of Stono River."[338]

While there had been only a brief sighting of the enemy, the march was not without challenges. The reporter went on to say that:

the weather has been exceedingly warm, the thermometer at times ranging as high as 110 degrees. Bearing in mind the intense heat, and the fact of there being very few shade trees on the line of march, it is a wonder how the troops succeeded-- unaccustomed as they are to marching – in getting over the extent of ground they did. John's Island is by no means a country abounding with fertile fields and rich pastures. On the contrary, it is a miserable tract of low ground, at the southern end marsh and producing nothing beyond clumps of underbrush and isolated trees ... Every portion of the island is infested with fleas, musquitoes [sic] and vermin..."[339]

When the reporter left the troops on John's Island he did not foresee the events of the next day. The leadership of the force crossing John's Island was caught off guard when they resumed the march on Thursday, July 7th and the results were devastating. On August 17, 1864, the *New York Tribune* published an account of the battle, written by someone identified by the initials J.H.S, which picked up where the earlier reporter had left off on July 6th.

In the forenoon of that day [July 7th] Colonel Silliman called the officers to him, and told them they would have a chance that afternoon to show themselves. A

rebel battery had been discovered two miles to our
right, and the commanding general had selected the
26th. U. S. C. C. to charge it. [340]

The men of the 26th started on time and after about a half hour on the move there was a brief stop before being ordered forward. The correspondent described the terrain yet to be traversed as "almost impenetrable thicket ... with the swampy nature of the soil rendered our progress slow, yet laborious..." The plan was that once the men reached the open area, they were to charge the enemy, but "the fatigue caused by our hard labor for the last hour, and the heat of the sun, rendered the men fit for anything but charging a battery..." Regardless of their exhaustion, the writer describes the determination of the troops once the order to charge was issued.

And never had I seen troops old or new, act with a
cooler determination ... They went forward as though
they were certain there were no rebels at their front.
They advanced under a heavy fire of musketry and
artillery... We charge five times against their four
pieces of artillery and eight hundred support, when
orders come from the rear, for us to retreat. The men
did it reluctantly.

The two-day Battle of Bloody Bridge ended with the retreat of the Union forces from the Island. Over 300 men were killed, wounded or missing.[341] Among the dead was Joseph Waters (Company F), of Genoa, Cayuga County, New York. The twenty-one-year-old had enlisted, along with his twenty-year-old brother, William, on December 23, 1863 and was mustered in at Auburn, New York on the 4th of January 1864. Waters entered the battle with the rank of Corporal, having received the promotion on June 23rd. Joseph and William were the sons of John and Matilda Waters, who had settled in the town of Venice, Cayuga County about 1840, within a circle of sympathetic Quakers.[342]

Elisha Swan and Henry Selby of Ithaca, Tompkins County, New York were both wounded during the battle. Swan was able to return to duty in December 1864, but Selby remained in the hospital until his discharge with a Certificate of Disability on February 13, 1865. Apparently in the eyes of the medical staff his extended stay in the hospital was not due to his wounds, but to his "old age and debility." The doctor rendered his reason for the discharge as follows:

> *He is, in my opinion, at least fifty-four years of age, and very feeble. He has done no duty for more than three months, nor will he ever again be able to perform the duties of a soldier and should be discharged [from] the service of the United States. The disability existed prior to his enlistment.*

Private Selby gave his age as 44 years at the time of his enlistment and was able to pass a physician's examination for fitness at that time.[343] Selby may not have known his exact age as he was very inconsistent when providing the census taker with that information. In the 1850 and 1860 census his age was listed as 46 and 44 years respectively.[344] Regardless of his age, it was his intent to serve in the army. If it had not been for his being wounded in the Battle of Bloody Bridge, he may have been able finish what he had started. The surgeon apparently had little sympathy for a man who would choose to serve, in spite of his advanced age.

The 26th USCT saw action again the end of November 1864 in the Battle of Honey Hill, South Carolina. General William T. Sherman, planning his move toward Savannah, Georgia, after capturing Atlanta, sent word to the War Department that he wanted action taken to cut the Savannah to Charleston railroad which would prevent supplies and reinforcements from reaching Confederate forces at Savannah. It would also remove a potential avenue of escape for the defenders of Savannah. On November 29th a force left Hilton Head, with orders to land at Boyd's Landing and march the nine miles to the railroad and to then tear up the tracks, burn railroad buildings and destroy nearby railroad bridges. Again, the execution of the plans fell short of the intended goal.

Once on land the troops were marched and counter-marched in search of the railroad. After a day of wandering, the troops ended the day seven miles from the railroad. The delay of the Union forces allowed the Confederate troops to plan for a defense of the railroad and on Wednesday the 30th of November the southerners were in position to repulse the northerners. The battle did not go well for the Union forces and at dusk they began their retreat from the field. The Union forces reported casualties of 88 killed, 623 wounded and 43 missing. The commanding officer of the 26th USCT, Colonel William Silliman, was severely wounded during the battle and died from his wounds a month later.

In both battles the men of the 26th USCT did not shirk from their duty. Private William Waters of Co. K wrote to the *Christian Recorder* in April, 1865 providing a summary of the actions of the 26th USCT:

Dear Editor: -
As nobody seems to take any interest in the 26th Regiment U. S. Colored Troops, I will endeavor to write a few lines for the benefit of all concerned, hoping our friends at the North, whom we have left behind while we went forward to fight for the defence [sic] of our Union, would be glad to hear from us.

We left our homes, our firesides, and our families, to fight for our country's cause, which we have done nobly. Twice we have been called upon to face the hot steel of the rebel batteries, which we did with unflinching bravery, and the energy of true soldiers, and lovers of our country. On John's Island, in the month of July 1864, the 26th won laurels for herself worthy to be recorded on the pages of history. The 26th has done noble deeds, and will do nobler, if she has a chance. At the battle of Honey Hill we lost our Colonel, who was leading his brigade through the field of battle, when a rebel shell struck his leg... The 26th admired and trusted in him, as a friend and a brave man...

We have often heard it said that the negro would not fight, - would not stand fire, - was only intended to stand behind the white man's chair. I deny the assertion. Has not the negro proved to be a true soldier? Has he not done the task assigned him? ... Yes, my fellow countrymen, the negro will fight. It has been proved. I defy either whites or black, to deny it.[345]

Private Waters enlisted alongside his brother Joseph in December 1863, representing hometown of Genoa, Cayuga County, New York. He lost his brother at the Battle of Bloody Bridge.

The 26th USCT was engaged in several other skirmishes during the month of December 1864. Just a few days before Christmas thirty-eight-year old Edward Sorrell of Dryden, Tompkins County was killed at Graham's Neck, South Carolina. Captain William H. Tracy wrote to the Pension Commissioner in September 1865 describing the events of December 22nd:

I was on picket with my Co. ('B', 26 U.S.C.T.) between the Tilifiring & Pocotaligo rivers South Carolina. At sunrise I was attacked by a party of the enemy and a skirmish ensued in which Edward Sorrell a Private of Co. 'B' ... was shot through the head and instantly killed by a ball from a short Enfield Rifle.[346]

Private Sorrell's eighteen-year-old-son, John, was also a private in Company B and most likely informed his mother of the death of her husband of twenty years. Private Edward Sorrell was born in Northumberland County, Virginia and his son was born in Baltimore, Maryland. The family migrated to Dryden, New York from Baltimore, Maryland about 1860.

There were many more deaths due to disease than armed combat in ranks of the 26th USCT. There would be a total of six deaths from the ranks of the men who enlisted in the regiment from Ontario County, New York, leaving three widows and six minor children, ages six months to 12 years. Charles H. Freeman was the first of the men from Ontario County to die in South Carolina. Private Freeman of Company D, fell victim to acute dysentery on July 25th 1864. When Freeman left Canandaigua just six months before his death, he said good-bye to his wife Eliza and his month-old daughter, Henrietta. His daughter would never get to know her father. Eliza (Dorsey) Freeman and her girlhood friend, Mary E. (Mayberry) Clark, would both mourn the loss of a husband that year. Corporal Stephen Clark, a soldier serving in the 8th USCT, died at Yellow Bluffs, Florida of intermittent fever the very same day as Private Freeman died in Beaufort, South Carolina.[347]

Two deaths of men from Ontario County followed in August. Corporal Isaac Holland, aged 22, died on August 17, 1864 of congestive fever and was buried in a military cemetery in Beaufort, South Carolina. An inventory of his effects included two great coats, one blouse, one pair of trousers, two caps, one knapsack, and two blankets. Upon his death Holland owed the government $1.85 for lost camp and garrison equipage; while the government owed him pay from July 1st plus an additional $24.00 due him for service from January through April.[348]

There was a large Holland family in Ontario County, but to which branch Isaac belonged has not been determined. A William Holland, most likely the progenitor of the family, was brought north as a slave by Judge Daniel Dorsey from Maryland about 1800 to what is now Wayne County, New York. Records indicate that William Holland was born about 1786 in Elkridge, Baltimore County, Maryland and gained his freedom about 1815 in Canandaigua, Ontario County. William Holland was listed as a free person of color and head of a household in the 1820 census of the town of Canandaigua that included five children under the age of fourteen.[349]

One day after the death of Corporal Holland, doctors at the Regimental General Hospital in Beaufort, South Carolina recorded the death of Martin Van Buren Fletcher, of Naples, Ontario County. Private Fletcher was listed as "sick in regimental Hospital" on the Company Muster Roll of May and June 1864, but the cause of death was not listed in his military record.[350] Two and a half months later Martin's younger brother Charles Morris Fletcher succumbed to pulmonary consumption at the same hospital.[351] The young men were the sons of Archelaus Fletcher, Jr. and were not the first nor last to die in the Fletcher family during the Civil War.

Another brother, David R. Fletcher, died in Camp Parapet, Louisiana in June 1864 while serving in the 11th USCHA. Two other Fletcher men from Ontario County – Roderick and Samuel – who were also members of the 11th USCHA died in Louisiana. Roderick died on July 1, 1864 and Samuel died a year later on July 5, 1865. They were related to the three brothers, but whether they were half-brothers or cousins is not known. Archelaus Fletcher, Sr. was born in Massachusetts, where he served during the Revolutionary War. He moved his family from Massachusetts to Ontario County about 1810.

One more Ontario County soldier in the 26th USCT died in South Carolina. Forty-year old John Hardy of Geneva died on October 5, 1864, leaving a wife Permelia and daughters Jane, Anna, and Phebe to mourn his loss. In November 1871 Benjamin Jupiter of Geneva, New York provided a deposition in regard to the pension application of Permelia Hardy, widow of John Hardy, which provided a small glimpse into the illness of his friend of twenty-five years:

> *John Hardy while there with the Company D & 26th Regiment were in two Battles ... that John Hardy the deceased soldier participated & took an active part in said fights ... upon his return to Bufort [sic] in & about the month of September 1864 said John Hardy was taken sick with what the surgeon of the Hospital at the Post (No. 10) Called Bone Feaver [sic]. The Surgeons name was Marvin Shoe who had charge of the hospital – that deponent saw said John Hardy when he was taken to the Hospital of the Regiment & after was to the Post Hospital – that said Hardy died within seven or eight days thereafter with what the Doctors & Surgeon called the Bone fever which disease he contracted while there in the Service. That said Hardy was Hale & Hearty man always down to the time of the Sickness at Bufort...*[352]

The fear of bad news from the war front plagued the households of every soldier regardless of race. When multiple members of a family were in the army, the terror was multiplied. Word of the death of Jeremiah Conway of Cayuga County, New York on October 5, 1864 was most likely sent to his wife, Nancy, by her brother Gabriel Davis who also was serving in the 26th.[353] It was the second death in the family within a month. Nancy Conway's brother, Hannibal Davis was a member of the 14th Rhode Island Heavy Artillery (11th USCHA), serving in Louisiana, when he died on September 5th.

Isaac Holland, Martin Fletcher, Charles Fletcher and John Hardy were all buried in Beaufort National Cemetery. Photos by George Perez.

Sixteen months after the 26th USCT had left Riker's Island, the surviving soldiers were on their way home. Mustered out on August 28, 1865 at Hilton Head, South Carolina, the unit was the first of the New York regiments to be released from duty. As the men made their way home they must have been filled with joy, anticipation and a bit of trepidation. Among those returning to Canandaigua were Thomas C. W. Clark and his twenty-two-year-old son, George W. Clark. On the day after Christmas in 1863, the elder Clark had been the first to enlist,

206

making his mark documents declaring his intention to volunteer. He claimed to be forty-five years old but was probably about fifty-five years of age at the time.

George Clark was only twenty-one-years old when he signed his enlistment papers on January 4, 1864. Both men were mustered into the service at Canandaigua on January 5th and were sent on to Riker's Island where they were mustered into Company D at the organization of the regiment on February 27th. By the time the regiment was ready to leave New York, George Clark had been named a musician in his company, a position he held until his promotion to Principal Musician on May 1, 1864, which was accompanied by his transfer to the regiment's non-commissioned staff.[354] The company and regimental musicians were key to the communication network of the army during the Civil War, providing critical means of sending orders while in the midst of battle. Being a principal musician meant that Clark would have played an important role during the Battles of Bloody Bridge and Honey Hill.

Thomas Clark was returning to his wife Margaret and daughter Julia, age 13. George Clark's wife, Mary and two-year old daughter Ida were also living in Canandaigua. The two families were listed together in the same dwelling in the 1870 census and living next door to each other in the 1875 census.[355] George did not give up his music once he was out of the army. Brass band music had taken hold in American life in the mid-1850s and would continue to be a prominent part of many communities through the end of the century.

The Canandaigua newspaper reported in July 1875 that the Canandaigua Colored Cornet Band had formed under the leadership of George Clark with twelve members.[356] He continued to make music until his untimely death from typhoid on October 23, 1878. The *Ontario County Journal* stated that he "was an upright and respected citizen, and his death will be deeply felt in the circle in which he moved as well as by the community generally."[357] George Clark was survived by his wife Mary, seven children, and his father, Thomas. Thomas Clark died in Canandaigua on September 14, 1886 and was buried in Woodlawn Cemetery.[358]

The Peter and Charlotte Peterson family of Leicester, Livingston County, New York welcomed home two of three sons they had sent to war in early 1864. The three young men – Peter Jr., age 20, John, age 19, Edward, age 18 - had enlisted together on December 31, 1863 and were all assigned to Company I. Peter was listed as "sick in hospital" on the May and June 1864 Company Muster Rolls. His death was recorded on August 23rd of acute diarrhea.[359]

Four members of the extended Gayton family of Ontario County, New York had signed on to serve in the army during December 1863 and January 1864. Thirty-six-year-old George Gayton was the only one not assigned to the 26th USCT. In fact, although he was officially part of the 20th USCT, he never left Elmira, New York where he served as a teamster until his discharge in 1865.[360] George Gayton's younger brother Aaron of Phelps, New York, cousin William C. and nephew Samuel Gayton went with the 26th USCT to South Carolina and all lived to come home.

William C. Gayton rose to the rank of Sergeant in Company D by November 1864. The *Compiled Military Records* provide very few clues to his life as a soldier, but it is likely that he participated in the Battle of Bloody Bridge and Honey Hill, as well as other engagements. When mustered out, Sergeant Gayton paid $6.00 to keep his rifle and other equipment. He was owed a bounty of $300 plus another $25.68 for his unused clothing allowance. There is no indication in the record that he had been sick or absent from duty for the entire time the regiment was in South Carolina. Yet William C. Gayton died on October 16, 1866, barely a year after his return home. Aaron and his brother George returned to Phelps, New York, with George moving to Cattaraugus County, New York about 1870. Within a few years, his brother Aaron joined him in the southern tier, where they both worked as farm laborers. Their nephew, Samuel Gayton, led a wandering life after the war, living in Geneva, Seneca Falls, Lockport and Auburn, where he died in 1921.[361]

The transition back into the old routines was not always easy for the returning soldiers and some were never fully able to "fit in" again. In 1863, thirty-five-year old Benjamin Jupiter was a married family man with his own barber shop in the town of Phelps, Ontario County, New York, located about fifteen miles from his hometown. Born in Geneva, New York to Anthony and Susan Jupiter, he was part of a close-knit family that had lived in the area for forty years. The war had a profound impact on the Jupiter family. Disease took the life of Jupiter's younger brother, Harvey, a soldier with the 20th USCT in Louisiana, on May 5, 1864. Four months later his nephew Dwight Jupiter (alias Dwight Ray), a private in the 8th USCT, was killed in action at Darbytown, Virginia. Meanwhile Benjamin Jupiter found himself in South Carolina facing the unpredictable threats of disease and battle.

In October 1864 at the post hospital Corporal Jupiter attended to his friend John Hardy as he lay dying from bone fever. Jupiter himself was taken sick in mid-November and was listed on hospital muster rolls as a patient in the hospital in Beaufort until the end of March. His recovery may have been sooner, for on March 22, 1865 he was promoted to Chief Nurse and Assistant Steward at the Regimental Hospital, a job he held until he was granted an early discharge for disability on June 28, 1865.[362] There is nothing in the records to indicate what the disability was that convinced the surgeon to send him home early. Was his disability tied to the illness that had sent him to the hospital in November 1864? Or was there some other reason?

From some accounts, Ben Jupiter returned to Geneva, New York a changed man. While he was in the army, his wife had moved the family to Geneva from Phelps to be closer to her in-laws, Anthony and Susannah Jupiter and Harriet Foster. Once home in Geneva, Jupiter tried to revitalize his business and opened a barber shop. Financially the family was struggling and sometime about 1870 Jupiter sold his shop and started to work for other barbers in the area. It is during this time that the life of Jupiter began to unravel. Many years later Jane (VanDyne) Jupiter began the process of applying for a Civil War pension. In an affidavit dated September 25, 1896 she outlined basic reasons for her claim:

> About 23 years ago, while living in Geneva, N.Y. my husband Benjamin W. Jupiter, left me and I have never heard anything from him since. He was a barber by trade and accustomed to going away from home to work in other places, sometimes telling me that he was going and sometimes not doing so. The last time he went, I had no intimation where he was going & even did not know that he intended going, until I found him gone. I waited some time in Geneva for him to return and then came to Boston, Mass where I have been ever since, but at no time since his departure twenty-three years ago, have I received one word on intelligence from him, so I concluded that he must be dead. We had always lived happily together, so when I found that he had gone, I supposed that he gone to look for work, as he had been accustomed to do, but whether, in fact he did go for this purpose I do not know...

This set-in motion a five-year search for verification that Benjamin W. Jupiter was in fact dead and that Jane V. Jupiter was indeed eligible to receive a pension as his widow. There is no doubt that the Special Examiners assigned to the case were thorough and were eventually able to solve the mystery of what happened the old soldier. In February 1898 Mrs. Jupiter was asked to give a deposition in which she gave additional information:

We were married in New Haven, Conn in 1853 & we lived together till he went into the army...I was keeping house at Geneva ... & when my husband came home & we continued to live in Geneva till he went away... Geneva was a small place & my husband was out of work & started out to hunt work. He was in the habit of going away to different towns & working a week or so & would often take his tools & walk from place to place...I heard one indirectly that he died suddenly at Hazeldell, Pa. but I wrote to the hotel man there & he wrote me that he had made inquiries & could learn nothing of it – This was about two years ago. When I went to Geneva to see his sister ... she said she had made every effort to learn of his whereabouts ... When my husband left we had four children ... our domestic relations had been happy. We had no trouble. My husband was a drinking man – but not what I would call a dissipated man ... I haven't any particular theory as to what has become of him... He was a man who loved his family & his parents & sister & there was no reason in the world for him to stay away unless something happened to him...

A year later a Special Examiner was once again asking Mrs. Jupiter to try to verify her earlier statements. She stated that she left Geneva with only her youngest child, Alfred, in 1874 and had chosen to move to Boston because she had a sister living there and felt she would be able find work in the city. Mrs. Jupiter denied that she had "left" her husband, but that she had only moved from Geneva after being abandoned by him. The Examiners were not about to approve a widow's pension application without proof of the soldier's death. Tracking down false lead after false lead, the examiners finally were able to end their search. Mr. and Mrs. John V. Bonnert of Rasselas, Pennsylvania provided an affidavit dated December 21, 1900 stating that in 1889 they ran a hotel in town and "became acquainted with Benjamin W. Jupiter, a colored man, who ... was employed by us as a helper around the hotel. One evening in September or October of 1889 he was taken suddenly ill ... in the morning...found Benjamin W. Jupiter dead in bed ..." An affidavit by Dr. J. H. Wells of Wilcox, Elk County, Pennsylvania confirmed that he had been called to the hotel and found the "body of a colored man, called Jupiter" and determined that he most likely died from heart trouble. In a later deposition Mr. Bonnert added new information about Benjamin Jupiter.

> *We always called him Ben. At first he was just staying at the hotel as a guest & afterwards he worked for me doing chores. He told me something of his family affairs. He spoke of having a wife – it seems to me he called her Jane. I don't recall whether he said anything about any children. He said they lived in Boston...He never said why he left home. I supposed things were all right at home from what he said. He wrote several letters while at my place but I don't know with whom he corresponded. He spoke of having been in the army during the war ...He often spoke to the boys about his experiences in the army. I don't remember what battles he said he was in...There were no papers in his*

possession indicating who he was except a few letters that came addressed to him as Benjamin Jupiter. I don't know what became of them... Jupiter was buried by the town...He was very jovial and talkative..."

Benjamin Jupiter lived for fifteen years after he abandoned his family in Geneva. The Pension examiners' investigation pieced together an overview of his life during those years which does include at least one visit to Geneva about 1887 and limited contact with his sister and nephew at that time. Most of the "sightings" of Jupiter during the time period were by fellow barbers as he worked his way around the southern tier of New York State and northern Pennsylvania. A fairly complete summary of Jupiter's life was given by George H. Burghardt, a barber in Kane, McKean Co., Pennsylvania when he was deposed in November 1901:

I first became acquainted with Benjamin Jupiter in 1876 at Attica, New York. He worked for me there in my barber shop for about five months ...The next time I saw Ben was at Perry, N.Y. where he again worked for me for a short while. This was along in the '80s – early. Then he went to Arcade... the next time I saw him was here at Kane, about twelve years ago last June. He was not working here & did not appear to be drinking at all. He told me he had been stopping principally over at Smithport, Pa, with a relative named Ray ... Ben told me that he was travelling around through the country, doing a little barber work when he could get it or sharpening razors, & that he made a practice of going round to these small towns... The first I heard of Ben's death was through Marcellus Ray, about a year or more after I last saw Ben... died over at Rasselas...."

The pension of Jane V. Jupiter was approved in 1902 and the application file contains part of the story of the soldier's life following his time in the army.[363] What it does not reveal is the "why" behind the journey that led this once industrious and apparently devoted family man to leave the security of his family and hometown to become a "wandering barber."

The 31st USCT Goes to War

The Union League Club was hopeful that they would be able to fill the ranks of the third New York regiment for the United States Colored Troops, but the flood of recruits arriving at Riker's Island slowed to a trickle. By late April there were only enough men for three companies – seven shy of what was considered a full regiment. None the less, the regiment was ordered to join the Army of the Potomac which was about to launch the spring campaign. It appears that less than 25 recruits from Western New York were among the ranks sent south.

Within a few weeks another three hundred men, raised for the 30th Connecticut (Colored) Infantry, were merged into the regiment and strengthened its ranks. Assigned to the Ninth Corps, 4th Division, 2nd Brigade, the regiment played a support role as the Army of the Potomac battled its way south toward Richmond. By the end of June the Federal forces set up siege operations around Richmond and Petersburg, Virginia. The 31st USCT took up its position outside of Petersburg. On the morning of July 30, 1864 the lives of the soldiers of the 31st USCT were forever changed at what has become known as the Battle of the Crater.

It all started with the idea that the Federal forces could tunnel under the Confederate lines, plant explosives which when set off would create a gap in the defenses of Petersburg. The Union forces would then rush through the lines, forcing

Robert E. Lee to abandon the Confederate capitol and capitulate. The plan apparently looked doable on paper and sounded good to General Burnside, but the execution failed with disastrous results.

Major Thomas Wright of the 31st USCT, writing on August 2, 1864, provided an account of the battle which was included in the *Union League Club Report*, published in October 1864:

> *On the night of the 29th we were in a position on the extreme left. We were drawn in about 9 P.M., and marched to General Burnside's headquarters... We there received official notice that the long looked for mine was ready charged, and would be fired at daylight next morning. The plan of storming was as follows: One division of white troops was to charge the works immediately after the explosion, and carry the first and second line of the rebel entrenchments. Our division [4th Division comprised of nine regiments of the USCT) was to follow immediately and push right into Petersburg, take the city, and be supported by the remainder of the Ninth and the Twenty-Eighth Corps. We were up bright and early, ready and eager for the struggle to commence I had been wishing for something of this sort to do for some time to gain the respect of the Army of the Potomac... At thirty minutes after five the ball opened...*[364]

There was no doubt that there was enough explosive material in the tunnel to make a very big noise, but what seemed to escape the planners was that it would create a massive crater, measuring over 150 feet long, 60 feet wide and 30 feet deep in the area that was to be traversed by the Federal forces. Not only was there a huge hole, but the field was strewn with piles of debris hurled in every direction across the terrain. Three divisions of white troops were the first sent in after the explosion and were driven back into the crater. It was now the turn of the 31st USCT to take the field. As part of the fourth division, comprised of nine black regiments with approximately 4,200 officers and men, they entered the fray about 8 am.

We waited anxiously expecting every moment to be ordered in, until 8 A.M., then our orders arrived to move forward, which was promptly obeyed, but owing to the difficult ground to pass, we did not reach our front line until 8:30. On reaching the front line, we at once pushed forward under a galling cross fire, thinning our ranks terribly, before reaching the crater. On reaching the crater we at once pushed through as well as the tangled mass of human beings and uprooted earth would permit. It caused considerable confusion ... By 2 P.M., all that we had gained in the morning, was lost.[365]

Sketch of the Battle of the Crater made by Alfred R. Waud, artist and correspondent. The line of troops entering the battlefield were part of the second charge and included soldiers of the 31st USCT. Library of Congress.

The loss of the regiment's Lieutenant-Colonel, followed by the wounding of Major Thomas Wright, and finally the capture or wounding of Captain Robinson who had been the last to assume command dealt a fatal blow to the organization of the regiment. This chaos was repeated up and down the line for troops, black and white alike. The men tried to retreat to the Union lines, others sought refuge in the enemy bombproofs and in the crater itself, while others, surrounded by Confederate troops, tried to surrender.

It was more than just a battle plan gone awry that set the Battle of the Crater apart from other engagements between the two armies. The overall losses for the Federal troops numbered over four thousand dead, wounded and missing. It was the massacre of wounded black soldiers as well as black prisoners that set this battle apart in the annals of history. Historian Bruce A. Suderow had described the events of July 30, 1864 as "The Civil War's Worst Massacre." Initial statistics reported by the army of casualties for the nine regiments of Colored Troops indicate that there were 219 men killed in action; 682 wounded in action; 410 missing or captured. Numbers of the 31st USCT listed 20 killed in action; 41 wounded, 64 missing or captured. When the dust settled, the Confederates reported having in their hands only 85 African American prisoners (wounded and unwounded), significantly less that the preliminary numbers listed as missing or captured by the Federal army. Suderow's research estimated the actual losses for the 31st USCT at 71 dead, 46 wounded, and 12 taken prisoner.[366] There are enough contemporary accounts by eyewitnesses to bolster the case of Suderow that wounded black soldiers and those that surrendered were given "no quarter."

Two of those taken prisoner at the Battle of the Crater were men with connections to Ontario County, New York. Twenty-four-year-old George H. Watts (Co. F) had enlisted at Canandaigua in late December and made preparations to leave his wife Ellen and two young daughters, Mary and Julia, behind in the care of his father-in-law, Francis Drake. The family had already sent off one member to war earlier that year. Ellen's brother, Nathan Drake, had been drafted into the 8th USCT. Private Watts was described in his enlistment papers as being 5' 6", with black complexion, black hair and black eyes, working as a carter in the village of Canandaigua.

George Watts was listed as missing in action as of July 30, 1864 on Company Muster Rolls beginning in July and August 1864 and would remain as such until the muster roll of March and April 1865, when notified by officials at Camp Parole at Annapolis, Maryland that George H. Watts had been among prisoners exchanged at North East Ferry, North Carolina on March 13, 1865. It was reported that Private Watts had been captured at Petersburg on July 30, 1864; was confined in Libby Prison, Richmond, Virginia on August 13th; transferred to Salisbury, North Carolina in November 1864, where he was admitted to the hospital on December 30th because of wounds; on February 1, 1865 was returned to quarters at Salisbury Prison before being moved to Goldsboro, North Carolina and finally paroled six weeks later.[367] Private Watts did live to come home to his wife and daughters, but was plagued with illness for the remainder of his life. The cause of his death in May of 1880 was ascribed to anasarca, a medical condition that can result from severe malnutrition, which he no doubt suffered from during his time as a prisoner.[368]

Edward Jackson, son of David and Susan (Riley) Jackson, was born in Ontario County about 1840, enlisted on December 31, 1864 in Lodi, New York and was forwarded to Riker's Island where he was assigned to Company E. The Company Muster Roll of August 1864 listed Jackson as killed in action on July 30th and that status remained the same through the date of the mustering out of the regiment in November of 1865. It would be almost two years later that the records would be amended to reflect that Edward Jackson had been taken prisoner during the Battle of the Crater and had died on December 28, 1864 at Danville, Virginia, due to chronic diarrhea.[369]

Among the wounded who escaped capture and execution was Private James H. Peterson, another member of Company E. Peterson was a twenty-seven-year-old cabinet maker who had enlisted on December 21, 1863 at Scio, Allegany County, New York. A gunshot wound to the right shoulder was treated at the General Hospital at Alexandria, Virginia where he succumbed to his wound on September 15, 1864 and was buried in Freemen's Cemetery (later Alexandria National Cemetery) the following day. [370]

The 31st USCT continued in place around the perimeter of Richmond and Petersburg through early April of 1865 when they joined the pursuit of Lee's Army which ended with the surrender of the Confederate General at the Appomattox Court House on April 9th. The final orders for the regiment took it to Texas where it served along the Rio Grande, along with the 8th USCT, before being mustered out at Brownsville, Texas on November 7, 1865.

As was the case throughout the ranks of the troops on both sides of the conflict, disease wreaked havoc among the men who were in the 31st United States Colored Troops. Of the three recruits from Canandaigua, two did not return home to their families. Twenty-four-year-old Alexander Blake and thirty-five-year-old Adam Holland both died of typhoid fever in September and October 1864, respectively. Two wives and five children were without the support of their primary breadwinners. Private Blake, son of Rev. David and Mrs. Elizabeth Blake, was born in New York City and had lived in Canandaigua since a child. He married about 1860 and at the time of his death was survived by his wife, Lucy, and one child. Private Holland was, very likely, the son of William Holland, who had once been enslaved by Daniel Dorsey and brought north from Maryland when his owner settled in Lyons, New York. Holland married Annis E. Prince, daughter of Festus Prince, in September 1850 and the couple had four children – Emma, George, William and Fanny.[371]

One of the recruits who did return home, was also one of the last to join the regiment. Forty-year-old William Wilson enlisted on July 30, 1864 as a substitute in Rochester, New York and was forwarded to the much depleted 31st USCT, arriving there in early September. Assigned to Company I, Wilson was almost immediately promoted to the rank of corporal. Unfortunately, Corporal Wilson was taken ill in May of 1865 and sent to the hospital at Fort Monroe, Virginia, from where he was mustered out of the service a month later.[372]

Wilson, a resident of Wayne County, New York, was the oldest son of Almira (Smith) Gregor and the fifth of her sons to join the Union Army. Mrs. Gregor sent off her youngest child, Abraham (Abram), one month after bidding good bye to her oldest. Besides his mother and step father, Wilson had at home a wife, Sarah Elizabeth, and four children – James A., William, Sarah J., and Ida, aged one to ten years old.[373] William's wife, Sarah, died within a few years of his return home and he married the Harriet Gregor, widow of his half-brother, Elijah Gregor, who had died from illness while serving in the 8th USCT.

They Too Served

The African American soldiers from Western New York were concentrated in regiments formed in Massachusetts, Rhode Island, and New York, as well as 8th United States Colored Infantry. Yet, there were others from the region, scattered among other units of the United States Colored Troops (USCT) and the Navy, who also served. It is only fitting that some of their stories should also be heard.

Connecticut Vies for New York Enlistments

Connecticut had been toying with the idea of forming a black regiment during much of 1863 and had gone so far as to begin recruitment in August, even before it had received approval from the War Department to raise a unit. With state and federal approval finally accomplished in mid-November 1863, recruitment began with added fervor. The black military-age population of Connecticut had already been depleted by recruitment into units of Massachusetts and Rhode Island, but with New York State still sitting on the side-lines, Connecticut felt certain that it would be able to fill the rosters for an infantry regiment, with recruits from its own state and the neighboring state of New York. What had not been foreseen was that in December, New York State would set out to create its own regiment of African American soldiers and try to block Connecticut from recruiting in the state. Connecticut had a decided edge in this battle for enlistees, promising a bonus package, valued at $685 - $310 from the state; $75 from the county from which the men enlisted; and $300 from the United States government. Connecticut also continued the tradition of paying bonuses to "agents" who brought in recruits. As with many bonus incentives, the promise was not always fulfilled.

Whatever the incentive, on January 2, 1864, three men from Wayne County, New York arrived at New Haven, Connecticut to enlist in the 29th Connecticut. Brothers William and Porter Wooby, of Lyons, New York, ages twenty-two and nineteen years old respectively, were assigned to Company I. Their companion, William Newport of Sodus, New York was attached to Company H. The men were connected through marriage of Newport's younger sister, Mary, to John Wooby, an older brother of William and Porter.

The Wooby and Newport families traced their roots to former slaves, who had arrived in Western New York during the pioneer era. John Wooby, patriarch of this family, is said to have been born a slave in New Jersey, but a freeman when he was brought north by Gideon Granger to Canandaigua, New York about 1803. In 1826, he married Clarissa Jacobs, who was formerly a slave of Daniel Dorsey, of Lyons, New York, being brought north from Maryland about 1799, as an infant.[374] It is thought that the parents of William Newport, William and Sarah (Plumber) Newport, arrived in the town Sodus, New York as free persons of color about 1812, residing in a settlement founded by former slaves, located on the outskirts of what is now the village of Sodus Point, New York. Although free when they arrived in Sodus, it is very likely that they or their parents had once been held in slavery in western Massachusetts, Connecticut, or eastern New York.[375]

William Newport gave his age on enlistment papers as twenty-years-old, but he was actually closer to thirty-two-years old. He and his wife, Margaret, were parents to six children, with an additional two children in their household from Margaret's first marriage. His twenty-one-year-old step-son, Thomas Lloyd, was already in the service, having enlisted in the 8th United States Colored Infantry (USCT), as a substitute, in July 1863. Of the three men from Wayne County, New York, Private Newport had the most difficult military service, due to illness that plagued him beginning as early as August 1864. By August 25th he was a patient in the Point of Rocks Hospital in Virginia. The Company Muster Rolls mark him as present in November and December 1864, but his reprieve was short-lived. Newport was back in the hospital in late February 1865 and remained a patient until his discharge on October 28, 1865 from De Camp General Hospital, located on David's Island in the New York Harbor.[376]

His pension file suggests that he contracted typhoid fever and suffered from exposure, resulting in the development of chronic diarrhea, a common debilitating illness associated with Civil War soldiers. William Newport returned home to Sodus, New York after his discharge and his sister, Margaret Potter, later recalled that "he was sick when he came home with chronic Diareah [sic] and was sick nearly a year." In 1870, William and Margaret are living separately, with William in the town of Marion, working as a hired man and Margaret in Sodus, with six of her children. According to his pension file, William Newport left Wayne County about 1870 and moved to Northampton, Massachusetts, where, in 1872, he married Eliza Bateman Sands. He continued to live in western Massachusetts until it was reported that he had been "killed by cars" in November 1889. But there is one more wrinkle in trying to tell the whole story of William Newport.[377]

It is true that the town records for Holyoke, Massachusetts include the death of a man identified as William Newport and it is true that the pension office dropped William Newport from its rolls in 1889, due to his not responding to correspondence. Yet, there is a report in the Clyde Times of October 17, 1904, that George Newport of Huron was "entertaining his father, Mr. Newport, from Connecticut".[378] George Newport was the oldest son of William and Margaret Newport. Now for the unanswerable questions. Did William Newport disappear from Massachusetts in 1889 and settle in Connecticut, or did he die in Massachusetts in 1889? And if he died in 1889, who was visiting George Newport from Connecticut in 1904?

The Wooby brothers made an interesting contrast in physique upon arrival at New Haven, Connecticut in January, 1864. William, the older brother, was described as being almost five feet, nine inches tall, while Porter was barely five feet, three inches tall. Much to the relief of their mother, who it is said was opposed to the enlistment of her youngest son, they were fortunate to make it through their two-year stint in the service, relatively unscathed, given that their regiment saw considerable action while it was stationed near Richmond and Petersburg between August 1864 and April 1865.

William and Porter Wooby were mustered out of service at Brownsville, Texas on October 24, 1865 and traveled with the regiment to Hartford, Connecticut, arriving on November 24, 1865, where they received final payments and discharge papers. Within a year of his return to Lyons, New York, Porter Wooby married Hannah E. Johnson, daughter of David and Maria (Smallwood) Johnson. Three years later, his brother William, married Hannah's younger sister, Mary Louise Johnson. The two men continued to live in Lyons until their deaths. Porter died in 1878, described in the newspaper as a "well-known jockey," leaving a wife and no children. William died in 1909 and was given a G.A.R. burial in the Lyons Rural Cemetery. He was predeceased by his wife, Mary Louise, and children, Clara Belle, Porter, Mary Ellen, Hannah Louise, Bessie and James. Surviving were two sons, William, of Buffalo, New York and Frederick, of Lyons.[379]

The amount of the bounty may have been the reason that convinced Alonzo Frank and Elijah Baker to enlist in the 29th Connecticut. Frank enlisted in Hartford, Connecticut on December 5, 1863 and he presents an interesting case. According to his *Compiled Military Records*, within three days of his enlistment, Frank was admitted to Knight General Hospital by order of E. W. Blake, Surgeon, who judged him to be insane. On December 11th, Blake wrote to Brigadier General L. C. Hunt, stating "the said Frank is <u>insane </u>and that there is good reason to support that his insanity existed prior to his enlistment." It was suggested that Frank's situation be referred to the Provost Marshal.

On December 17th, Lucius Goodrich, Captain and Provost Marshal of the 1st District sent on letters from Blake and General Hunt to Major D. D. Perkins, asking what was be done about Alonzo Frank's enlistment. He stated that Private Frank "has yet received no bounties except the $10, from the State, payment of his check for $300, having been stopped." On December 23rd, Provost Marshal Lucius Goodrich wrote to General L.C. Hunt stating that it was determined that neither he nor Major Perkins had the authority to discharge Private Alonzo Frank and suggested that the regiment's colonel be assigned the task. Goodrich added that "Neither the Dr. nor myself discovered anything wrong about the man. We are both of us pressed very much with the business of the office and cannot detect all the frauds that come before us."

It may be that Goodrich included a copy of the report by Dr. H. A. Grant, dated December 22nd, which outlined his findings regarding Alonzo Frank's situation:

I have the honor to respectfully report to you; that I examined carefully said volunteer, put him through a Thorough course of Exercise, and close examination by questions in regard to his birth, occupation, length of time he had lived with various persons & different places – His general health – the amt. of wages he had recd.pr month etc. all of which questions he answered rationally and apparently truthfully – There was no wandering either in his Eye or manner, or any thing

225

*that would indicate at that time Insanity - Said he had
never been subject to fits or any ailment of the kind –
There were no signs of Insanity present and nothing at
that time which would indicate that he had been
subject to that infirmity - ...*

The doctor did concede that "I can easily conceive that
with the unlimited indulgence in alcoholic stimulus the
Volunteers are given by Brokers before & after they pass the
Surgeon, that a man who ever had been insane, a recurrence,
would almost surely quickly if not immediately be reproduced."
The case was not concluded. On January 6, 1864, four doctors
at Knight General Hospital in New Haven signed a statement
that after their "careful examination" of Alonzo Frank it was
their unanimous opinion "that he is unfit for military service
by reason of great mental weakness, amounting to Imbecility."

Accompanying this statement was a letter from Acting
Assistant Surgeon S. G. Hubbard confirming the opinion that
Frank "is an imbecile & of unsound mind – harmless &
incurable." On February 15, 1865, Private Frank was issued a
Certificate of Disability for Discharge, having been unfit for
duty "since the day of enlistment" due to "unsoundness of mind
and imbecility." He was discharged "without final statements
& loss of all pay & allowances, by reason of fraudulent
enlistment."[380]   Was Alonzo Frank an imbecile?   Was he
insane?   Was he a fraud?   If Frank had faked insanity and
imbecility in order to get out of his enlistment and still receive
the bounty, his plan failed miserably.

There is still one more unanswered question. Who was
Alonzo Frank? He claimed to have been born in Rome, Oneida
County, New York about 1835.   There were three African
American families with the surname of Frank living in Oneida
County in 1840, with two households having males under the
age of 10. Following the Frank families of Oneida County from

1850 through 1860, none have a son with the name of Alonzo. No Alonzo Frank, born between 1830 and 1840, is found in the 1850, 1860, or 1870 census, anywhere in the United States. There is no record of an Alonzo Frank registering for the Civil War draft in any state during the summer of 1863. Of course, it is possible that Alonzo was not his first name, or maybe Frank was not his last name.[381]

Twenty-seven-year-old Elijah Baker enlisted on January 9, 1864, stating he was single and born in Scipio, New York. Two months later, Private Baker was granted a pass and never returned to camp. He was listed as having deserted on March 5, 1864 and the remarks in the *Company Descriptive Book* concluded that he was, in fact, a married man and he was "supposed to have gone to Canada." Baker was living in Syracuse, New York in 1860, with his wife Louisa and two-year-old son, Charles. It is not clear whether he received his state bounty prior to his desertion.[382] Nothing more is known about the fate of Elijah Baker and we are left with only a small piece of his story.

Finding Substitutes

As the Civil War progressed into late 1864 and into 1865, there was a growing number of men, fearing that they would be drafted into the army, who set out to find substitutes to serve in their stead. At this phase of the war, the person who was willing to serve as a substitute, was required to prove that he was not subject to the draft. Male citizens, married and single, between the ages of 20 and 35 years old, as well as unmarried men, ages 36 to 45 years of age, were all in the pool of possible draftees. Married men, between the ages of 35 and 45 years old, were put into a second class, to be called upon only if communities could not meet their quota of recruits. As a result, the substitutes were often very young. This is just a small sampling of the African Americans who went to war as substitutes, mostly in the place of white men.

One of the first of these young substitutes to sign up was seventeen-year-old Henry Dewitt of Savannah, New York. Using the alias of Henry D. Thompson and giving his age as eighteen years on his official enlistment papers, he enlisted on August 10, 1864 in Auburn New York, agreeing to serve a term of one year. Henry may have been trying to avoid any challenges to becoming a soldier. He had agreed to be a substitute for twenty-six-year-old Henry McGonigal of Butler, New York. Henry Dewitt, the son of John and Susan (Hill) Dewitt, was one of six children and the oldest son. *A Muster and Descriptive Roll*, dated February 16, 1865 indicates he was in Elmira, New York waiting to be forwarded to the 25th United States Colored Troops (USCT). He never reached his destination. Henry Dewitt, died in New Orleans of disease on April 2, 1865, before he could join the unit. Where he had been between August 1864 and February 1865 is not explained in his military records. His family had not been notified of his death as late as June 1865, when the census taker visited the home of his parents and listed Henry as "in army."

One month after Henry Dewitt enlisted, John McGonigal married Marcella Johnson in Savannah, New York. The couple had two daughters, Mary and Ethel. John McGonigal became active in business and Republican politics in Wayne County, New York, eventually serving as County Clerk. He died in Lyons, New York in February 1914 and was buried in the Butler-Savannah Cemetery.[383]

In the summer of 1864, two members of the James and Almira Gregor family of Walworth, New York, entered the army as substitutes. Forty-year-old William Wilson, son of Almira and step-son of James Gregor, enlisted on July 30, 1864 in Rochester, New York for a three-year term of service. A month later, his seventeen-year-old half-brother, Abraham Gregor, youngest son of James and Almira Gregor, joined the army. William Wilson went as a substitute for Peter Robison of Gaines, Orleans County, New York. Wilson, a resident of Sodus, New York, was married and had four children at home – James, William, Sarah J. and Ida. Technically, he was not eligible to be a substitute, even with second class status, but he appears to get around that by claiming to have been born in Canada. A search for Peter Robison in Orleans County, New York was unsuccessful, but there was a Peter Robinson, age about 28 years old in 1864, living in Rochester, New York. When he registered for the draft in July 1863, Robinson indicated he was single and a carpenter. According the 1865 census for Rochester, New York, Peter Robinson was living at home with his mother, Martha Robinson and not in the army. His younger brother, Samuel was identified as serving in the navy at the time. It is possible that this is the person who hired William Wilson as a substitute. Peter Robinson, of Rochester, New York never married, died in 1885 and was buried in Mt. Hope Cemetery.

William Wilson was sent first to Elmira and then to Hart's Island in New York Harbor, where he was assigned to Co. I in the 31st USCT on August 25th. The ranks of the 31st USCT were in desperate need of replacements after suffering great losses at the Battle of the Crater, which took place in the trenches near Richmond on July 30th. Wilson joined the regiment on the siege line of Petersburg, Virginia in early September, and was quickly promoted to rank of Corporal for his company.[384]

Abraham Gregor, a substitute for William E. Gould, of Ontario, Wayne County, New York, enlisted on August 29, 1864 for a one-year term of service. William Gould, the twenty-five-year-old son of Israel Gould, had requested an exemption and was notified on July 15th, that to be eligible for the exemption, he must "file a written statement … verified by affidavit" with the Town Clerk of Ontario, New York, on or before August 15th. The Gould family had ties to the Quaker faith, but it is not known if Gould sought an exemption based on his religious beliefs. Many members of the Gould family had been active participants in the anti-slavery movement and local lore says that their homes were used as safe havens for freedom seekers, traveling the Underground Railroad.

Instead of securing an exemption, William E. Gould paid Abraham Gregor the sum of $600 to be his substitute. The money was turned over to his parents, for their support while Abraham was in the army. At the time of Abraham's enlistment, the Gregor family was fully invested in the Civil War. He was the sixth son of the Gregor family to enlist in the army to fight in the Civil War and the third son to enter as a substitute. In addition to his half-brother, William Wilson, an older brother, Bradley Gregor, joined the 8th USCT in July 1863, as a substitute for his brother-in-law, Dexter Taylor of Huron, New York. Private Bradley Gregor was killed at the Battle of Olustee in February 1864.

On October 8, 1864, Abraham Gregor was in Elmira, New York, awaiting transfer to the 43rd USCT, which was stationed on the siege line against Petersburg and Richmond. He arrived in camp on October 15th and was assigned to Company A. The 43rd USCT was a battle-tested regiment, having participated in the Wilderness Campaign during June 1864 and the Battle of the Crater, on July 30, 1864, in which the regimental losses included 29 men killed, 104 men wounded, and 12 men missing. Private Gregor remained with the regiment in Virginia until May 12, 1865, when he was admitted to the hospital, suffering from "Cont. Fever." Two days later he was transferred to the General Hospital at Fort Monroe, Virginia with diagnosis of "Incipient Phthisis" or more commonly known as tuberculosis.

Interestingly, William Wilson had been admitted to the same hospital on March 28, 1865, for treatment of the same disease as his brother Abraham. It is not known if the two ever realized their stays at the hospital overlapped or if they were aware that their regiments were in such close proximity. Corporal Wilson was discharged from the army on June 5, 1865 and returned home to his wife and children, who were living with his parents in Walworth. It must have been a household bulging at the seams. The census taker who visited the home in June 1865, recorded the names of thirteen persons, belonging to four different generations, ranging in age from 95-year-old, Rachel Gregor, mother of James, to one-year old Ida Gregor, daughter of William Wilson. William's wife Sarah, died before 1870 and he then married his half-brother's widow, Harriet. William Wilson died in Canandaigua, New York on October 29, 1878 and was buried in Woodlawn Cemetery. [385]

Information in pension file records indicate that Abraham Gregor was returned to duty on August 1, 1865 and transferred to Philadelphia on October 12, 1865, but his military record reports him "absent' and in hospital during July and August, 1865. By August 1865, the 43rd USCT was stationed in Texas and it would seem unlikely that with less than a month left in his term of service, they would have sent him to join his regiment. It is more likely that he was transferred to a hospital in Philadelphia, Pennsylvania and that his illness delayed his discharge until December 5, 1865, three months beyond his one year of service. He too returned to the family home in Walworth, but his health was so compromised that he died on March 9, 1866. There is a tombstone in the Gould Family Cemetery, with the inscription "Abram Gregor Enlisted in the U.S. Colored Troops Sept. 9, 1864." The date does not match enlistment date on military records, but perhaps it reflects the day he left home.

Tombstone erected in Gould Family Cemetery, Walworth, New York, bears inscription "Abram Gregor, Enlisted in U.S. Colored Troops Sept. 9, 1864."

In October 1867, Almira Gregor began a pension application as "dependent mother" based on the service of her youngest son, Abraham Gregor. Mrs. Gregor asserted in her claim, that her husband was an invalid and unable to work and that prior to his enlistment, her son had contributed his earnings as a farm laborer to the support of the family. Dr. Edson Whitcomb confirmed that James Gregor, husband of Almira and father of Abraham "is afflicted with Paralysis Agitans [Parkinson's disease], which renders him unfit for performance of any kind of manual labor" and that the "disability is chronic and has existed for a number of years." It was twenty-one years before Abraham's mother received her pension, retroactive to March 9, 1866. She received a payment amounting to a little more than $2,200 from the Pension Office sometime after April 19, 1888. James Gregor died in April 1885 and Almira Gregor died in Penfield, Monroe County in July 1889, aged about 80 years. One can only imagine how much that pension would have meant to her and her husband during those years after 1866.[386]

In the summer of 1864, Charles Bennett, of Williamson, New York, was forty-two years old and married, making it unlikely that he was about to be drafted. Yet, on September 1st, Reuben Pollett (also known as Pollard), an eighteen-year-old laborer from Virginia, appeared before the County Clerk of Wayne County, New York to sign his enlistment papers having "agreed with Charles Bennett, Esq. of Williamson...to become his SUBSTITUTE in the Military Service for a sufficient consideration paid and delivered to me ..." Private Pollett joined Company D of the 43rd USCT on October 15, 1864. He very likely traveled from Elmira, New York in the company of Abraham Gregor, of Walworth, New York, who also joined the 43rd USCT on October 15th. Twelve days later, Pollett was wounded in action at the Battle of Hatcher's Run, near Petersburg, Virginia, and sent to the L'Ouverture U.S. General Hospital in Alexandria, Virginia, arriving there on October 31st.

He remained a patient in the hospital until his discharge on September 7, 1865, "in consequence of impaired use of the right hand the result of a gunshot wound of right forearm." His discharge papers listed his address as Williamson, New York. There were no clues found as to where Reuben Pollett was prior to his enlistment in September 1864 or how he came to be living in Williamson, New York in 1864. He made an application for a pension, beginning on September 14, 1865, but did not live long enough to receive a certificate. He was buried with the name of Reuben Pollard in the Bogart family plot of the Palmyra Village Cemetery, sometime between 1865 and 1868.

Charles Bennett continued to live in Williamson until his death in 1907. He was buried in Pleasantview Cemetery in that same town.[387]

Twenty-five-year-old James Bias, of Seneca Falls, New York, was another substitute to join the 43rd USCT on October 15, 1864. Mr. Bias had been on the opposite side of a substitute transaction in July 1863, when, after being drafted, he arranged to pay Calvin Van Hazen (aka Calvin Hazel), of Oneida County, New York to take his place. Van Hazen, who claimed by be twenty-one-years old, but was closer to sixteen, enlisted in the 8th USCT. Private Van Hazen was killed on September 3, 1864, while on picket duty near Petersburg, Virginia. Just two weeks prior to Van Hazen's death, James Bias enlisted for a one-year term, at Seneca Falls, as a substitute for Henry J. Riegle, a thirty-one-year old farmer of the same town.

In order to establish that he could serve as a substitute, Bias was deposed by the Justice of the Peace in Seneca Falls, stating "that he is not enrolled on the United States Enrollment in said town or elsewhere and that he is not liable to be drafted into the Military Service of the United States for the reason that in July 1863 he was duly drafted into said service for the term of three years and that he procured a Substitute for said term, who was duly accepted in deponents stead."

Private Bias, assigned to Company F, was mustered out at Brownsville, Texas at the expiration of his term of service on August 23, 1865. After his service, James Bias settled in Geneva, New York, with his wife, the former Christina Arnold, who he had married in August 1863. He died at the Soldiers and Sailors Home in Bath, New York on March 29, 1919 and was buried in the Bath National Cemetery. Henry J. Reigle continued to live in Seneca Falls until his death on March 10, 1904.[388]

The 25th USCT received two new recruits from Western New York in April 1865, both serving as substitutes. William Cleggett left his home in Rochester in late December, along with a friend, Frank Rowe, with the intention of enlisting. According to an affidavit provided by Frank Rowe in 1902 they "enlisted away from home so our mothers could not find us." Both boys were only seventeen years old and each enlisted using an alias. William Cleggett's alias was "James Brown" and Frank adopted the name of James Johnson. Frank Rowe never made it to the 25th USCT, after taking sick while still at Elmira, New York, waiting to be sent south. One could understand why William Cleggett's mother might object to his joining the army. Mary Cleggett's husband, David Cleggett, died in 1852, leaving her with two minor children – Isaac and William – and she was increasingly dependent on her sons for her support.

William Cleggett enlisted on December 22, 1864 in Avon, Livingston Co., New York to serve a one-year term, as a substitute for Sears E. Brace, a married, thirty-two-year-old grocer from Mt. Morris, Livingston County. James Gibbs, of Macedon, New York, enlisted on January 10, 1865 as a substitute for Noah Sherwood of New Hudson, Allegany Co., New York. The oldest child of Redding and Mary E. Gibbs, James was born in Warsaw, Wyoming County on November 29, 1847, making him barely seventeen years old when he agreed to serve a three term in the army. His leaving the family would have been a hardship, as at home was his recently widowed mother and four younger siblings. Perhaps the incentive was the money he received from Mr. Sherwood. Cleggett and Gibbs left Elmira on February 16, 1865 for the 25th USCT, which was then stationed near Pensacola, performing garrison duty. Private Cleggett, or more correctly, Private James Brown, joined Company H. on April 13, 1865 and Private Gibbs joined Company K a day later, April 14th.

According to the regimental history, during the spring and summer of 1865, the men of the 25th USCT "suffered terribly from scurvy, about one hundred and fifty dying and as many more being disabled for life. The mortality rate at one time amounted to from four to six daily. This was the result of want of proper food." Private Gibbs did not escape from effects of this malady. The pension application of James E. Gibbs, includes a statement from his mother that he "wrote to me twice from the army that he ached in his limbs so that he could not sleep; also, that there was something the matter with his mouth and face. When he got home he told that he had had an army scurvy, that his teeth had been loose, and when his teeth set they set crooked..."

In early December 1865 the regiment was ordered to Philadelphia, Pennsylvania and on the 6th of December it was mustered out of service. In 1888, James' mother recalled that her son returned home in Macedon between Thanksgiving and Christmas in 1865 and that he remained with her for one year, working with local farmers, before setting out on his own. William Cleggett returned to Rochester, New York, where he married and started to raise a family. In 1897, he filed an application for a pension, but died in 1905 without having completed the process.[389]

Three members of the Prime Cortright family, of Huron, New York set out from home in December, 1863, joining the 14th Rhode Island Regiment Heavy Artillery, also known as the 11th USCHA. Prime Cortright and two sons, John W. and George W, served in Company M. The fourth family member to join the army was fifteen-year-old William Freeman Cortright, enlisting on March 28, 1865 for a one-year term. While William Cortright added three years to his age to qualify as a substitute, his father, Prime, lowered his age by almost ten years in order to enlist. The military record of Cortright indicates he was to serve as a substitute for William D.

236

Burroughs. a twenty-nine-year-old married man and hotel keeper in the town of Ontario, New York, who was able to secure his substitute after receiving notification of his being drafted. The abstracts of the *New York Muster Roll* give the name of James A. Rush of Sodus as the person for whom Cortright was serving as substitute. Rush the son of Hickson and Nancy Rush was about twenty-five years old and single in 1865.

William F. Cortright reported to Elmira, New York within a few days of enlistment and awaited transfer to a regiment. His military records indicate that he remained an "unassigned recruit" until July 8, 1865, when he joined Company A, of the 38th USCT, which was moved to Texas the previous month. Private Cortright was mustered out of the service on March 26, 1866 and returned to Wayne County, New York. A year later he married Caroline A. Taylor, also of Huron, New York, and started raising a family. William F. Cortright died in Syracuse, New York on April 12, 1928, sixty-three years after his enlistment. According to an obituary in the Syracuse Herald, Mr. Cortright was an active member of Root Post #151, of the Grand Army of the Republic and Merriam Camp #52 of the Sons of Veterans of the Civil War, both headquartered in Syracuse, New York. William D. Burroughs moved from Ontario to Webster, New York about 1870, where he continued to be a hotel keeper.[390]

James A. Potter and Company K of the 1st USCT

Thinking they were missing out on the adventure and comradery of war, young men often were eager to find ways to join the army. James A. Potter was not a young man, but he too was eager to join the army, not so much for the adventure, but to be part of a cause to end slavery. To tell his full story, it is best to start prior to his enlistment on September 3, 1864. James A. Potter, son of James and Chloe Potter, was born in

Hillsdale, Columbia County in 1825. His family moved to Sodus, New York between 1830 and 1840, where his father earned a living as a weaver.[391]

Here, the Potter family became neighbors and friends with the family of Josiah and Elizabeth Rice, ardent anti-slavery activists. The sentiment of the parents was also shared by the Rice children – Lewis, Valorus, Sophronia, Judson, Myron and Albert. Apparently, Sophronia was so outspoken on the issue of slavery, that after teaching a term in the Williamson-Sodus School District #18, the district voters issued notice on October 9, 1860 that "we shall never hire any of the Rice family or any other abolitionist for our teacher."[392] It was the ties to this family that may help to explain his determination to enlist at the age of thirty-nine, leaving behind his pregnant wife, Margaret, and six children, ages one to eleven years old.

Just a few months into the Civil War, nineteen-year-old Judson Rice, enlisted on September 13, 1861 as sergeant in Co. D of the 8th New York Cavalry, a regiment recruited mainly in the vicinity of Rochester, New York. The cavalry unit left Rochester in late November 1861, to much fan-fare, but without horses for all, except the officers. The regiment settled into very poor living quarters outside of Washington, D.C. where it remained until March, 1862. The enlistees may have had visions of dashing cavalry charges, but the reality of their initial army life included no horses, and months of picket and guard duty on the outskirts of the capitol city. The regiment finally became "mounted" in the spring of 1862 and was moved to the area around Harper's Ferry.[393]

In July of 1862, Lewis B. Rice, Judson's older brother, enlisted at Auburn, New York, joining a unit that would eventually be named the 9th New York Heavy Artillery Regiment. Sent to Washington, D.C., the regiment became part of the line of defense for the city and was still in place during the spring of 1863. In the early months of 1863, Sergeant Judson Rice contracted typhoid fever and was given a discharge due to illness. He did not return home, but stayed around Washington, D.C. as he decided what his next step would be. In May, both Judson and Lewis Rice were exploring the possibility of joining the newly established United States Colored Troops as officers. Judson and Lewis Rice were both assigned to Company K, in the 1st United States Colored Troops, Judson with rank of Captain and the Lewis as Second Lieutenant. On July 4 1863, Judson wrote home from Washington, that it was all settled.

> *I am now a Soldier in the regular Army, a Soldier for life. I have my commission in my pocket and my uniform upon my back. I shall take command of company on Monday. We probably shall remain in this place for some time yet as they are raising --- a brigade here and --- the first Regt. I have nothing to do with recruiting my Company It is already raised and I must command it Lewis & I have been highly favored in every undertaking and I hope that we shall ever prove true to the friends who have helped us there has not been two young men before the Board for examination who has brought as much influence as we have.*

> *Lewis will be in the same Company with me, but it will be a few days before he can go around as he has got to be discharged from the Regt where he now is.*

> *I would not really advise Philip or any other of the boys down there to come yet, as it is hard to tell how they can succeed I would gladly have Philip as Orderly in my company but I don't think that he wishes to enlist for five years and those are the terms of enlistment in our Regt* [394]

This last comment very likely refers to interest among some in the African American community of Sodus, New York, to join Judson and Lewis Rice as members of the 1st USCT. "Philip" was most likely Philip Newport, who would have been considered an "old-timer" if he had joined, being about forty-three-years old in the summer of 1863. He was also the father of five children. One of the "other boys" mentioned by Judson was probably James A. Potter, who was no boy, but a man of almost forty-years old.

Captain Rice referenced James Potter in a letter dated March 24, 1864, asking his parents "has James enlisted yet." Potter had yet to enlist, but he did so at Sodus, New York on September 3, 1864, for a one-year term. His enlistment papers describe him as thirty-nine years old, five feet and eight inches tall, of dark mulatto complexion, with black eyes and hair. It was over three months before Private Potter was forwarded from Elmira, New York to join the 1st USCT. If Potter's intent by enlisting was to join the Rice brothers, he must have been sorely disappointed once he arrived in camp near Fort Fisher in North Carolina on December 30, 1864.[395]

In early November, the Rice family had been notified that Judson was wounded and missing in action after a skirmish with Confederate forces on October 27, 1864 near Fair Oaks, Virginia. At first it was thought he may have been taken prisoner, but his status was later changed to "presumed dead." It was reported that his Orderly attempted to remove him from the field, but that Rice said, "Leave me. Save yourselves. I am mortally wounded."[396] Three days prior to this event, Captain Rice requested a "leave of absence of twenty days on account of sickness." The request was accompanied by a letter from the regimental surgeon, stating that the captain "is suffering from general debility, the sequel of severe dysentery in August last." Lewis Rice was also not well for much of his time with the 1st USCT. He was in the hospital at Fort Monroe, Virginia, when his brother was wounded in October. Lewis was discharged for disability on November 28, 1864, so he too was not on duty to welcome James Potter to the regiment and Company K, which was then located near Fort Fisher in North Carolina. One can only wonder, if Private Potter's army experience would have been different, if his friends had still been in command of Company K.[397]

The Union army was putting pressure on all fronts from Georgia to southern Virginia. By December 1864, Sherman's March to the Sea had reached Savannah, Georgia and was headed to Charleston, South Carolina. Forces stationed on the coastal islands near Charleston and Beaufort, South Carolina were moving inland to support the movement of Sherman's army on its march north. In early December, General Grant dispatched forces to capture Fort Fisher, the last coastal stronghold protecting the port of Wilmington, North Carolina.

After the destruction of Fort Fisher, Grant's plan was to force the Confederate forces, led by General Joseph E. Johnston, into submission. With Johnston's army defeated, what was left of the Confederate Army under the command of General Robert E. Lee, would have nowhere to go and would have to surrender. The 1st USCT regiment was one of the units sent from the Richmond-Petersburg siege lines to the North Carolina coast.

Only a few days before Private Potter joined his unit, the men of the 1st UCST took part in an unsuccessful attempt to capture Fort Fisher, with deadly results. Potter was in the trenches for the second Battle of Fort Fisher which took place between January 7th and 15th, 1865. The fort fell to Union forces on January 15th and one month later, James Potter wrote to his wife the following letter:[398]

Fort fisher North Carolina
february th 16 1865
my dear wife i take this opportunity
write you a few lines to let you now
how i am i am as well as can be
expected considering the place i am in
i hope that these few lines may
find you all well i received your
letter dated february th 1 i have had
tou of your letters since i have been
here i cant say anything about this
place it is oso god forsaken that
i dont wish to say anything about
we have a got the rebs before us and
have got drive them by inches their
riffle pits are about ten rods
and they have to be charged an our
loass is heavy they have got ten or
fifteen thousand colord troops her
and we dont get only halfe rations
and no clothes we are naked i have not
had on a clean shirt since the first
of January and dont now when

Portion of letter written by James A. Potter to his wife, Margaret, dated February 16, 1865. From private collection of the Wallace family, descendants of James and Margaret Potter.

My dear wife   i take this opportunity write you a few lines to let you now [know] how i am   i am as well as can be expected considering the place i am in i hope that these few lines may find you all well i received your letter dated February the 1   i have had tow of your Letters since i have been here   i cant say anything about this place it is so god forsaken that i dont wish to say anything about   we have got the rebs before us and have got to drive them by inches   their riffle pits are about ten rods apart and they have to be charged an[d] our Loss is heavy   they have got ten or fifteen thousand Colored troops her] and we don't get only halfs rations and no Clothes we are naked I have not had on a Clean shirt since the first of January and don't now when i shall.

i am in a dreadful condition   i have no tobacco nor haven't had this two months   i have one special favor to ask and that is i want you to send me some tobacco get a cigar box and pack it full of plug tobacco and two pounds of fine cut   get the best kind of plug i can get rations for tobacco but I cant get it for greenbacks   if you can get up something in the way of eating to put into the box   a good Loafe of inelian [?] bread and a Little Butter   i want a pair of Boots   Just see what you can get   three pairs   for one pair of No 8   not the heaviest kind soldiers Boots french calfe   one pair of No 9 Light calfe tops on the out side   one pair of No 10 regular soldier Boots   them is for the old man himself my Boots are pretty good yet But i thought i had Better begin think about another pair. i had to leave my kapscack [sic] in virgin[ia] and i Left my evelopes [sic] in it   it is almost impossible to get one here   money wont get theme and hard tack we don't have to spare so this is poorest time i ever saw or ever wish to see again in this world   no one need say that this war is carried for a good purpose it is nothing but develishnes[s]

the next time i rite if i don't get cut down i will tell you something about this fort fisher you can Judge what music we had   the gun Boats to [two]days and tonight storming it and one Little monitor throud [?] tow [sic]thousand five hundred shells shot and there was fifty gun Boats that was engaged and some of the Largest magnitude

do not Bother with the Boots   send on the Box   put in some postag stamps an envelopes and paper   i shant have anything in my knapsacks when i get it   I must draw my Letter to A close   i expect to go out on picet [picket]to night and the sun is getting low

No more at this time
From your affectionet Husband James A. Potter

There was little time to reflect on the success at Fort Fisher, as the army moved on to capture Wilmington, North Carolina on February 22, 1865. In March, the 1st USCT joined with Sherman's army as part of "Carolinas Campaign." Again, the men trudged northward toward New Bern, North Carolina, all the while attacking the forces led by General Joseph E. Johnston, the only viable savior of General Lee's army surrounded in Richmond. It is unlikely that the conditions described by Private Potter to his wife in February, 1865 had improved, and in fact, there is plenty of proof that the soldiers continued to suffer great deprivations on the march.

244

In a letter dated April 18, 1865, Margaret Potter received the news no wife wants to hear during any war. It was written by James H. Waugh, Sergeant with Company K, 1st U.S.C. Troops, from Raleigh, North Carolina:[399]

Respected Friend, it is with regret that I announce the following information to you although I feel it my duty as Sergeant and a member of the Same Company K, 1st U.S.C.T.

I here Say that on the 9th day of this month April your loved and esteemed, husband James A. Potter, died of neumonia at Warsaw Station, N.C. we saw him well Cared for, and properly buried, we then had to march the Same day, or I should have written to you before for it was his request for me to write to you and his Children and to tell you that he was happy and at rest and to tell you that he has taken a part in a good Cause for his family and race, Mrs Potter I was with him until he drew his last breathe hear on earth, and I truly hope and Believe that he has gone to a better land of Rest where truble is no more.

So you must not Greive for it was the lords will that his Sorrow Should be over You must rite and let me know if you get this So I will Close by Saying I am your Friend James H. Waugh, Sergt.
Mrs J. Potter
Direct
Sergeant Jas. H. Waugh Co K 1st U.S.C. troops 1st Brigade 3rd div 10th A.C.
Care of G. H. Rich Lt. Col Ralleigh N.C.

Camp 1st U.S.C. troops
Raleigh N.C. Aprile 19th 1865.

Mrs Potter

Respected Friend, it is with regret that I announce the following information to you although I feel it my duty as Sergeant and a member of the Same Company K, 1st U.S.C.T.

I here Say that on the 9th day of this month, Aprile your loved and esteemed, husband James A, Potter died of newmonia at Warsaw Station N.C. we saw him well cared for, and properly burried we then had to march the Same day, or I should have written to you before for it was his request for me to write to you and his Children and to tell you

Page one (1) of letter from James H. Waugh, Sergeant of Co. K, 1st USCT to Margaret Potter. Found in Civil War Pension File, submitted by Mrs. Potter.

It seems difficult to imagine that the words of Sergeant Waugh could bring much comfort to Margaret Potter and their surviving children, Sylvester, age eleven, Benjamin, age nine, Fanny, age six, Clara, age four, and newborn son James, named for his father and grandfather, less than a month old when his father died in April 9th. Ironically the date of his death is the same as the day General Lee surrendered his army to General Grant. Mrs. Potter's burden was great, having already suffered the loss of two children in the previous year – Lester and Mary Ann, both under the age of two years when they died. Myron H. Rice, younger brother of Judson and Lewis Rice, wrote to his family on May 27, 1865: "I received the welcome letter yesterday containing the sad news of james death. I thought if he was not killed he would surely stand the climate but its seems different. I am sorrow for his family he has a couple boys now that can more than ern [sic] their living."[400] Myron's age, at only twenty years old, may excuse him from expecting an eleven and nine year old to be able to take on the job of supporting a family, but on the surface he seems to lack any depth of sympathy for the hardships ahead for the Potter family.

Margaret E. Potter provided a declaration for a widow's Army pension on August 15, 1865, giving the basic information of her husband's enlistment, their marriage date, names and birthdates for her minor children. She signed her name to the document, witnessed by Josiah Rice and her sister Mary (Newport) Wooby. Lewis B. Rice provided a deposition that he had been First Lieutenant in Co. K, 1st. U.S.C.T., "that he was acquainted with James A. Potter ... that he knew him before his enlistment that said Potter maintained a strictly moral Character before entering and after he had enlisted the Army that he was strictly temperate in his habits..."[401]

In 1868, Margaret Potter and her brother-in-law, Richard McKinney jointly purchased a house and lot, located on Rice Street in Lyons, New York. It is possible that the financial obligation of this purchase was too much for Mrs. Potter as in 1874, she sold her share of the property to Conrad Englehart, who held the mortgage. Mr. Englehart then sold the property to Richard McKinney in December of 1875, who lived in the house until 1915. Mrs. Potter died in Lyons of typhoid fever on April 4, 1889. She was buried in Sodus, New York, most likely in Rural Cemetery, where a stone was erected for her husband. Her death occurred just five days shy of the twenty-fourth anniversary of her husband's death. It is not known if the body of Private Potter was removed from his burial site in Warsaw Station, North Carolina and placed in the Sodus Rural cemetery. As late as 1883, his burial place was thought to have been Warsaw Station.[402]

Tombstone erected in Sodus Rural Cemetery with inscription "James A. Potter, 1st U.S. Col. Inf, Died Apr 9, 1865.

Margaret Potter purchased the cemetery lot in November 1864, shortly after the death of her daughter, Mary Ann, who died on October 30, 1864. There are no other tombstones on the lot, but it may be the burial place for Margaret Potter and her children Mary Ann, Lester, and James.

Photo by Janet Wallace, 2001.

The children of James and Margaret Potter remained in Lyons, New York until the late 1800s, before moving to near-by communities in Syracuse, Batavia, and Rochester, New York. There is no record of the child James beyond a baptism in June 1870, and the family oral history is that he died young. Clara married George Bacome, a transplant from Tennessee, in 1881 and they had seven children; Benjamin married Mary J. Jackson, of Chatham, Ontario, Canada, also in 1881, and they had three girls and a boy. The son, named James, for his grandfather, died as an infant. Fanny married Charles William Harris in 1883. Sylvester waited until he was fifty-years-old before tying the knot, marrying Ida Johnson in 1903 and three years later becoming the father of one daughter, Julia.[403]

Thomas Mathews – A Strange and Sad Tale

Thomas Mathews, of Springport, Cayuga County, New York enlisted for one year in the army at Rochester, New York on September 16, 1864 and was credited to the quota of the Town of Gates, Monroe County, New York. The twenty-four-year-old recruit, son of Peter and Amy Mathews, worked as a boatman either on Cayuga Lake or the Erie Canal prior to his enlistment. The Mathews family had been residents of Springport since about 1815, making them among the earliest settlers in the area.

Mathews was in Elmira, New York on December 5, 1864, awaiting transfer to the 1st United States Colored Cavalry. What happens to him next is very confusing. His name does not appear on any *Company Muster Rolls* for the regiment between January and October 1865. During that time period, the regiment was on duty at Newport News, Portsmouth and in the District of Eastern Virginia through May 1865, when they were moved to City Point, Virginia in preparation for transportation to Texas on June 10th.

In late October 1865, a full month after Private Mathews should have been discharged from the army, he showed up in Lexington, Kentucky at the headquarters of the 6th United States Colored Cavalry and no one seemed to know what to do with him. On October 23rd, Lt. Col. Albert Coats wrote General James F. Wade, Commander of the regiment:

Herewith enclosed I have the honor to transport to you a partial Description List of J. Mathews, who has reported at these Head Qrs. As belonging to the 6th U.S.C.Cav. – Mathews says that he Volunteered at Rochester [crossed out] Auburn [inserted above Rochester] New York, for one year, on the 15th day of Sept. 1864: was mustered into service at Rochester, N.Y. on the 16th day of Sept. 1864 – He does not remember by whom – and assigned to the 6th U.S.C.Cav by the Prov. Marshal at Rochester – He has been on duty at Washington City, Alexandria, Columbus, Ohio, and Baltimore, Maryland, and was latterly sent to Texas to join this Regiment, but not finding it there he returned and joined the Regiment at Lexington, Ky. A few days ago. I would respectfully request that the Provost Marshal at Rochester be instructed to forward the man's muster & Descriptive Roll to these Head Qrs.

By November 15th, Provost Marshal offices in Rochester, Buffalo and Elmira had all responded that they had no record for a J. Mathews, but did have a record for a Thomas Mathews, who was mustered into service at Rochester, New York and assigned to the 1st USC Cavalry in September 1864. There are so many questions. Had Thomas Mathews ever joined the 1st USC Cavalry unit? He claimed to have done duty in Washington City, Alexandria, Columbus, Ohio and Baltimore, Maryland, yet the 1st USCC had not been stationed in those places. No cavalry unit of the United States Colored Troops

250

was ever stationed near Washington, D.C. during the war. The 5th Massachusetts (Colored) Cavalry was stationed at Point Lookout, Maryland from July 1864 to March 1865, but that location is not what would be considered close to Baltimore or Washington, D.C. None of these cavalry units included a person named Thomas Mathews on their roster. Mathews also indicated his regiment had been sent to Texas and it is inferred that he did not accompany the unit but was sent to Texas at a later time. The 1st USC Cavalry was moved to Texas in early June 1865.

If Thomas Mathews did not join the 1st USC Cavalry, did he join another unit? If so, which unit? And why on earth did he include Columbus, Ohio in his list of duty sites? There was a Union prisoner of war camp in Columbus, and is it possible his unit was once assigned to guard the camp? So far, none of these questions have been answered. Finally, on December 29th, 1865 it appeared that Thomas Mathews was about to be sent home. General James F. Wade, Commanding Officer of the 6th USC Cavalry wrote to Lt. W. H. C. Joyner [?] at the St. Francis River District in Helena, Arkansas that Mathews

> *had come to the 6th C. Cav. while the regt was in Kentucky the authorities forwarding him, supposing that he belonged to this regt. His term of service has expired and he is desirous of being mustered out. Lt. Col Coats while in command of the reg't wrote to the authorities at Washington, in relation to the man & rec'd the papers which I herewith endow. I suppose he will have to be forwarded to Washington ...*

Thomas Mathews made it as far as Helena, Arkansas, but no further. On January 15, 1866 Dr. John Rulgely, Post Surgeon, wrote to Lt. Joyner that Thomas Mathews, had died in the Small Pox Ward of the Post Hospital at Helena on January 14th. With so little known about Thomas Mathews, it is possible that his family in Springport, New York was never notified of his death. Thomas' brother, Peter, had enlisted in the 20th USCT at Auburn, New York on August 10, 1864 for a one-year term. He survived his year in the army and returned to Cayuga County in August 1865.[404]

Theodore and George Shears of Manchester, New York Join the Army

The story of Theodore S. and George C. Shears, sons of Tillman and Melissa Shears, challenges the prevailing policy during the Civil War that restricted African Americans from serving as soldiers in what were considered "white" regiments. The Shears (aka Brashears) family traced its roots to Maryland and slavery, with the matriarch of the family, Araminta Shears, brought to Ontario County about 1800. Several Maryland families migrated to the area of Manchester and Farmington with their slaves between 1800 and 1805, but it has not been determined which of the families may have been the enslaver of Araminta or "Minta," as she was also known. Minta, born about 1782 in Maryland, was the mother to two children, both born in Ontario County – Christa, born about 1805 and Tillman, born about 1807.

The first public record for the Shears family in Ontario County may have been created by John Shekell, Jr., who on December 28, 1807, registered the birth of Tilman Jacobs, born on May 25, 1807 in the town of Farmington to an unnamed slave. The unusual first name and the year of birth match what we know about Tillman Shears, but that alone is not sufficient proof that they are one in the same person. The next public records, more clearly related to the Shears family, were deeds transferring property, located in Lot #70 in the town of Manchester from Mary McGowen to Christa and Tillman Brashears, in 1828 and 1832 respectively. When the property is sold the surname was given as Shears. In 1836, Christa

Shears moved to a log house, located on the outskirts of Sulphur Springs (now Clifton Springs). Three years later, Tillman and Melissa Shears purchased property in Manchester Center, a thriving mill community, where he found work as a carpenter. Their property adjoined that of David Cook and Pompey Grayson, two African American families with ties to the Orme and Shekell families.[405]

Christa Shears and her mother lived together until the death of Minta, between 1865 and 1870. Christa, who never married, continued to live on that property until her death on March 9, 1889. Tillman and Melissa Shears were parents of six children – Theodore S., Augusta, Josephine J., Helen A., George C., and Jonathan C., born between 1839 and 1857. Tillman Shears died about 1860 and his wife, Melissa passed away about 1863, leaving three minor children.[406]

Theodore S. Shears was the first son to enlist. The twenty-three-year old joined the newly formed 126th New York Volunteers at Manchester, New York on August 8, 1862, leaving behind his widowed mother to care for his younger brothers and sisters. There is little chance that his fellow soldiers in Company H were not aware of his racial heritage, as well over fifty percent of the unit were from his home town. His close neighbor, William F. Lemunyon, and his future brother-in-law, Frederick Bayne were also in the same company. While Shears' mother may have been white, his father, Tillman and the children were usually identified in the census records, through 1865, as mulatto. The probate file of Christie Shears listed the children of Tillman Shears as her nieces and nephews, and Miss Shears was also identified as mulatto or black in census records.

The 126th New York Infantry regiment left the state on August 26, 1862 and less than three weeks later, it went into battle at Harper's Ferry, Virginia. The untrained recruits were at a terrible disadvantage, especially as they had received their rifles only a few days previous to the fight. The regiment surrendered and was branded as the "Harper's Ferry Cowards," a moniker that would follow them until their stellar performance at Gettysburg in July 1863. Theodore Shears was wounded in Harper's Ferry, "struck by a minié ball from the enemy said ball striking him in the left shoulder, passing directly through his shoulder and coming out at the back." Private Shears was treated first at the hospital at Harper's Ferry and then at the Naval School Hospital at Annapolis, before being sent to the Parole Camp at Alexandria.

In December 1862, Shears rejoined his regiment, which was then assigned to the defenses of Washington, D.C. During the first four days of July 1863, the 126th was again in the heat of battle, this time in Gettysburg, Pennsylvania. The regiment was better prepared for this encounter, yet the total losses from the battle included forty dead, 181 wounded and ten missing. The reputation of the 126th was restored, being part of the Union forces to hold the line against Picket's charge on July 3rd. Although Private Shears escaped injury at Gettysburg, he was not so lucky in May, 1864 during the Wilderness Campaign, when he was wounded at Spotsylvania Court House, Virginia. Shears was transferred to several hospitals, before arriving at Slough Hospital in Alexandria, Virginia. On September 25, 1864 he was transferred to the U.S. Veteran Reserve Corps, where he remained until his discharge on August 22, 1865, having completed his three-year term of service. Theodore S. Shears returned to Manchester, New York and began the process of applying for an invalid's pension on August 13, 1866. The last known record for the soldier was a deed, dated May 3, 1867, in which he and his siblings sold the property purchased by their father, Tillman Shears, in 1839. It is very likely that Theodore Shears died before he could complete his pension application.[407]

George C. Shears was only fourteen years old, when his brother, Theodore, left home with the 126th New York Volunteers, but he was determined to go to war. According to his statements for a pension, he first tried to enlist in Rochester, New York in December 1862, but was rejected. In February 1863, now fifteen years old, George made a second attempt, enlisting at Phelps, Ontario County, New York, but got only as far as Canandaigua, New York, before being rejected by the examining surgeon because of his age. In the summer of 1864, he was barely sixteen years old and working on the Erie Canal for Samuel Stacy, out of Port Gibson, New York and according to his account:

> *I told Capt. Stacy that I intended to enlist, but he objected and tried to discourage me. I stayed on the boat until at the 'Locks" at Newark, N.Y., I asked for my pay, but in trying to hold me the Captain have me one half ($20) & told me to visit home & get over the notion of enlisting. Did visit home for a short time, then returned to Newark, N.Y. and got a job on the boat 'Chas. D. Mills' and came on it to Buffalo, N.Y., then took a trip on train to Rochester, N.Y. and then to Lockport, N.Y. where I enlisted. ...*

Shears explained that he went first to Rochester to enlist, but decided that would not be a good idea, having already been rejected once before in that city. He then started back to Buffalo, getting off at Lockport upon seeing recruiting posters.

> *I went in and enlisted, but as I had been rejected twice on account of being too young, I thought I might be rejected again should I give my right name, I therefore assumed the name of George Miller ...*

This was on September 3, 1864. George C. Shears, now George Miller, was assigned to the Third New York Independent Battery, Light Artillery and went first to Elmira, New York and from there to the siege line before Petersburg, Virginia, arriving there in October.[408] Private George Miller was discharged from the service on June 24, 1865 at New York City and returned to Manchester, New York, where he made his home with his sister, Josephine J. Bayne, wife of Frederick Bayne. He returned to using the name of George C. Shears and went back to work on the Erie Canal for the next thirty years, before settling permanently in Buffalo, New York. After 1865, George and his siblings began to self-identify as white on census records.

During the pension application process for George Shears, fellow soldiers were asked if they recognized the man in this photo as the person who served with them as "George Miller." The' pension file included depositions of several men who answered in the affirmative. Providing a description of himself at time of enlistment, Shears said, "I was then, I would judge 5' 9" or 10" high... had light or hazel eyes, brown hair and my complexion was tanned by out door work."

Both Josephine and Helen married white men and continued to live in the vicinity of Clifton Springs, where their family was well-known. The youngest of the Shears family, John, enlisted in the United States Army at Buffalo, New York on December 2, 1879 for a five-year term of service. Private Shears served first at Fort Sanders in the Wyoming Territory and in 1882 his unit was moved to Fort Thomas in the Arizona territory. He was discharged on December 1, 1884 at Fort Thomas and returned to Buffalo, New York.[409] In 1902 George Shears married Susan (Anger) Ford, sister-in-law of his brother Jonathan. George C. Shears, Sr. died in Buffalo on August 28, 1928.

Navy Men

The United States Navy had a long tradition of accepting African American sailors into its ranks and once the Civil War began it greatly expanded its recruitment. The task of blockading the Confederacy, along the east and gulf coastlines, required a massive naval initiative and the need for manpower exploded. It is estimated that over 18,000 African Americans served in the Union Navy during the Civil War, making up almost 20% of the total naval force. Recent research has found that the sailors hailed almost equally from Union and Confederate states. Maryland, New York, Pennsylvania, New Jersey and Massachusetts were home to the majority of northern recruits. From the south, it is likely that many were former slaves, sometimes labeled "contrabands," who lived along the coastline between Virginia and Louisiana or on the Mississippi River who sought refuge with Union Naval forces. In November 1861, the Secretary of the Navy, Gideon Welles, issued orders that enlisted "contrabands" be relegated to the rank of "Boys" (First, Second and Third Class), the lowest rank and pay in the Navy hierarchy, usually assigned to boys over thirteen and under eighteen years old. [410]

Among the northern recruits were two members of the Cleggett family of Rochester and Geneva, New York. The younger of the two was the first to enlist. Seventeen-year-old James Henry Cleggett left his home in Rochester, New York in March, 1862 and traveled to New York City. One of three sons of James and Maria (Jackson) Cleggett, orphaned with the deaths of their mother in 1850 and father in 1855, James may well have been on his own and looking for an adventure. What he endured during the next three and a half years was not the adventure he may have imagined.[411]

James H. Cleggett enrolled on March 14, 1862 for a three-year term of service as a landsman, the rank given to recruits with little or no experience at sea. He joined the crew of the *USS Morning Light*, which had recently arrived in New York from duty along the east coast, searching for Confederate blockade runners. The sailing vessel left port in late March, loaded with provisions for the West Gulf Blockading Squadron, under the command of Admiral David G. Farragut. Once the *Morning Light* arrived in the Gulf of Mexico, Admiral Farragut ordered it to perform picket duty off Ship Island, Mississippi, while Farragut's fleet advanced on New Orleans. For the next several months, *Morning Light* and its crew performed blockade duty off Pensacola, Florida; Mobile Bay, Alabama; and Velasco, Texas.

In January, 1863 the United States Navy was under attack along the coast of Texas. The Battle of Galveston on January 1st, resulted in their loss of Galveston, which had been occupied by Union forces, and the capture of the *Harriet Lane*, one of the Union vessels defending the harbor. Admiral Farragut was none too pleased with the conduct of his officers, referring to the "shameful conduct of our forces at Galveston has been one of the severest blows of the war to the Navy."[412] Reports followed that Confederate vessels were passing with ease along the entire Texas coastline and on January 21ˢᵗ, the *USS Morning Light* received orders to join the *USS Velocity* in patrolling the area around the Sabine Pass, a small stretch of water leading from Sabine Lake into the Gulf of Mexico, located on the border between Mississippi and Texas. Two days later, two Confederate vessels exited the Sabine Pass, approached the two American ships, which sat with their sails down on a calm sea, and after a brief exchange of gunfire, captured the *Morning Light* and the *Velocity.* A total of 109 men were captured, among them were twenty-nine black sailors, including Landsman James Henry Cleggett.

The ordeal of the African American crew members was just beginning. The prisoners were moved from Sabine to Houston on January 24th and there the black sailors were separated from their fellow crew members. The white officers and sailors were eventually sent to Camp Groce in Texas. The fate of James H. Cleggett was decided in what can only be described a surreal legal maneuver. On April 24, 1863 a writ was issued, ordering him to appear in court of the Seventh Judicial District at Houston on May 7ᵗʰ to answer the petition of the State of Texas. The petition stated that the Sheriff of Harris County, Texas had in custody

> *persons of color ... captured by the Military Authorities of the Confederate States ...and that said persons of Color were coming into the State of Texas with an armed force of the United States Government ...and then found in the ranks of our enemies giving them aid and comfort. Said persons of Color part of whom I aim to be free and part slaves...are here in contravention of Law...and that they be dealt with as the Statute requires...*[413]

The petition included the names twenty persons considered escaped slaves and ten persons deemed to have been free men. In the end it did not matter, as all were sentenced to "hard labor." The prisoners were assigned to the Negro Labor Bureau, which was in charge of building fortifications along the Texas coastline, specially at the port of Galveston.[414] Mr. Cleggett outlined his experiences in several statements for his pension application. On February 16, 1881 he wrote that his injuries were "caused from over work while in enemy's hands as prisoner ..., while sick ... compelled to carry heavy rail road iron and was otherwise abused..."

In a document dated February 5, 1884 he stated:

That he was confined in jail at Houston, Texas for several months the exact period he has forgotten. From thence he was removed to Galveston, Texas where he was compelled to work on the confederate fortifications for a long time and where he sustained the injury for which he claims pension...he was with other prisoners sent to Madagorda, Texas. That of the twenty-four prisoners sent from Galveston to Madagorda, Texas with him, he recollects the names of the following person, viz: James Reddan, Wm. L.G. Smith, William Peterson, James Johnson and David Satifield and that soon after his arrival in Matagorda, Texas he was separated from the other prisoners and was taken by the two Confederate Captains named Brown and Marmier, who were friendly towards me to Pass Cavallo, Texas and there released on the 3rd day of June 1865 by these same captains and was taken aboard the U.S. Steamer Virginia or Virginians by a boat crew belonging to said steamer ... came to New York, N.Y. arriving in New York on or about the 11th day of July 1865. That he was discharged from the Naval Service in the Brooklyn Navy Yards July 11th 1865.

After the war, James H. Cleggett, became a traveler, supporting himself as a hairdresser, importer of human hair and manufacturer of hair goods. According to his pension file, his first stop after his discharge was in Syracuse, New York, where his aunt, Harriet (Jackson) Myers, lived. From there he made a short stopover in his hometown of Rochester, before heading west. He was in Chicago in 1866, Janesville, Wisconsin in 1867, and in Green Bay and Ripon, Wisconsin from 1869 to 1884. Then he returned to Chicago where he lived between 1884 and 1899. Not long after that he moved to Chatham, Ontario, Canada, before leaving for London, England in 1907, where he would make his home until 1920. On October 7, 1920 Mr. Cleggett applied for a passport, stating that he planned to return to his hometown of Rochester, New York.

His departure may not have been at his own request. In November 1919, Frazier Smith, of the London Branch of the American Civil War Veterans, wrote to the U.S. Pension Commissioner in Washington, D.C. concerning behavior attributed to Mr. Cleggett, who "during the last 2 years has developed Hallucinations (a brain trouble) which has become serious lately ... A few weeks ago he took a dislike to his Flat & would not sleep there. But rode about in Busses & trains most of the night, sleeping on benches or chairs anywhere during the day." Mr. Smith had been able to place the pensioner in the Wentworth Borough Infirmary and wanted advice on how to proceed. The Pension Office replied that if pensioner is mentally incompetent to receive and handle the pension checks, it would be necessary to appoint a guardian.

Photograph of James H. Cleggett, from his passport, issued on October 7, 1920 by the United States Embassy in London, England.

Whatever had afflicted James Cleggett while in London, he seems to have recovered enough to be interviewed by reporters for the *Rochester Democrat & Chronicle* at the end of November 1920. Although his memory may have been faulty on some matters, he remembered well the details of his service with the United States Navy.[415] Cleggett's traveling days were not over. In 1927 he wrote the pension office from Boston, Massachusetts to provide a new address. In June 1929, Mrs. Etta E. Shoecraft of Chicago wrote the pension office that James H. Cleggett had died in that city on June 12th, 1929.[416]

Thirty-five-year old barber, Benjamin F. Cleggett, from Geneva, New York, joined the navy as a landsman at the Brooklyn Naval Yard on September 14, 1864. Mr. Cleggett, son of David Cleggett, was very likely a relative of James H. Cleggett, but the exact relationship is yet to be determined. The Cleggett family plot in Mt. Hope Cemetery in Rochester, New York contains burials for fathers of both Benjamin F. and James H. Cleggett, giving the implication of a family connection. David, father of Benjamin F. Cleggett died in 1852 and the father of James H. Cleggett died in 1855.[417]

Between the mid-1829s and late 1840s, David Cleggett, a shoemaker and self-emancipated slave born in Maryland about 1796, moved his family often. In 1830 he was in Amboy, Oswego County, New York; in 1836 he purchased land in Manchester, Ontario County, New York, which he sold six months later; and about 1837 he took his family to Toronto, Canada, where he continued his trade as shoemaker. The family returned to the United States about 1847, settling in Rochester, New York, where James Cleggett, father of James H., had established himself, working as a whitewasher by 1840. The *Rochester City Directory* of 1847-1848 included listings for Benjamin F. Cleggett, barber in Arcade Hall, boarding with E. W. Walker, and David Cleggett with his son Otis Albert, shoemakers, living at 134 Mt. Hope Ave.[418]

On September 5, 1849 Benjamin F. Cleggett married Frances Nell, sister of William C. Nell, who was working with Frederick Douglass as printer and publisher of the *North Star* newspaper. Mr. Nell, native of Boston, Massachusetts, had relocated to Rochester in late 1847, giving up his position with the *Liberator*, the anti-slavery publication operated by William Lloyd Garrison. Between 1847 and 1856, Mr. Cleggett played an active role in the civic life of Rochester, New York's African American community. In one instance he served as secretary at a meeting in 1853 in which the "colored citizens of Rochester" met to challenge the Board of Education's appointment of a teacher for their school. Among the resolutions passed that evening was a statement that "we will continue to agitate until our rights are respected." In 1856 the family, consisting of wife Frances and two small children, moved to Geneva, New York, a village located about sixty miles east of Rochester, where he set up his barbershop.[419]

According to his Civil War pension file, Benjamin F. Cleggett served on five vessels during his thirteen months in the Navy, being discharged from the *USS Vanderbilt* in Philadelphia Naval Yard on October 13, 1865. He returned home and with the exception of a brief time spent in Washington, D.C. in the early 1880s, working for Charles J. Folger, during his tenure as Secretary of the Treasury, remained a resident of Geneva until his death in January 1917 at the age of 89 years. On the morning of his death, Mr. Cleggett had gone to work in his barbershop as usual. He returned home for his noon meal and "before he could remove his outside garments he fell to the floor and expired of heart disease." One obituary identified him as the "oldest barber in the State." As a testament to his commitment to education, his prized library was bequeathed to two of his daughters, to be divided equally. [420]

On the same day Benjamin Cleggett joined the Navy in September 1864, twenty-seven-year-old Charles Shorter, of Wayne and Cayuga counties, New York, signed on for a two-year stint in New York City as a landsman. He joined the crew of the USS *Tallapoosa*, a steamer built in 1863 and outfitted with heavy guns for intercepting blockade runners, working his way up to steerage steward, before he was discharged in New York City on November 19, 1866. Shorter had three brothers who served in the army during the Civil War. His brother, John, joined the 54th Massachusetts; Alfred served in the 26th USCT, a New York regiment; and William enlisted in the 102nd USCT, a Michigan regiment. Charles Shorter returned to Western New York, eventually settling permanently in Syracuse, New York where he owned and operated a restaurant until his death in 1907. [421]

New York Transplants in Michigan

In the 1850s the families of Judson Grayson and Thomas Gayton joined the great migration from New York to Michigan, in search of better lives for themselves and their families. Both families trace their roots to an earlier migration from Maryland and Virginia that brought slavery into what was then called the "Genesee Country." Congo and Esther Grayson, parents of Judson, were formerly enslaved by the John Shekell, Sr. family, which left Maryland about 1800 and settled in Manchester, Ontario County, New York. Judson Grayson, born about 1808 while his parents were still in slavery, married Lucy Ann Griswold, of the town of Galen, about 1837. It appears that Judson and Lucy may have traveled to Calhoun County, Michigan soon after their marriage, where on September 10, 1838, he deposited a certificate with the land office at Bronson, Michigan, stating that he had purchased eighty acres of land.[422] Their stay in Michigan at that time was short, for they are back in Ontario County, New York when they were enumerated in the 1840 census for the town of Manchester.

Thomas Gayton was born into slavery about 1799 in Virginia. In 1801 he, his parents, siblings, and other enslaved families were brought north to northern shores of Seneca Lake, near Geneva, New York, by Robert S. Rose, who was hoping to "tame" the frontier with the use of slave labor. Thomas and his brother were finally set free by Mr. Rose in 1822. It is likely that Thomas married Judah Mason about 1825 and began to raise their family near Geneva, New York. The family was enumerated in the town of Huron, Wayne County, New York in 1840 and 1850. By 1850 the household included nine children, ranging in age from one to nineteen years old. In 1853, Thomas and Judah Grayson sold their farm in Wayne County in preparation for their move to Arlington, Van Buren County, Michigan.[423]

Between 1851 and 1854, Judson and Lucy Grayson also traveled to Michigan, taking with them eight children – Albert O., Charles H., Charlotte, Amos, Mary Jane, John W., Willard C. and Harriet. An additional three children were born into the family after the move to Michigan. In the fall of 1863, the Civil War came calling on the Grayson family, and they answered with the enlistment of four of their sons – Albert, Charles, Amos and John. The four brothers were members of Company H of the 102nd USCT, originally known as the 1st Michigan Colored Infantry. There they were joined by a cousin, Harry Grayson, whose parents, Pompey and Matilda Grayson had also moved from Manchester, New York to Michigan in the 1850s.[424]

The Grayson family did not fare well while in the army, with three deaths and one discharge because of disability. The first to die was the youngest of the brothers, John W. Grayson, age eighteen. He died of typhoid fever on July 5, 1864 at the Regimental Hospital at Beaufort, South Carolina. Twenty-three-year-old Charles H. Grayson's death was caused from chronic diarrhea and occurred at the same hospital on November 11, 1864. Amos S. Grayson died of disease in Beaufort, South Carolina on May 16, 1865. Cousin Harry Grayson was hospitalized for all but two months between March 1864 and June 8, 1865, the date he was given a disability discharge. The only brother to come out of his army experience in relatively good health was twenty-five-year-old Albert O. Grayson.[425]

It is difficult to imagine the grief experienced from the death of one child in war, but Judson and Lucy Grayson faced not only the grief for three deaths, but also the serious blow to the family's economic well-being. In 1865, remaining at home were five minor children, ages four to fifteen. Prior to his enlistment, Charles Henry Grayson had purchased a small farm of sixty acres for his parents, making a down payment with his bounty money. The balance was covered by a mortgage, which he intended to pay once he returned from army service. The property was only partially developed, with large portions covered with marshland.

With his death, the debt fell on the parents, which they found difficult to pay. It was also at this time that the health of Judson Grayson began to fail. Beginning about 1858, this once hearty able-bodied worker began to feel the severe effects of rheumatism and with each successive attack, he became more and more disabled. In 1867, Lucy Grayson began the application for a Civil War pension, as a dependent mother of Charles H. Judson, who, because of her husband's

267

disabilities, was the main source of support for her and the minor children at the time of his enlistment.

Lucy was initially successful in securing a pension, but in 1871, there was an accusation that altered their lives. On November 1871, Griffin Paddock of Dansville, Michigan, alerted the Pension Office that he had identified four cases of pension fraud, one of which involved Lucy and Judson Grayson. In regards to the Grayson claim, he wrote that in his estimation "there was not the least doubt" about it being fraudulent and that Mr. Grayson "is an able bodied man, ... was never in the least dependant [sic] upon either of his Sons for his support, and in fact the only one of his Sons that ever done anything for him is now at home..."

Mr. Paddock did allow that the Grayson case may not have been deliberate fraud, rather placing the blame with their lawyer, William Martin, whom he described as "not very consciencious about gitting claims allowed against the government he has or did have a pension himself for a pretended injury in the Mexican War, and it can be Shown that the injury for which he gits his pension was done him when a boy." Paddock went on to explain why he was writing:

There is now no law So Subject to abuse as the law granting pensions to dependant mothers. The $8 per month brings up dependant mothers, who only for that would never have been thought of as Such in reporting these I have no other motive then to See Justice done and I hope that either of the cases will be merely droped. I do not believe that either one is in either the Spirit or letter of the law entitled to a pension and it is Said there are quite a number that can be droped and no injury done and if I am not mistaken in these there are other names that can be given if report tells the truth...[426]

268

The self-appointed investigator, Griffen Paddock, may have thought he was just doing his duty to expose fraud and abuse, but to the Grayson family his accusations had serious implications. Pension payments were discontinued beginning in December 1871 and Lucy Grayson was dropped from the rolls in June 1873.

In 1875, Lucy Grayson applied for restoration of her pension. Her neighbors and friends rallied behind the couple, with fifteen signing the following statement:

> *We the undersigned hereby certify that we are well acquainted with Lucy Ann Grayson (mother of Charles H. Grayson deceased) and know her circumstances financially and know that she is poor and needy but industrious And sustains a good moral character. We therefore pray that her pension which has been for some time with-held from her be again paid to her.*

It was not enough to reinstate the pension and Judson and Lucy Grayson continued to struggle to hold onto their farm and support themselves. Judson Grayson died on April 4, 1882 in Ingham County, Michigan and Lucy was forced to sell the farm. In 1886, Lucy Grayson made another attempt to restore her pension. Once again former neighbors came to her aid. Morris Topping and John Wasson, both who had signed the above statement in 1875, repeated their support, stating that they "think her name should be retained on the Pension Rolls we further have good reason to believe that her name having been drooped [sic]from said roll was caused by evil designing person and was unjust."

The pension examiner saw it differently and reported "that the claimant was not dependent upon her son Charles H. Grayson at any time and that her husband Judson Grayson was able to and did support her up to a few years before his death."

One last attempt in the mid-1890s was also unsuccessful, but at least the special examiner recommended there be no attempt to recover the payments received by Lucy Grayson between 1867 and 1871.[427]

Albert O. Grayson, the one brother who survived the war, initially remained in Michigan, where he worked as a barber. In the early 1880s he returned to his roots, settling in the village of Phelps, Ontario County, New York, just a few miles east of where he grew up. On January 12, 1892 he married Emily Frances (Haley) Hollingsworth at the Trinity Episcopal Church in Geneva, New York. Mr. Grayson died in Phelps on October 8, 1912 of Bright's disease. According to the pension application of his widow, she did not believe that he had been previously married, but most of the file is filled with a special examiner trying to sort out the life of Albert Grayson after he left the service and before he moved to Phelps. It is from this application that we also learn that his mother, Lucy Grayson, lived to the ripe old age of 100 years, dying in Chicago, Illinois on July 31, 1917. She was buried next to her husband in the Hawley Cemetery, located in Mason, Ingham County, Michigan.[428]

Cousin Harry Grayson's years after the service were difficult to say the least. According to the regiment's surgeon, Dr. Wesley Vincent, while at Annapolis, Maryland in April 1864, the soldier suffered from severe exposure and that the "sickness resulting from said exposure gave development to a large abscess ... terminating in a fistula in ano and a permanent disability for which he was discharged." The condition worsened over the years and by the 1875, Grayson was suffering with paralysis of the lower extremities, caused by condition contracted during his service and heart disease. He died in April 1894 in Bellevue, Eaton County, Michigan. His widow, Sarah (Varnum) Grayson died two years later and there is no indication that she applies for a pension.[429]

The family of Thomas and Judah Gayton also contributed to the Union cause during the Civil War. On October 21, 1863, twenty-six-year old Allen Gayton and his twenty-one-year old brother, Nicholas, enlisted in Kalamazoo, Michigan and were assigned to Co. B of the 102nd USCT. They must have been an imposing pair, with Allen being described as five feet, eleven inches tall and his younger brother topping him by two inches. Both were with the regiment when it left Detroit in late March, 1864. Less than a month later, Private Allen Gayton died at the General Hospital at Annapolis Junction, Maryland. The cause of death was given as Phthisis, or consumption. Nicholas Gayton survived the war and returned to Michigan, dying in Grand Rapids, Michigan in 1909.[430]

Conclusion

... And me and my brother were happy as you please
Thinking we were fighting for Democracy's true reign
And that our dark blood would wipe away the stain
Of prejudice, and hate, and the false color line –
And give us the rights that are yours and mine.
They told us America would know no black or white:
So we marched to the front, happy to fight...

Langston Hughes.
Excerpt from "The Colored Soldier"[431]

Langston Hughes was writing about a different war when he penned "The Colored Soldier" in 1919, but it could just as easily apply to the sentiments of soldiers who fought in the Civil War. Approximately 180,000 African American men served in the Union Army and another 18,000 served in the Union Navy during the Civil War, representing ten percent and twenty percent of the respective services.

Choosing to look at African American soldiers of Western New York, offered me an opportunity to tell the bigger story of the Civil War with a focus on the individuals who lived in that region and went to war. It allowed me to personalize the experience of war for each person. Overall, the stories told in this book represent every soldier who goes to war. The soldiers who fight our wars are mostly young; often have not traveled far beyond the borders of their community before joining the military; and leave behind parents, spouses, children, brothers, sisters, and friends who will worry about them. Once at war they bond with their brother soldiers; yearn for home; complain about the food and their officers; and try to detach themselves from the horrors of battle. Back home from the war they will struggle to pick up their old lives and strike out to claim their hard-won status as veterans. Yet, the story of each soldier is unique. Each story deserves to be told and we need to listen – no matter how uncomfortable it makes us.

The African American soldiers from Western New York went to war for a variety of reasons, ranging from compulsion by draft to wanting to fight against slavery to joining up just because everyone else was. But even the most cynical among these soldiers felt that because they had served their country in its time of need, their lives would be better after the war.

Reality did not match up to the dreams of equality. Langston Hughes and his fellow soldiers of World War I were still yearning for the illusive "equality" that motivated the soldiers of the Civil War. African American soldiers have been on the field of battle for the United States of America since its formation and this book was an effort to tell the story of a small group of men who fought during the Civil War.

End Notes

To streamline the source notations the following abbreviations have been applied:

CWMR - Compiled Military Service Records of Volunteer Union Soldiers, 1861-1865, National Archives and Records Administration, (NARA), Record Group 94, Microfilm identified by letter M followed by Microfilm Series Number and Roll Number (i.e. M1821-10).

Civil War Pensions – Case Files of Approved Pension Applications, 1861-1934; Civil War and Later Pension Files; Dept. of Veterans Affairs, Record Group 15; National Archives and Records Administration, Washington, D.C.

U.S. Census – In most cases accessed via online images of NARA microfilm located on www.ancestry.com. Identification of Microfilm Series Number and Roll Number, prefaced by letter M or T. (i.e.T9-213). If from manuscript copies in local archives, it will be noted.

NOTE: First name and surname spellings have been standardized in the text, but documents often provide alternative spellings. For example, in the text the surname of Bogart is used for consistency, but various spellings on documents include Bogert, and Boget. The spelling as found on the document is referenced in the endnote.

Introduction

[1] *Douglass' Monthly*, May 1861, Vol. III, No. XII, 452:2-3; online images, www.accessible.com .
[2] *Douglass' Monthly*, September 1861, Vol. III, No. XIV, 516:1.
[3] *Douglass' Monthly*, March 1862, Vol. IV, No. IX, 613:1.
[4] *Record of the Action of the Convention Held at Poughkeepsie, July 15th and 16th, 1863 For the Purpose of Facilitating the Introduction of Colored Troops into the Service of the United States* (New York: Francis & Loutrel Steam Printers and Stationers, 1863.)
[5] *Union League Club Report of the Committee on Volunteering, October 13, 1864* (New York: Union League Club, 1864), 8.
[6] Ibid, 9-10.

[7] Whitney R. Cross, *The Burned-over District: The Social and Intellectual History of Enthusiastic Religion in Western New York, 1800-1850*, (Ithaca, Cornell University Press, Reprint, 1982), vii.

[8] *The Colored American*, 2 February 1839, 3:1; 18 May 1839, 2:1; www.accessible.com.

[9] Phyllis F. Field, *The Politics of Race in New York: The Struggle for Black Suffrage in the Civil War Era*, (Ithaca, Cornell University Press, 1982), 19, 126-129.

[10] Joseph C. G. Kennedy, *The United States in 1860; Compiled from the Original Returns of the Eighth Census Under the Direction of the Secretary of the Interior*, (Washington, D.C., Government Printing Office, 1864), 322-347.

Go East Young Men

[11] *Douglass' Monthly*, March 1863, Vol. V, No. VI, 801:1-3,

[12] *Republican Advocate*, Batavia, New York, 14 April 1863, 2:2, www.fultonhistory.com.

[13] CWMR, Louis F. Douglass, M1898-5; Charles R. Douglass, (Co. I, 5th Massachusetts Cavalry), M1817-80, (Cpl., Co. F, 54th Massachusetts), M1898-5.

[14] CWMR, Samuel J. Robinson (Co. D., 55th Massachusetts), M1801-12.

[15] CWMR, John Shorter (Pvt. Co. G, 54th Massachusetts), M1898-14. *Wayne Co., NY Vital Records, 1847-49*, Galen, NY, Wayne Co. Historian, Lyons, NY. 1860 U.S. Census, New York, Wayne Co., Galen, M653-876, 235, Family #920, Sarah Ann Prine; Ontario, 594, #46, Alfred Shorter; Cayuga Co., Aurelius, M653-729, 703, #801, Jane Sherter [Shorter]. Civil War Pension, John Shorter, (Pvt., Co. G, 54th Mass.), Cert. #47.332. *Massachusetts: Vital Records, 1841-1910*; Boston, Vol. 366, 294, www.americanancesters.org.

[16] CWMR, Miles Moore, (Musician, Co. H, 54th Massachusetts), M1898-11. 1850 U.S. Census, Painted Post, Steuben Co., NY, M432-598, 27A, #390. 1855 NYS Census, Corning, Steuben Co., ED 1, 34, #286. 1865 NYS Census, Elmira, Chemung Co., p.13, #83.

[17] Irene Schubert and Frank N. Schubert, *On The Trail of the Buffalo Soldier: 1866-1917*, (Rowman & Littlefield, 2nd ed., 2004), 206.

[18] 1880 U.S. Census, New Orleans, Orleans Co., LA, T9-464, ED 90, 462D, #250. 1900 U.S. Census, Saratoga Springs, Ward 3, Saratoga Co., NY, T623-1159, ED 130, 18B, #430. Dennis Segilquest Post, http://civilwarthosesurnamesblogspot.com/2012_05_2-_archive.html. *U.S., Find A Grave Index*, Greenridge Cemetery, Saratoga Springs, NY; www.ancestry.com.

[19] CWMR, Cornelius Harding, (Co. G., 54th Massachusetts), M1898-7. Civil War Pension, Cornelius Harding, (Pvt. Co. G, 54th Massachusetts), Cert. #552.073.

[20] Virginia M. Adams, Editor, *On the Altar of Freedom: A Black Soldier's Civil War Letters from the Front* (Boston: University of Massachusetts Press, 1991), 4.

[21] CWMR, George H. Lee, M1898-10.

[22] *Massachusetts Vital Records, 1841-1910*, New Bedford, Vol. 162, 91, Record #14, www.americanancestors.org.

[23] Kathryn Grover, *Make a Way Somehow: African-American Life in a Northern Community, 1790-1965* (Syracuse: Syracuse University Press, 1994), 79, 111, 286-7: Note 29.

[24] 1850 U.S. Census, Seneca, Ontario Co., NY, M432-572, 442A, 477B. 1860 U.S. Census, Boston, Ward 5, Suffolk Co., M653-521, 425, #224/359. *Massachusetts: Vital Records, 1841-1910*; Hyde Park, Vol. 320, 233. *Census of Inmates in Almshouses and Poorhouses, 1875-1921*; New York State Archives, Albany, NY, Microfilm A1978-159; Record Number: 534. Ontario County, *NY Poor House Records of Inmates, 1875-1908*, #534.

[25] CWMR, Walter Gayton (Co. E., 54th Massachusetts), M1898-6. Grover, 22. *U.S. Census Mortality Schedules: New York, 1850-1880*, NYS Archives, Microfilm M4; Census Year1869, Seneca, Ontario Co., NY, 50. 1860 U.S. Census, Seneca, Ontario Co., NY, M653-831, 50, #386. *Non-Population Census Schedules for Massachusetts, 1850-1880*, NARA, T1204-23, 1869: Boston, Ward 3, Suffolk Co., MA, Walter J.W. Gayton; online images, www.ancestry.com. *Massachusetts: Vital Records, 1841-1910*, Vol. 222, 156. *U.S. City Directories, 1822-1995*, Boston, MA, 1869, Thomas and George H. Lee, online database, www.ancestry.com.

[26] CWMR, John F. Harrison (Co. D, 54th Massachusetts), M1898-7; Edwin Lukes (Pvt., Co. D, 54th Massachusetts), M1898-11.

[27] CWMR, Oscar Sesor (Co. C, 55th Massachusetts), M1801-12.

[28] *Index, Rochester Newspapers Published 1818-1898*; Osken Sesser, *Union and Advertiser*, May 4, 1866, 2:1; *Mail Robberies*, Oscar Sessor, *Union and Advertiser*, May 15, 1866, 2:4; www.libraryweb.org. 1870 U.S. Census, Auburn, Cayuga Co., NY, M593-910, 168B; *U.S. Army, Register of Enlistments, 1879-1914*, Oscar Sessor; www.ancestry.com.

[29] CWMR, John E. Davis (Co. D, 54th Massachusetts), M1898-4, (Co. A, 55th Massachusetts), M1801-3.

[30] CWMR, Ephriam Freeman (Pvt., Co. I, 55th Massachusetts), M1801-5.

[31] Louis F. Emilio, *A Brave Black Regiment: The History of the 54th Massachusetts, 1863-1865* (1894; reprint, Da Capo Press, 1995), 55-59, 344-349, 373-378, 383-388.

[32] CWMR, Anthony Schenck (Pvt., Co. H, 54th Massachusetts), M1898-14. CWMR, Henry Dennis, (Cpl., Co. H. 54th Massachusetts), M1898-4. Civil War Pension, John Dennis (Cpl., Co. H., 54th Massachusetts), Mother's Pension, Cert. #27.924.

[33] CWMR, Thomas P. Riggs (Pvt., Co. D, 54th Massachusetts), M1898-14. Civil War Pension, Thomas P. Riggs (Pvt. Co. D, 54th Massachusetts), Sarah Riggs, Mother's Pension Cert. #179.313.

[34] CWMR, George W. Moshroe (Pvt., Co. F, 54th Massachusetts), M1898-12. *Civil War Prisoners Database*, www.civilwarprisoners.com.

[35] CWMR, Nathaniel Hurley (Pvt., Co. E, 54th Massachusetts), M1898-8. *Civil War Prisoners Database*, www.civilwarprisoners.com.

[36] CWMR, Charles Kane (Pvt., Co. A, 54th Massachusetts), M1898-10. 1850 U.S. Census, Kaskaskia, Randolph Co., Illinois, M432-125, 127A, #38/48. *Illinois Servitude and Emancipation Records, 1722-1863*, Vol. 1, 17, Illinois State Archives, www.ilsos.gov.

[37] CWMR, George Washington (Pvt., Co. E., 54th Massachusetts), M1878-17. Civil War Pension, George Washington (Pvt. Co., E, 54th Massachusetts), Mary F. Washington, Widow's Pension Cert. #102.291. CWMR, Charles K. Reason (Pvt., Co. E, 54th Massachusetts), M1898-13. 1860 U.S. Census, Onondaga, Onondaga Co., New York, M653-8295, 35, #209.

[38] CWMR, William R. Lee (Pvt., Co. F, 54th Massachusetts), M1898-10. William R. Lee (Pvt., Co. F, 54th Massachusetts, Civil War), Sarah J. Lee, Widow's Cert. # 41.935.

[39] CWMR, George Holmes (Pvt., Co. F., 54th Massachusetts), M1898-8. Civil War Pension, George Holmes, (Pvt., Co. F, 54th Massachusetts), Mary A. Holmes, Widow's Cert. # 25.072.

[40] Emilio, 105.

[41] "Letter to Major G. L. Stearns," *Douglass' Monthly*, August 1863, Vol. V, No. X, 849:1-3, www.accessible.com.

[42] Charles B. Fox, *Record of the Service of the Fifty-Fifth Regiment of Massachusetts Volunteer Infantry* (Boston, 1868), 11-13; digitized; www.archive.org.

[43] Emilio, 173.

[44] Report of Col. Edward N. Hallowell, March 1, 1864, www.battleofolustee.org/reports/hallowell.htm.

[45] CWMR, Stephen A. Swails, Lt., Co. F, 54th Massachusetts, M1898-16. Find a Grave Memorial, Stephen Atkins Swails, Humane and Friendly Society Cemetery, Charleston, South Carolina, www.findagrave.com. "Black Civil-War Soldier Gets Overdue Honors", Nov. 1, 2006, www.npr.org/templates/story/story.php?storyId-6417951. 1865 NYS Census, Elmira, Chemung, Co, Ward 3, 59, #433. 1870 U.S. Census, Kings, Williamsburg Co., SC, M593-1511, 78B. #291/304.

[46] CWMR, Albert D. Thompson, Sgt., Co. D, 54th Massachusetts, M1898-16. "Marriage in High Life", *Buffalo Daily Courier*, 28 December 1868, 2:1, www.newspapers.com. Obituary, Albert D. Thompson, *Buffalo Commercial*, 18 October 1878, 4:3, www.newspapers.com. "In Memoriam to Late Hon. B.F. Randolph", *The Christian Recorder*, 5 December 1868, www.accessible.com. "To the Masonic Fraternity," *The Christian Recorder*, 3 October 1878, 1:3, www.newspapers.com. Civil War Pension, Albert D. Thompson (Sgt., Co. D, 54th Massachusetts), Cert. #152.321.

[47] CWMR, Isaac S. Hawkins (Corp., Co. D, 54th Massachusetts), M1898-7. 1855 NYS Census, Ridgeway, Orleans Co., ED 2, #332/325. 1865 NYS Census, Ridgeway, Orleans Co., ED 2, #291/319, #291/320.

[48] Civil War Pension, Isaac S. Hawkins (Co. D., 54th Massachusetts), Cert. #136.515. 1870 U.S. Census, Washington, Ward 4, District of Columbia, M593-124, 866B, #3569. *U.S. City Directories, 1822-1995*, District of Columbia, 1870, Isaac S. Hawkins, www.ancestry.com.

[49] Emilio, 174-175.

[50] Noah Andre Trudeau, ed., *Voices of the 55th: Letters from the 55th Massachusetts Volunteers, 1861-1865*, (Morningside House, Inc. Dayton, Ohio, 1996), 81.

[51] "A Soldier's Letter," *The Christian Recorder*, 9 July 1864, 1:6-7, www.accessible.com.

[52] CWMR, Albert O. Robbins (Co. F, 55th Massachusetts), M1801-11.

[53] Letter from John H. W. N. Collins, *The Christian Recorder*, 23 July 1864, 1:3, www.accessible.com.

[54] Noah Andre Trudeau, *Like Men of War: Black Troops in the Civil War, 1862-1865*, (Boston, Little Brown and Company,1998), 254-5

[55] Emilio, 227-228.

[56] Trudeau, *Voices of the 55th: Letters from the 55th Massachusetts*, 150.

[57] CWMR, Levi Carter (Co. F, 54th Massachusetts), M1898-3. 1865. NYS Census, Elmira, Chemung Co., Ward 3, 25, #179. 1880 U.S. Census, Elmira, Chemung Co., New York, T9-817, ED 72, 309A, #126/138.

[58] CMMR, Andrew Miller (Co. F, 54th Massachusetts), M1898-11. Civil War Pension, Andrew Miller (Co. F, Corp. 54th Massachusetts), Phebe A. Miller, Widow's Pension, Cert. #69.763, www.fold3.com.

[59] CWMR, Alexander W. Renkins (Co. D, 54th Massachusetts), M1898-13.

[60] CWMR, Andrew Deforest (Co. E, 54th Massachusetts), M1898-4. 1855 NYS Census, Syracuse, Ward 7, Onondaga Co., #21/32; 1860 U.S. Census, Syracuse, Ward 7, Onondaga Co., NY, M653-830, 967, #635/823. Various spellings for this surname include DeForest, Deforrest.

[61] CWMR, Henry F. Stewart (Co. E, 54th Massachusetts), M1898-16.

[62] CWMR, George Alexander, (Co. H, 54th Massachusetts), M1898-1.

[63] CWMR, Lorenzo T. Lewis, (Co. I, 54th Massachusetts), M1898-11. 1850 U.S. Census, Taylor, Wayne Co., Michigan, M432-366, 386B, #24/24; 1860 U.S. Census, Dearborn, Wayne Co., Michigan, M653-564, 699, #67/65; *Michigan, Death Records, 1867-1950*, Jane P. Lewis, 1901 and Robert E. Lewis, 1904, online images, www.ancestry.com.

[64] CWMR, James P. Johnson, (Co. F, 54th Massachusetts), M1898-9; James H. Postley, (Co. F, 54th Massachusetts), M1898-13; Andrew Miller, (Co. F, 54th Massachusetts), M1898-11.

[65] CWMR, John R. O'Neil (Co. D, 54th Massachusetts), M1898-12.

[66] CWMR, Frank Boyer, (Co. F, 54th Massachusetts), M1898-2.

[67] Emilio, 316-322.

[68] Fox, 83-84.

[69] Steven M. LaBarre, *The Fifth Massachusetts Colored Cavalry in the Civil War,* (Jefferson, North Carolina, McFarland & Company, 2016), 47.

[70] CWMR, James W. Collins, (Co. A, 5th Massachusetts Cavalry), M1817-79. Civil War Pension, Juan DeColaines, alias James W. Collins, (Co. A, 5th Massachusetts Cavalry), Cert. #948.669. *Vermont, Vital Records*, Montpelier, Vermont, 1873, online database, www.ancestry.com. 1880 U.S. Census, Montpelier, Washington, Co., Vermont, T9-1348, ED 210, 147D, #58/80.

[71] CWMR, John Nelson (Co. A, 5th Massachusetts Cavalry), M1817-87.

[72] CWMR, Irenas J. Palmer (Co. A, 5th Massachusetts Cavalry) M1817-88. Iranas J. Palmer, Deposition, 27 April 1886, Civil War Pension File, Solomon Peterson (Pvt., Co. A, 5th Massachusetts Cavalry), Cert. # 328.793. Obituary, Irenas J. Palmer, *Olean Evening Herald*, 7 June 1919, 5:4.

[73] CWMR, Charles R. Douglass (Cpl., Co. F, 54th Massachusetts), M1898-5; (Sgt., Co. 1, 5th Massachusetts Cavalry), M1817-80.

[74] LaBarre, 50.

[75] LaBarre, 88.

[76] CWMR, John S. Peterson (Co. A, 5th Massachusetts Cavalry), M1817-88. Civil War Pension, John S. Peterson, (Pvt., Co. A, 5th Massachusetts Cavalry, Civil War), Harriet A. Peterson, Widow's Pension, Cert. #84.409. 1855 NYS Census, Wirt, Allegany Co., #241/251. *U.S. Burial Registers, Military Posts and National Cemeteries. 1862-1960,* online database, www.ancestry.com. *U.S. National Cemetery Interment Control Forms, 1928-1962*, online database, www.ancestry.com.

[77] CWMR, Alfred W. Butler (Co. A., 5th Massachusetts Cavalry), M1817-79.

[78] CWMR, Charles R. Douglass (Co. I, 5th Massachusetts Cavalry), M1817-80.

[79] Ross M. Kimmel and Michael P. Musick, *"I Am Busy Drawing Pictures": The Civil War Art and Letters of Private John Jacob Omenhausser, CSA.* (Annapolis: Friends of the Maryland Archives, 2014), 91-93.

[80] LaBarre, 127,134.

[81] CWMR, William Elebeck (Co. A., 5th Massachusetts Cavalry), M1817-81. 1850 U.S. Census, Buffalo, Ward 4, Erie Co., NY, M653-746, 653, #1030/1347. 1865 NYS Census, Buffalo, Erie Co., NY, 29, #114/141.

[82] Civil War Pension. William Elebeck (Co. A, 5th Massachusetts Cavalry), Mother's Cert. #328.936.

[83] CWMR, Solomon Peterson (Co. A, 5th Massachusetts Cavalry), M1817-88. 1855 NYS Census, Olean, Cattaraugus Co., 119, #279/279. 1860 U.S. Census, Olean, Cattaraugus Co., NY, M653-726, 816, #493/476., Solomon Peterson. 1865 NYS Census, Olean, Cattaraugus Co., p. 3, #20. 1870 U.S. Census, Olean, Cattaraugus Co., NY, M593-909, 405A, #323/310.

[84] *The Buffalo Commercial*, 25 Mar 1896, www.newspapers.com. *Find a Grave*, www.findagrave.com.

8th USCT and The Draft

[85] *Rochester Union and Advertiser*, 7 April 1863; 8:7.

[86] Doris Kearns Goodwin, *Team of Rivals: The Political Genius of Abraham Lincoln*, (Simon & Schuster, 2005), 537.

[87] *Civil War Newspaper Clippings*, Cayuga County, New York, New York, NYS Military Museum website http://dmna.ny.gov/historic/reghist/civil/counties/cayuga/cayuga_CWN.htm ; *Auburn Advertiser and Union*, 22 July 1863, transcription.

[88] Eugene Converse Murdock, *Patriotism Limited, 1862-1865: The Civil War Draft and the Bounty System* (Kent State University Press, 1967), 210.

[89] Lewis H. Clark, *Military History of Wayne County, New York* (Sodus: Lewis H. Clark, Hulett & Gaylord, 1883), 423.

[90] *Geneva Gazette*, 14 August 1863, 2:1; online images, www.nyshistoricnewspapers.org.

[91] *New York State Town Clerk Records, 1865*, LeRoy, Genesee County; online images, www.ancestry.com.

[92] *U.S., Civil War Draft Registrations Records, 1863-1865*, online database and images, www.ancestry.com.

[93] *Civil War Newspaper Clippings*, Broome County, New York, NYS Military Museum website, http://dmna.ny.gov/historic/reghist/civil/counties/broome/broome.CWN.htm.

[94] *Geneva Gazette*, 31 July 1863, 2:5-6, www.nyshistoricnewspapers.org.

[95] Civil War Clippings, Cayuga County, New York, New York State Military Museum website, http://dmna.ny.gov/historic/reghist/civil/counties/cayuga/cayuga_CWN.htm.

[96] Clark, 417-445.

[97] New York State Archives, Albany, New York; *New York Civil War Muster Roll Abstracts, 1861-1900*; Abstracts of Muster Rolls for Colored Enlisted Men Unassigned to Any Unit During the Civil War, 1863-1865; Archive Collection #B0812-85; Box #1; Roll #1; online images, www.ancestry.com.

[98] War Department, Adjutant General's Office, General Orders, No. 143, May 22, 1863; http://ourdocuments.gov/document_data/document_images/doc_035.big.jpg.

[99] CWMR, William T. Dorsey (Pvt., Co. B, 8th USCT), M1821-5.

[100] 1850 U.S. Census, Sodus, Wayne Co., NY, M432-612, 1868, #934; 1860 U.S. Census, Sodus, Wayne Co., NY, M658-876, 472, #1461; Ontario Co., NY Surrogate Court, Probate, Film #118/25, Peregrine Fitzhugh, 1813; Wayne County, NY, Surrogate Court, Will Book D, 480 and Probate File #0279, Abraham Bradington; R.C. Smedley, *History of the Underground Railroad in Chester and the Neighboring Counties of Pennsylvania*, ((John A. Hiestand, Lancaster, PA, 1888), 357-358.

[101] Wayne County, NY Deed Books, 88/515 (Molly Lee to Madeline Dorsey) and158/521 (Grantee Charles R. Dorsey, heir at law of Madeline Dorsey).

[102] Donald Scott, Sr., *Camp William Penn, 1863-1865: America's First Federal African American Soldiers' Fight for Freedom* (Atglen, Pennsylvania: Schiffer Military History, 2012), 79.

[103] CWMR, Levi A. Preston (Pvt. Co. B, 8th USCT), M1821-12.

[104] CWMR, Theodore Duffin, (Pvt. Co. B, 8th USCT), M1821-5.

[105] CWMR, William P. Woodlin, (Pvt. Co. B, 8th USCT), M1821-16.

[106] CWMR, Edgar G. Fryman, (Co. B, 8th USCT), M1821-6.

[107] CWMR, Charles H. Cooper, (Co. B, 8th USCT), M1821-4.

[108] CWMR, Robert Mann, (Co. B, 8th USCT), M1821-10.

[109] CWMR, Edwin H. Brown, (8th USCT), M1821-2.

[110] William P. Woodlin, *Diary of an African American Soldier in the 8th Regiment of the United States Colored Troops, Co. G.* Gilderman Lehrman Institute for American History.

[111] Ibid.

[112] 1850 U.S. Census, Ledyard, Cayuga Co., NY, M432-483, 245B.

[113] 1855 NYS Census, Ledyard, Cayuga County, Family #166; www.familysearch.org.

[114] Woodlin, *Diary*, February 20, 1864.

[115] Civil War Pension, George Van Schaick (Private, Co. G, 8th USCT), Aurelia Van Schaick, Mother's Pension Certificate #120.903. Various spellings for surname include Van Schaick, Van Schoick, Van Shaick, Van Shank.

[116] *Battle of Olustee Battlefield and Reenactment* website, www.battleofolustee.org.

[117] Oliver Willcox Norton, *Army Letters, 1861-1865*, (Chicago: O.L. Deming, 1903); 198, 202; digitized by Google.

[118] Woodlin, *Diary*, 5 July 1864,

[119] CWMR, George Alexander, (Co. B, 8th USCT), M1821-1. 1855 NYS Census, Corning, Steuben Co., ED #2, 5, #34; online images, www.familysearch.org.

[120] CWMR, Henry Charles, (Co. F, 54th Massachusetts), M1821-3.

[121] CWMR, Bradley Gregor, (Co. B, 8th USCT); Elijah Bradley, (Co. B., 8th USCT), M1821-2. Civil War Pension, Bradley Gregor (Co. B., 8th USCT), Almira Gregor, Widow' Pension App. #886.863.

[122] CWMR, Henry Thompson, Corp., (Co. B, 8th USCT), M1821-14.

[123] "Letter, A. P. Heichhold to Supervisory Committee for Organization of Colored Regiments, Philadelphia, Pennsylvania" transcription, *The Christian Recorder*, 12 March 1864, www.accessible.com.

[124] CWMR, James Fayette, (Co. B, 8th USCT), M1821-5. Civil War Pension, James Fayette (Co. G, 8th USCT), Martha Fayette, widow's pension, Cert. #109.607, online digital images, www.fold3.com.

[125] Grover, 33-35.

[126] CWMR, Thomas Lloyd, (Co. B, 8th USCT), M1821-9.

[127] Letter, A. P. Heichhold, *The Christian Recorder*, 12 March 1864;, www.accessible.com.

[128] Letters, Pvt. James Jordon to "My Dear Louisa", 21 February 1864; Cpt. Henry Shackelford to "My Dear Mother", 20 February 1864; transcriptions; www.battleofolustee.org/letters.

[129] Brig. Gen. Joseph Finegan to Headquarters, District of East Florida, report, 23 February 1864; transcription; www.battleofolustee.org/reports.

[130] "Our Hilton Head Correspondence; Prisoners Held by the Rebels," *New York Times*, 19 April 1864, transcription, www.nytimes.com/1864/04/19/news/our-hilton-head-coresspondence-prisoners-held-rebels-capture-valuable-prize-one.html.

[131] *Civil War Prisons Database*, www.civilwarprisoners.com.

[132] CWMR, William O. Lewis, (Corp., 8th USCT), M1821-9.

[133] 1865 NYS Census, Catharine, Schuyler Co., 39, #292, www.familysearch.org.

[134] CWMR, John Thompson, (Co. B, 8th USCT), M1821-14. New York State Archives:, Albany, New York; *Town Clerks' Registers of Men Who Served in the Civil War, 1861-1865*; online images, www.ancestry.com.

[135] CWMR, Paul G. Blackman, (Co. G, 8th USCT), M1821-2. Civil War Pension, Paul G. Blackman (Pvt., Co. G, 8th USCT), Harriet A. Blackman, widow's pension, Cert. #222.464.

[136] CWMR, Richard Chancellor, (Co. B, 8th USCT), M1821-3. Civil War Pension, Richard Chancellor (Sgt., Co. B, 8th USCT), Cert. #181.028.

[137] CWMR, Joseph Ford, (Co. B, 8th USCT), M1821-6. Civil War Pension, Joseph Ford (Pvt., Co. B, 8th USCT), Pension Cert. #111.201.

[138] Oliver Willcox Norton, *Army Letters, 1861-1865*, (Chicago: O.L. Deming, 1903); 203; digitized by Google.

[139] Norton, 202.

[140] Norton, 212.

[141] Letter, Rufus Sibb Jones, transcription, *The Christian Recorder*, 7 May 1864, www.accessible.com

[142] Woodlin, *Diary*, 6 May 1864.

[143] Civil War Pension, George Van Schaick (Private, Co. G, 8th USCT), Aurelia Van Schaick, Mother's Pension, Cert. #120.903.

[144] Norton, 214.

[145] Woodlin, *Diary*, May 21, 1864.

[146] Woodlin, *Diary*, 24 July 1864.

[147] Civil War Pension, George Van Schaick (Private, Co. G, 8th USCT.

[148] Ibid.

[149] Civil War Pension, Stephen W. Clark (Corp. Co. G, 8th USCT), Mary Elizabeth Clark, Widow's Pension Cer. #44.237.

[150] Woodlin, *Diary*, 12 August 1864.

[151] Woodlin, *Diary*, 13 August 1864.

[152] R.J.M. Blackett, Editor, *Thomas Morris Chester: Black Civil War Correspondent, His Dispatches from the Virginia Front*, (1989; Reprint, New York, New York: Da Capo Press, 1991), 135-6.

[153] CWMR, Calvin Van Hazel, (Co. B, 8th USCT), M1821-15. New York State Archives; New York, *Civil War Muster Roll Abstracts, 1861-1900*; Calvin Van Hayen; www.ancestry.com.

[154] 1855 NYS Census, Camden, Oneida Co., #265; Calvin Hazel; online digital images, www.familysearch.org.

[154] CWMR, Allen Hazel,(Co. I, 11th USCHA), M1821-15.

[155] Civil War Pension, Calvin Hazel (Private, Co. I, 8th USCHA), Susan Hazel, Mother's Pension Application #114.528.

[156] Civil War Pension, Joseph R. Smith (Private, Co. B, 8th USCT), Helen M. Smith, Widow's Pension Cert. #48.030.

[157] Woodlin, *Diary*, 28 September 1864.

[158] CWMR, Milton Frank, (Co. G, 8th USCT), M1821-6.

[159] Civil War Pension, Robert Frank (Private, Unassigned, 31st USCT), Delano Frank, Widow's Pension Cert. #74.420.

[160] CWMR, Richard Burke, (Co. G, 8th USCT), M1821-3.

[161] 1865 NYS Census, Ridgeway, Orleans Co. Dist. #2, 46, #319, digitized images, www.familysearch.org. 1880 U.S. Census, Medina, Orleans Co., New York, T9-912, ED 151, 242B, #227.

[162] CWMR, Samuel Dennis, (Co. G, 8th USCT), M1821-5.

[163] CWMR, James Butler, (Co. G, 8th USCT), M1821-3.

[164] Woodlin, *Diary*, 7 October 1864.

[165] Bracket, 148.

[166] Woodlin, *Diary*, 12 October 1864.

[167] CWMR, Dwight Jupiter, (Co. B, 8th USCT), M1821-9.

[168] Grover, 68-9.

[169] Brian M. Thomsen, Editor, *The Civil War Memoirs of Ulysses S. Grant*, Reprint (2002, Tom Doherty Associates, LLC, New York, New York), 439-40.

[170] "An Acknowledgement", *The Christian Recorder*, 22 July 1865, 2:6-7, www.accessible.com.

[171] Ibid.

[172] Norton, 259.

[173] Ibid, 263-4.

[174] Ibid, 267.

[175] CWMR, Thomas Brown, (Co. B, 8th USCT), M1821-2. Thomas Brown, (Co. H, 20th USCT), M1823-2. Thomas Brown, (100th USCT), NARA RG 94-Box 07; online digital images, www.fold3.com.

[176] CWMR, Dennis Low, (Co. G., 8th USCT), M1821-10.

[177] CWMR, Elijah Gregor, (Co. B, 8th USCT), M1821-6. Civil War Pension, Elijah Gregor (Private, Co. B, 8th USCT), Harriet Gregor, Widow's Pension, App.#161.253.

[178] Woodlin, *Diary*, 10, 11, 12 and 28 December, 1863; 8 January 1864.

[179] "Florida Expedition", Letter from Rufus Sibb Jones, *The Christian Recorder*, 7 May 1864, transcription, www.battleofolustee.org.letters_rufus_jones_8thusct_cr_02_html.

[180] 1840 U.S. Census, St. Martin's Parish, Louisiana, M704, p. 297, www.ancestry.com. Palfrey Family Papers, Louisiana State University, https://www.lib.lsu.edu/special/research/manuscripts/guides/plantations?combine=&page=44. John Gorham Palfrey Papers, Andover-Harvard Theological Library, https://guides.library.harvard.edu/hds/john-gorham-palfrey/slavery. 1850 U.S. Census, Ledyard, Cayuga Co., NY, M432-483, p. 245B, #1149; Walworth, Wayne Co., NY, M432-612, 82B, #73; Farmington, Ontario Co., NY, M432-572, 278, #6, 280B, #44.

[181] *The Advent Review & Sabbath Herald*, 17 September 1889, 15:2, https://adventisdigitallibrary.org.

[182] 1880 U.S. Census, Battle Creek, Calhoun Co., MI, T9-574, ED 44, 119C, #70. 1900 U.S. Census, Bowling Green, Warren Co., KY, T623, ED 101, 2, #39. "Tennessee River Conference", *The Advent Sabbath Review Herald*, 29 Jan 1901, 13:3, https://adventistdigitallibrary.org.

[183] *New York, Town Clerks' Registers of Men Who Served in the Civil War*, Smithfield, Madison Co., online images, www.ancestry.com. CWMR, Orange C. Thompson, (Co. B., 8th USCT), M1821-14. Edwin S. Redkey, ed. *A Grand Army of Black Men: Letters from African-American Soldiers in the Union Army, 1861-1865*, (Cambridge University Press, Reprint, 1993), 132.

[184] Civil War Pension, Orange C. Thompson, (Co. B, 8th USCT), Cert. #1.007.073; Widow's Pension, Emma C. Thompson, App. #862.897. "Court Proceedings", *Times-Picayune*, New Orleans, LA, 18 Sept. 1902, 14, www.genealogybank.com. *The Weekly Messenger* (St. Martinsville, LA), 28 June 1903, 3:3, http://chronicleingamerica.loc.gov. St. Martin's Parish, LA, *Clerk of Court Official Records, Criminal Book* 10, 525,546,547.

[185] CWMR, Garrett S. Russell, (Co. B, 8th USCT), M1821-13. Civil War Pension, Gerrit S. Russell, (Principal Musician, Co. B, 8th USCT), Cert. #712.899. Obituary, Gerritt Russell, *The Clinton Advertiser*, 1 December1906, 1:4, www.fultonhistory.com.

[186] Obituary, William F. Brown, *Geneva Courier*, 29 July 1874, 3:4. 1850 U.S. Census, Hagerstown, Washington, MD, M432-298, 155, #531.

[187] CWMR, Glenalvin Brown (Co. G., 8th USCT), M1821-2.

[188] Civil War Pension, Glenalvin Brown (Musician, Co. G, 8th USCT), Cert. #513549; Mother's App. #557.345. *Geneva Advertiser*, 31 May 1892, 3:3.

14th Rhode Island Heavy Artillery

[189] Kennedy, *The United States in 1860*, 442.

[190] *Report of the Finance Committee of the House of Representatives, on Bounty Frauds, etc.*, (Providence Rhode Island: H.H. Thomas & Co., Printers to the State, 1865), 151, 154; digitized by Google,

[191] Civil War Pension, George Washington Bogert (Pvt., Co. L, 11th USCHA), Lydia Bogert, mother; Cert. #64,222. NOTE: Various spellings of surname include Bogart, Bogert, Boget.

[192] *Geneva Gazette*, 27 May 1835, 3:6; www.nyshistoricnewspapers.org.

[193] *Ontario Repository and Freeman*, 10 May 1837, 3:6, www.nyshistoricnewspapers.org.

[194] *New-York Daily Reformer*, Watertown, New York, 25 May 1863, 3, www.genealogybank.com.

[195] *Report of Finance Committee …*, 76.

[196] *New-York Daily Reformer*, 19 September 1863, 2:4; www.genealogybank.com.

[197] *New-York Daily Reformer*, 3 October 1863, 3:2 www.genealogybank.com.

[198] Civil War Pension, George Washington Bogert (Pvt., Co. L, 11th USCHA), Lydia Bogert, mother's, Certificate # 64,222.

[199] Ibid. Deposition of David H. Ray, 13 December 1865.

[200] CWMR, Henry Fields, (Co. F, 11th USCHA), M1818-195.

[201] *Report of Finance Committee ...*, 11.

[202] Ibid, 18

[203] CWMR, Richard Champlin, (Co I, 11th USCHA) and George H. Champlin, (Co. I, 11th USCHA), M1818-192. *Vital Records, Jefferson County, NY, 1847-1849*, http://jefferson.nygenweb.net/vrecbrow.htm and http://jefferson.nygenweb.net/vrecwate.htm.

[204] CWMR, James F. Henry, (Co. M, 11th USCHA) and Richard T. Henry, (Co. H, 11th USCHA), M1818-212.

[205] CWMR, Jacob W. Redder, (Co. I, 11th USCHA), M1818-207.

[206] CWMR, Roderick S. Fletcher, (Co. L, 11th USCHA), M1818-195.

[207] CWMR, Thomas A. Wycoff, (Co. H, 11th USCHA), M1818-216.

[208] Civil War Pension, Prime Cortright (Pvt., Co. M, 11th USCHA), Cert. # 280.805. NOTE: Various spellings of this surname include Cortright, Courtright, and Cartwright.

[209] New York State Archives; Albany, New York: *Town Clerks' Registers of Men Who Served in the Civil War, ca 1861-1865*; Prime Courtright; online digital images, www.ancestry.com.

[210] Civil War Pension, Prime Cortright.

[211] Tombstone Inscription, Prime Cortright, Photo by Bill Huff, Jr.

[212] CWMR, William L.G. Freeman (Corp., Co. G, 11th USCHA), M1818-196.1860 U.S. Census, Phelps, Ontario Co., NY, M653-831, 615, #883. *U.S. Civil War Draft Registrations, 1863-1865*, Congressional Dist. #25, Phelps, New York, William L. Freeman, online images, www.ancestry.com. 1870 U.S. Census, Seneca Falls, Seneca Co., NY, M593-1093, 232, #964. *The Auburn Bulletin*, January 1894, 4:3, Obituary, William Freeman, www.fultonhistory.com. .

[213] CWMR, Philip Lenison, (Co G, 11th USCHA), M1818-203.

[214] J. M. Addeman, *Reminiscences of Two Years with The Colored Troops*, (Providence: N. Bangs Williams & Co., 1880), 12, www.archive.org.

[215] CWMR, David H. Ray, Jr., (Co. I, 11th USCHA), M1818-207.

[216] CWMR, Charles F. Taylor, (Co. L, 11th USCHA), M1818-212.

[217] CWMR, Benjamin Jones, (Co. M, 11th USCHA), M1818-202. George Carpenter, (Co. L, 11th USCHA), M1818-191.

[218] Chenery, 42.

[219] CWMR, Stephen L. Watkins, (Co. M, 11th USCHA), M1818-214.

[220] *Rochester, New York City Directories,* 1866, 1867 and 1868, online images, http://www3.libraryweb.org. 1870 U.S. Census, Rochester, Monroe Co., NY, M593-969, 1A.

[221] Chenery, 145-6.

[222] Ibid., 105

[223] *The Daily Milwaukee News,* 18 October 1865, 1:2; online digital images, www.newspapers.com.

[224] Chenery, 104-05.

[225] CWMR, Hezekiah Davis, (Co. M., 11th USCHA), M1818-192.

[226] 1865 NYS Census, Rochester, Ward 3 North, Monroe County, 34, #228, online digital images, www.familysearch.org.

[227] Civil War Pension, Hezekiah Dixon, Jr. (Pvt., Co. M, 11th USCHA), Hezekiah Dixon, Sr., father's pension application #264.242; mother's application #460.242.

[228] CWMR, John Sullivan, (Pvt., Co. G, 11th USCHA), M1818-211. Civil War Pension, John Sullivan (Pvt., Co. G, 11th USCHA), Sabrina Sullivan, widow's pension. Cert. #89,832; Frances Sullivan, widow's pension, App. #35.640.

[229] CWMR, Allen Hazel, (Pvt., Co. I, 11th USCHA), M1818-198.

[230] CWMR, David R. Fletcher, (Co. L, 11th USCHA), M1818-195.

[231] Civil War Pension, David R. Fletcher (Pvt., Co. L, 11th USCHA), Mary E. Fletcher, Widow's pension Cert. # 96.512; Emily A. Fletcher, Minor's pension Cert. #169.022.

[232] CWMR, Franklin Fisher, (Co. K, 11th USCHA), M1818-195. Civil War Pension, Franklin Fisher (Pvt., Co. K, 11th USCHA), Ellen Fisher, Widow's pension cert. #46.086.

[233] CWMR, Roderick S. Fletcher, (Co. L, 11th USCHA), M1818-195.

[234] CWMR, William H. Mann, (Sgt., Co. L, 11th USCHA), M1818-204. Civil War Pension, William H. Mann (Sgt., Co. L, 11th USCHA), Susan Mann, Mother's pension, Cert. #51.007.

[235] Civil War Pension, George W. Bogert (Pvt., Co. L, 11th USCT), Lydia Bogert, Mother's Pension, Certificate #64.222.

[236] CWMR, Hannibal F. Davis, (Co. G, 11th USCHA), M1818-193.

[237] 1850 U.S. Census, Lockport, Niagara County, New York, M432-560, 90A, #1383. 1855 NYS Census, Lockport, Niagara County, ED 2, #528; online images, www.familysearch.org.

[238] Civil War Pension, George Moore (Pvt., Co. M, 11th USCHA), Maria Moore, Widow's pension Cert. #89.924. CWMR, George Moore, (Co. M, 11th USCHA), M1818-205.

[239] CWMR, Amos A. Lunn, (Co. D, 11th USCHA), M1818-204.

[240] Civil War Pension, Amos Lunn (Pvt., Co. D, 11th USCHA), Helen E Lund/Lunn, Widow's pension Cert. #56461.

[241] *Palmyra Village Cemetery Records,* Transcriptions, Wayne County Historian's Office, Lyons, New York.

[242] Civil War Pension, Alfred W. Brewster (Pvt., Co. I, 11th USCT), Fannie Brewster, Widow's Pension, Cert. #59.714; online images, www.fold3.com.

[243] Civil War Pension, Charles H. Hardy (Pvt., Co. K, 11th USCHA), Cornelia Hardy, Widow's Pension, Cert. #78.486. Aaron Myers (Pvt., Co. M, 11th USCHA), Abbie A. Myers, Widow's Pension, Cert. #67.497.

[244] CWMR, Anthony T. White, (Pvt., Co. I, 11th USCHA), M1818-214.

[245] CWMR, William P. Anderson, (Pvt., Co. F, 11th USCHA), M1818-188.

[246] CWMR, John W. Cortright, (Co. M, 11th USCHA), M1818-192.

[247] CWMR, Hugh DePuy, (Co. K, 11th USCHA), M1818-193.

[248] Civil War Pension, William H. Clark (Pvt., Co. M, 11th USCHA); Rebecca Clark, Mother's Pension, Certificate # 80.777.

[249] Addeman, 24.

[250] Howard Westwood, "Company A of Rhode Island's Black Regiment: Its Enlisting, Its 'Mutiny', Its Pay, Its Service." *Black Troops, White Commanders and Freedmen during the Civil War*, (Carbondale: Southern University Library Press, 1992), 142-166.

[251] Ibid.

[252] CWMR, James Castles, (Pvt., Co. D, 11th USCHA), M1818-192.

[253] Ibid.

[254] Westwood, 155

[255] CWMR, James H. Taylor, (Pvt. Co. F, 11th USCHA), M1818-212.

[256] CWMR, John G. Graves, (Pvt., Co. G, 11th USCHA), M1818-197.

[257] Ibid.

[258] Ibid.

[259] 1865 NYS Census, Watertown, ED #2, Jefferson County, 15, #102.

[260] CWMR, David H. Ray, Jr., (Pvt., Co. 1, 11th USCHA), M1818-207.

[261] *Courier and Freeman* (Potsdam, NY), 15 April 1863, 2; *Ogdensburg Daily Journal*, 9 September 1867, 1:2. www.nyshistoricnewspapers.org.

[262] 1870 U.S. Census, Palmyra, Wayne County, New York, 358, #181/199, David H. Ray, Jr.; Wayne County Historian, Lyons, New York.

[263] CWMR, Winfield B. VanHorn, (Pvt., Co. L, 11th USCHA), M1818-213.

[264] 1870 U.S. Census, Rochester, Ward 3, Monroe County, New York, M593-969, 81A, #68.

[265] 1875 NYS Census, Saratoga Springs, Saratoga County, ED 2, 15, #123.

[266] CWMR, Webster Demann, Pvt., (Co. K, 11th USCT), M1818-194.

[267] *Michigan, Marriage Records*, 1867-1952, online images, www.ancestry.com.

[268] CWMR, Thomas Dorsey, (Co. K, 11th USCHA), M1818-194.

[269] CWMR, William A. Moore, (Co. K, 11th USCHA), M1818-203. *New Orleans, Louisiana, Death Records Index, 1804-1949*, William A. Moore, www.ancestry.com. 1880 U.S. Census, New Orleans, Orleans Co., LA, T9-464, ED 90, 461D, #250.

[270] Catherine S. Brown, *Abel Brown, Abolitionist*, Edited by Tom Calarco (Jefferson, North Carolina: McFarland & Co., Inc., 2006), 115, 119. *New York Town Clerk's Registers of Men Who Served in the Civil War, 1861-1865*, Town of Elbridge, Onondaga Co., online images, www.ancestry.com. 1855 NYS Census, Elbridge, Onondaga County, New York, ED 2, #382; www.ancestry.com. Rev. James Bulah (Beulah) House Site, Jordan, New York, www.pacny.net/freedom_trail/Buelah.htm.

[271] 1855 NYS Census, Avon, Livingston County, ED 1, #77. 1860 U.S. Census, Rush, Monroe Co., New York, M653-786, 664, #636. *U.S. Civil War Draft Registration Records, 1863-1865*, online database and images, www.ancestry.com. 1865 NYS Census, Ontario, Wayne County, 7, #39.

[272] CWMR, Joseph P. Bulah, (Co. M, 11th USCHA), M1818-191. Charles J. Duffin, (Co. M, 11th USCHA), M1818-193. John G. Hill, (Co. L, 11th USCHA), M1818-199.

[273] Civil War Pension, Joseph P. Bulah (Pvt., Co. M, 11th USCHA), Cert. #402.089

[274] *Buffalo City Directories*, 1876-1900, www.ancestry.com. 1875 NYS Census, Buffalo, Ward 4, Erie Co., 32, #286.

[275] Civil War Pension, Joseph P. Bulah.

[276] Civil War Pension, John G. Hill (Pvt., Co. L, 11th USCHA), Cert. #342.736.

[277] Civil War Pension, Joseph P. Bulah.

[278] *Forest Lawn Cemetery*, Buffalo, NY, www.forest-lawn.com.

New York Regiments

[279] Frederick Phisterer, *New York in the War of the Rebellion, 1861 to 1865*, (Albany, Weed, Parsons and Company, 1890), 14; digitized by Google.

[280] *Douglass' Monthly*, June 1863, Vol. V, No. VI, 840-841; online digital images, www.accessible.com.

[281] *Douglass' Monthly*, August 1863, Vol. V, No. X, 1:3; online digital images, www.accessible.com.

[282] *Record of the Action of the Convention Held at Poughkeepsie, N.Y., July 15th and 16th, 1863* (New York: Francis & Loutrel, Steam Printers and Stationers, 1863), 1.

[283] Ibid., 9.

[284] Ibid., 12.

[285] *The Christian Recorder*, 29 August 1863, 2:4, online digital images, www.accessible.com.

[286] *The Christian Recorder*, 5 September 1863, 2:4, online digital images, www.accessible.com

[287] Benjamin Quarles, *The Negro in the Civil War* (Reprint, Da Capo Press, New York, 1989), 189-90.

[288] *Union League Club, Report of the Committee on Volunteering, Presented October 13th, 1864* (New York, Club House, 1864), 7.

[289] Ibid., 9.

[290] Ibid., 18.

[291] Ibid., 13.

[292] Ibid., 12.

[293] Ibid., 14.

[294] CWMR, Oliver Comback, (Co. B, 20th USCT), M1823-4.

[295] Eugene Converse Murdock, *Patriotism Limited: 1862-1865*, (Kent University Press, 1967), 173.

[296] Union League Club Report, 19.

[297] CWMR, George Whitney, (Pvt. Co. D, 20th USCT), M1823-19. Festus Prince, (Pvt., Co. D, 20th USCT), M1823-14.

[298] Civil War Pension, Joseph Gillam, (Pvt, Co. D, 20th USCT), Cert. # 876.931.

[299] Harry Bradshaw Matthews, *African American Freedom Journey in New York and Related Sites, 1823-1870: Freedom Knows No Color* (Cherry Hill, New Jersey: Africana Homestead Legacy Publishers, 2008), 203.

[300] CWMR, Albert Ray, (Pvt. Co. G, 20th USCT), M1823-14.

[301] CWMR, William H. Goodman, (Pvt. Co. H, 20th USCT) and Harrison Hammitt, (Pvt. Co. D, 20th USCT), M1823-7. Alternate spellings of surname include Hammit and Hammitt. John A. Lee, (Pvt. Co. I, 20th USCT) and Thomas N. Nash, (Pvt. Co. I, 20th USCT), M1823-11. William Culbert, (Pvt. Co. I, 20th USCT), M1823-3.

[302] CWMR, Harvey A. Jubiter, (Pvt. Co. I, 20th USCT), M1823-10.

[303] CWMR, Amasa Carr, (Pvt. Co. G, 20th USCT), M1823-3. Thomas Craig, (Pvt. Co. A, 20th USCT), M1823-4. George H. Carr, (Pvt., Co. G, 20th USCT), M1823-3.

[304] Matthews, 204.

[305] Ibid., 206.

[306] CWMR, Harvey A. Jubiter.

[307] CWMR, Amasa Carr, Pvt. Co. G, 20th USCT, M1823-3.

[308] Union League Club, 47.

[309] Ibid., 47.

[310] CWMR, James Thomas, (20th USCT), M1823-17.

[311] CWMR, William VanHorn, (20th USCT), M1824-14.

[312] CWMR, John W. Garthen, (Unassigned, 20th USCT), M1823-6: William Garten, (Pvt. Co. D, 20th USCT), M1823-6. Civil War Pension, John W. Garthen, (Unassigned, 20th USCT), Mother's Pension, App. #137.487.

[313] CWMR, Martin Wigden, (Pvt., Unassigned, 20th USCT), M1823-19. Civil War Pension, Martin Wigden (Unassigned, 20th USCT), Permelia Wigden, Mother's Pension, App. #504.361.

[314] CWMR, George Bliss, (Pvt., Co. G, 20th USCT), M1823-2.

[315] Civil War Pension, George Whitney (Pvt., Co. D, 20th USCT), Charlotte Whitney, Widow's Pension, Cert. #84.840.

[316] Judith M. Wellman, *Uncovering the Freedom Trail in Auburn and Cayuga County, New York*, 2005, 299.

[317] CWMR, Thomas Hart, (Co. E, 20th USCT), M1823-7. Civil War Pension, Thomas Hart, (Pvt., Co. E, 20th USCT), Sarah Jane Hart, Widow's Pension, Cert. #122.857.

[318] CWMR, Harrison Hammit, (Pvt., Co. D, 20th USCT), M1823-7.

[319] CWMR, Simon L. Graham, (Co. E, 20th USCT), M1823-7. Civil War Pension, Simon L. Graham (Pvt., Co. E, 20th USCT), Lucinda Bennett, Mother's Pension, Cert. #74.081.

[320] CWMR, Samuel Carpenter, (Pvt., Co. I, 20th USCT), M1823-3.

[321] CWMR, William Alexander, (Pvt., Co. A, 20th USCT), M1823-1.

[322] Civil War Pensions, Joseph Gillam, alias Joseph Williams, (Pvt. Co. D, 20th USCT), Cert. #876.931. Grover, 277, Note 7.

[323] Civil War Pension, Festus Prince, (Pvt., Co. D, 20th USCT), Cert. #772.008.

[324] Civil War Pension, John Phillips (Sgt., Co. D, 20th USCT), Maria Phillips, Widow's Pension, Cert. #356.301.

[325] Thomas Cook, *Palmyra and Vicinity*, (Palmyra, NY, *Palmyra Courier-Journal*, 1930), 32.

[326] CWMR, Franklin Bogart, (Pvt., Co. B, 20th USCT, M1823-2. Civil War Pension, Frank Boget, (Pvt., Co. B, 20th USCT), Cert. #769.209.

[327] *Register of Deaths, Palmyra, New York, 1900-1913*, Benjamin Franklin Bogart, #1426. Palmyra Town Clerk.

[328] 1850 U.S. Census, Palmyra, Wayne Co., New York, M432-612, 21, #302.

[329] Eaton Surname File, Palmyra, NY Community Library.

[330] Foster Surname File, Palmyra, NY Community Library.

[331] CWMR, Andrew R. Foster, (Pvt., Co. D, 20th USCT), M1823-6. Civil War Pension, Andrew R. Foster (Pvt. Co. D, 20th USCT), Emma J. Williams, Minor's Pension, App, #485.446.

[332] CWMR, Edwin J. Watkins, (Cpl., Co. I, 20th USCT), M1823-18.

[333] Civil War Pension, Edwin J. Watkins (Cpl., Co. I, 20th USCT), Josephine Watkins, Widow's Pension, App. #1.173.688.

[334] *New York Times*, 28 March 1864; "Presentation of a Stand of Colors to the Twenty-sixth Regiment, U.S.C.T.", transcription, http://nytimes.com.

[335] Ibid.

[336] 1865 NYS Census, Canandaigua, Ontario Co., ED #1, 49, #244.

[337] CWMR, Augustus Smith, (Pvt., Co. I, 26th USCT), M1824-11.

[338] "Our James Island Correspondence," *New York Times*, 15 July 1864,; www.nytimes.com/1864/07/15/news/our-james-island-correspondence.

[339] Ibid.

[340] "From Department of the South. An Expedition – The Colored Troops – Bloody Bridge Battle," *New York Tribune*, Wednesday, 17 August 1864, p. 6; www.genealogybank.com,

[341] *"The Battle of Bloody Bridge"*, www.battleofchas.com/history2.htm.

[342] CWMR, Joseph Waters, (Cpl., Co. F, 26th USCT and William Waters, (Pvt., Co. K, 26th USCT), M1824-14. 1855 NYS Census, Venice, Cayuga Co., #353.

[343] CWMR, Elisha S. Swan, (Pvt., Co. B, 26th USCT), M1924-12. Henry Selby, (Pvt., Co. B, 26 USCT}, M1824-11.

[344] 1850 U.S. Census, Ithaca, Tompkins Co., New York, M432-606, 211A, #143. 1860 U.S. Census, Ithaca, Tompkins Co., New York, M653-868, 481, #700.

[345] "Letter From the 26th U.S.C.T.", *The Christian Recorder*, 15 April 1865, www.accessible.com.

[346] CWMR, Edward Sorrell and John H. Sorrell, (Pvt., Co. B, 26th USCT), M1824-12. Civil War Pension, Edward Sorrell (Pvt., Co. B, 26th USCT), Sydney A. Sorrell, Widow's Pension, Cert. #71.054.

[347] CWMR, Charles Freeman, (Pvt., Co. D, 26th USCT), M1824-5. Civil War Pension, Charles H. Freeman (Pvt., Co. D, 26th USCT), Eliza Freeman, Widow's Pension, Cert. #43.455.

[348] CWMR, Isaac Holland, (Pvt., Co. I, 26th USCT), M1824-6.

[349] *Certificate of Freedom*, William Holland, 24 April 1821; Records, Town of Canandaigua, New York, 1784- 1846; Ontario County Records and Archives Center, Hopewell, New York. 1820 U.S. Census, Canandaigua, Ontario County, M33-62, 213, online images, www.ancestry.com.

[350] CWMR, Martin V. Fletcher, (Pvt., Co. D, 26th USCT), M1824-5.

[351] CWMR, Charles M. Fletcher, (Pvt., Co. I, 26th USCT), M1824-5.

[352] Civil War Pension, John Hardy (Pvt., Co. D, 26th USCT), Permalia Hardy, Widow's Pension, Cert. #160.510.

[353] CWMR, Jeremiah Conway, (Pvt., Co. E, 26th USCT), M1824-3.

[354] CWMR, Thomas C. W. Clark, (Pvt. Co. D, 26th USCT) and George W. Clark, (Principal Musician, Co. D, 26th USCT), M1824-3.

[355] 1870 U.S. Census, Canandaigua, Ontario Co. New York, M593-1065, 86A, #847. 1875 NYS Census, Canandaigua, Ontario Co., ED #1, 47, #415.

[356] *Ontario Repository and Messenger*, 14 July 1875, transcription, www.ontario.nygenweb.net.

[357] *Ontario County Journal*, 25 October 1878, transcription, www.ontario.nygenweb.net.

[358] *Ontario County Journal*, 17 September 1886, transcription, www.ontario.nygenweb.net.

[359] CWMR, Peter Peterson, (Pvt., Co. I, 26th USCT), John Peterson, (Corp., Co. I, 26th USCT) and Edward G. Peterson, (Corp., Co. I, 26th USCT), M1824-10.

[360] CWMR, George Gayton, (Pvt., Unassigned, 20th USCT), M1823-6.

[361] CWMR, Aaron Gayton, (Pvt., Co. D, 26th USCT), Samuel Gayton, (Pvt., Co. D, 26th USCT) and William C. Gayton, (Sgt., Co. D, 26th USCT), M1824-5. Civil War Pension, Samuel Gayton (Pvt., Co. D, 26th USCT), Cert. #628.811. Ontario County, New York Probate Files, William Gayton, File #49, Microfilm #124, Batch 22, Frame 1059.

[362] CWMR, Benjamin W. Jupiter, (Pvt., Co. E, 26th USCT), M1824-8.

[363] Civil War Pension, Benjamin Jupiter (Pvt., Co. D, 26th USCT), Jane V. Jupiter, Widow's Pension Cert. #528.109.

[364] *Union League Club Report*, 49

[365] *Report of Major Thomas Wright, 31st USCT, of Operations June 4-November 6, 1864*, Transcription from Annual Report of the Adjutant-General of the State of Connecticut, for the Year Ending March 31, 1866, www.beyondthecrater.com.

[366] Bruce A. Suderow, "The Civil War's Worst Massacre" in *Black Flag Over Dixie: Racial Atrocities and Reprisals*, Gregory J. W. Urwin, Editor, (Southern Illinois University, 2004), 207-208.

[367] CWMR, George H. Watts, (Pvt., Co. F, 31st USCT), M1992-16.

[368] *New York, U.S. Census Mortality Schedules, New York, 1850-1880*, New York State Education Department, Office of Cultural Education; Albany,; Archive Roll Number: M13; Census Year:1880; Canandaigua, Ontario County.

[369] CWMR, Edward Jackson, (Pvt., Co. E, 31st USCT), M1992-8.

[370] CWMR, James H. Peterson, (Pvt., Co. E, 31st USCT), M1992-11.

[371] CWMR, Alexander Blake, (Pvt., Co. A, 31st USCT), M1992-2; New York, Civil War Muster Roll Abstracts, 31st USCT, A-G #379, Alexander Blake. CWMR, Adam Holland, (Pvt. Co. E, 31st USCT), M1992-7; Civil War Pension, Adam Holland (Pvt. Co. E., 31st USCT), Widow's Pension, Cert. #135.443.

[372] CWMR, William L. Wilson, (Corp., Co. I, 31st USCT), M1992-17.

[373] 1865 NYS Census, Walworth, Wayne County, New York, Family #304. Wayne County Historian's Office, Lyons, New York.

[374] Marriage, Wooby-Jacobs, 1826, St. John's Episcopal Church Records, Canandaigua, New York. Death Notice, John Wooby, *Lyons Republican*, June 1874, clipping, Wooby Surname File, Wayne Co., NY Historian; Obituary, John Wooby, Jr., *Wayne Democratic Press* (Lyons, NY), 1914, clipping, Wooby Surname File, Wayne Co., NY Historian.

[375] 1820 U.S. Census, Sodus, Ontario Co., NY, 121, M33-62.

[376] CWMR, William Newport (Pvt., Co. H, 29th Connecticut (Colored) Regiment), M1824-0064. 1860 U.S. Census, Sodus, Wayne Co., NY, M653-876, 381, #689. CWMR, Thomas Lloyd, (Pvt., Co. B, 8th USCT), M1821-9.

[377] Civil War Pension, William Newport (Pvt., Co. H, 29th Connecticut (Colored) Regiment), Cert. # 319.457. 1870 U.S. Census, Marion, Wayne Co., NY, M593-1112, 297, #105; Sodus, Wayne Co., NY, 497B, #830/845.

[378] *Massachusetts Vital Records, 1841-1910*, Vol. 245, p. 95, Vol. 400, 443, www.americanancestors.org. "Huron", *The Clyde Times*, 17 Oct 1904, 2:3.

[379] CWMR, William Wooby and Porter Wooby, (Pvts., Co. I, 29th Connecticut (Colored) Regiment), M1824-70. Civil War Pension, William Porter (Pvt., Co. I, 29th Connecticut (Colored) Regiment), Cert. #741.677; Porter Wooby (Pvt., Co. I, 29th Connecticut (Colored) Regiment), Widow's, Hannah E. Walters, Cert. #875.538.

[380] CWMR, Alonzo R. Frank, (Pvt., unassigned, 29th Connecticut (Colored) Regiment), M1824-58.

[381] 1840 U.S. Census, Western, Oneida Co., NY, M604-313, 150, 164.

[382] CWMR, Elijah Baker (Pvt., Co. K, 29th Connecticut (Colored) Regiment), M1824-54. 1860 U.S. Census, Syracuse, Ward 8, Onondaga Co., NY, M653-830, 971, #143.

[383] CWMR, Henry Dewitt Thompson (Pvt. 25th USCT); M1823-95. 1865 NYS Census, Savannah, Wayne Co., Family #67. Find a-Grave, John McGonigal, Butler-Savannah Cemetery, Savannah, NY, www.findagrave.com. Turner Family Tree, Ancestry Family Trees, https://www.ancestry.com/family-tree/person/tree/17930751/person/1521840028/facts?ssrc=, accessed 9 Mar 2018, www.ancestry.com.

[384] CWMR, William Wilson, (Co. I, 31st USCT), M1992-17. *New York Town Clerks' Registers of Men Who Served in Civil War*, Gaines, Orleans Co., www.ancestry.com. 1865 NYS Census, Rochester, Monroe Co., 69, #429/541. *U.S., Civil War Draft Registration Records, 1863-1865*, 28th Congressional District, NY, Peter Robinson. Mt. Hope Cemetery Records, Peter Robinson, 1885, www.lib.rochester.edu/IN/RBSCP/Database.

385 1865 NYS Census, Walworth, Wayne Co., #304. 1870 U.S. Census, Penfield, Monroe Co., NY, M593-973, 504B, #695. 1875 NYS Census, Brighton, Monroe Co., NY, ED 1, 27, #206. Civil War Pension, William Wilson, (Pvt. Co. I, 31st USCT), Dependent's Pension, Hattie Wilson Holcomb, App. #1.239.785.

386 CWMR, Abraham (Abram) Gregor, (Co. A, 43rd USCT), M1994-39. *New York, Civil War Muster Roll Abstracts, 1861-1900*, Abram Gregor, online images, www.ancestry.com. Civil War Pension File, Abraham Gregor, (Pvt., Co. A, 43rd USCT), Mother's Pension, Cert. #242.996. 1865 NYS Census, Walworth, Wayne Co. #285/304. Find A Grave, Abram Gregor, Gould Cemetery, Walworth, NY, https://www.findagrave.com/memorial/21232335/abram-gregor#view-photo=158131905.

387 CWMR, Reuben Pollett, (Co. D., 43rd USCT), M1994-48. *New York, Town Clerks' Registers of Men Who Served in the Civil War, ca. 1861-1865*, Town of Williamson, Wayne Co., online images, www.ancestry.com. Palmyra Village Cemetery Records, Wayne Co. Historian's Office, Lyons, NY. Civil War Pension Files, Reuben Pollett (Co. D., 43rd USCT), App. #88.707.

388 CWMR, James Bias, (Co. F., 43rd USCT), M1994-33. Civil War Pension File, James Bias (Pvt., Co. F, 43rd USCT), Cert. #964.117. *U.S., Burial Registers, Military Posts and National Cemeteries, 1862-1960*, James Bias, online images, www.ancestry.com. *U.S., Civil War Draft Registration Records, 1863-1865*, New York, Cong. Dist. #24, James Bias and Henry J. Reigle, online images, www.ancestry.com. Find a Grave, Henry John Riegel, Canoga Cemetery, Seneca Falls, NY, www.findagrave.com.

389 CWMR, James Brown, (Pvt., Co. H., 25th USCT), M1823-84; Civil War Pension, William Cleggett, alias James Brown, (Pvt., Co. H., 25th USCT), Cert. #1.201.448; *U.S., Civil War Draft Registrations Records, 1863-1865*, New York, Cong. Dist. #24, Sears E. Brace, online images, www.ancestry.com. CWMR, James E. Gibbs, (Pvt. Co. K, 25th USCT), M1823-486; Civil War Pensions, James E. Gibbs, (Pvt. Co. K, 25th USCT), Cert. #421.441.

390 CWMR, William Cartwright (Co. A., 38th USCT), M1993-56. Civil War Pension, William F. Courtwright (Pvt., Co. A, 38th USCT), Cert. #1.079.367. *U.S., Civil War Draft Registrations Records, 1863-1865*, New York, Cong. Dist. #24, William D. Burroughs, online images, www.ancestry.com. 1870 U.S. Census, Webster, Monroe Co., NY, M593-973, 462A, #480/500. 1875 NYS Census, Webster, Monroe Co., ED #2, 16, #139. New York, Civil War Muster Roll Abstract, 1861-1900, William F. Cortright, online images, www.ancestry.com. 1860 U.S. Census, Sodus, Wayne Co., NY, M653-876, 417, #988, James Rush.

[391] Susan G. Wallace, interview, 8 August 2001. 1830 U.S. Census, Hillsdale, Columbia Co., NY, M19-87, 197. 1840 U.S. Census, Sodus, Wayne Co., NY, M704, 95. 1850 U.S. Census, Sodus, Wayne Co., NY, M432-612, 176B, #741/779. www.ancestry.com.

[392] *The Minutes of the East Williamson, New York District School Meetings, 1843-1887*, transcribed by Harold J. DeBrine, Wayne County, NY Historian's Office, Lyons, NY.

[393] Robert Marcotte, *Where They Fell: Stories of Rochester Area Soldiers in the Civil War*, (Rochester, NY, Q Publishing, 2002), 84-88. Lewis H. Clark, *Military History of Wayne County, New York*, (Sodus, NY: Lewis H. Clark, Hullet & Gaylord, 1883), Appendix A, 143.

[394] Letter, Judson Rice to Family, 4 July 1863, Rice Family Collection, 1861-1865, Photocopies, Wayne Co., NY Historian, Lyons, NY.

[395] CWMR, James A. Potter (Co. K, 1st USCT), M1817-11.

[396] Clark, Appendix A, 143.

[397] CWMR, Judson E. Rice, (Capt., Co. K, 1st USCT); Lewis B. Rice (Lt., Co. K, 1st USCT), M1819-12.

[398] Letter, James A. Potter to Margaret (Newport) Potter, 16 February 1865, Private Collection.

[399] Civil War Pension, James A. Potter, (Pvt., Co. K, 1st USCT), Margaret E. Potter, Widow's Pension Cert. #118.877.

[400] Letter, Myron H. Rice to Family, 27 May 1865, *Rice Family Collection, 1861-1865*.

[401] Ibid.

[402] Wayne Co., NY Deed Books, 185/400, 114/19; *Register of Deaths, 1888-1903, Lyons, NY Town Clerk*, Margaret E. Potter, #801.

[403] *Lyons Presbyterian Church Records*, Baptisms, 25 June 1870, 42. Bette Wallace, Interview, September 2001. *Lyons Methodist Episcopal Church Records, 1860-1973*, Marriages, 22 Oct 1881, Benjamin Potter and Mary J. Jackson. *Register of Marriages, 1882-1888, Lyons, NY Town Clerk*, Fanny Potter-Charles Harris, #96. *Register of Marriages, Rose, NY Town Clerk*, 15 April 1903, Sylvester Potter to Ida Johnson.

[404] CWMR, Thomas Mathews, (1st USC Cavalry), M1817-9. 1820 U.S. Census, Aurelius, Cayuga Co., NY, M33-68, 38, Peter Matthews; 1855 NYS Census, Springport, Cayuga Co., NY, Family #208, Annie Mathews;1860 U.S. Census, Springport, Cayuga Co., NY, M653-729, 647, #371/372, Amy Mathews, www.ancestry.com. CWMR, Peter Mathews, (Co. K, 20th USCT), M1823-12. NOTE: Various spellings of this surname include Matthews and Mathews.

[405] *Slave Birth Register, Town of Farmington, Ontario County,* Ontario County, NY Records and Archives, Hopewell, NY. Ontario Co., NY Deed Books 47/275, 53/23, 60/484, 78/217. Will and Probate File, Priscilla Orme, 1809, Ontario Co., NY Surrogate Court Records.

[406] 1840 U.S. Census, Manchester, Ontario Co., NY, M704-319, 69, 84. 1850 U.S. Census, Manchester, NY, M432-572, 323, #324; 328A, #398. 1855 NYS Census, Manchester, Ontario Co., 30, #252; 36, #304. 1865 NYS Census, Manchester, Ontario Co., 13, #97; 17, #124. Probate File, Christie Shears, 1889, Ontario Co., NY Records and Archives.

[407] Civil War Pension, Theodore S. Shears, (Pvt., Co. H, 126th NY Volunteers), App. # 114.594. NY Military Museum & Research Center, https://dmna.ny.gov/historic/reghist/civil/infantry/126thinfMain.htm.

[408] Civil War Pension, George S. Shears (alias George Miller), (Pvt., 3rd NY Independent Battery, Light Artillery), Cert. #1.172.134. New York Military Museum & Research Center, https://dmna.ny.gov/historic/reghist/civil/artillery/3rdIndBat/3rdIndBatMain.htm.

[409] *U.S. Army, Register of Enlistments, 1798-1914*, online database and images, www.ancestry.com. 1880 U.S. Census, Fort Sanders, Albany Co., Wyoming Territory, T9-1454, 60B.

[410] Joseph P. Reidy, *Black Men in Navy Blue During the Civil War*, *Prologue Magazine*, Fall 2001, Vol. 33, No. 3, www.archives.gov/publications/prologue/2001/fall/black-sailors-1.html.

[411] 1850 U.S. Census, Rochester, Monroe Co., Ward 9, NY, M432-531, 456A. 1855 NYS Census, Rochester, Monroe Co., Ward 9, #114. Mt. Hope Cemetery Records, Mrs. Cleggett, 1850 and James Cleggett, 1855. *Rochester City Newspaper Index*, Marriage, Clagett-Jackson, *Rochester Daily Advertiser*, 10 Sept. 1840, 2:5, www.libraryweb.org/research. Note: Various spellings of surname include Cleggett, Clagett, Cloget.

[412] *The Official Records of the Union and Confederate Navies, 1861-1865*, Series 1, Vol. 19, 553.

[413] *Navy Survivors' Certificates, 1861-1910*, James H. Cleggett, (Landsman, U.S. Navy), Cert. #4738, online images, www.fold3.com.

[414] Danial Francis Lisarelli, *The Last Prison: The Untold Story of Camp Groce, C.S.A*, (Universal Publishing/uPUBLISH.com, 1999), 13.

[415] "Last Member of Family Once in Slavery in South", *Democrat & Chronicle*, Rochester, NY, 26 November 1920.

[416] *Navy Survivors' Certificates, 1861-1910*, James H. Cleggett, (Landsman, U.S. Navy), Cert. #4738.

[417] *U.S., Naval Enlistment Rendezvous, 1855-1891*, online images, www.ancestry.com. Mt. Hope & Riverside Cemetery Records, http://rbscp.lib.rochester.edu/3310.

[418] 1830 U.S. Census, Amboy, Oswego Co., NY, M19-215, 267. Ontario Co., NY Deed Book 61, 18-19. 1846-47 *Brown's Toronto City Directory*, 14, *Canada, City and Area Directories, 1819-1906*, online images, www.ancestry.com. 1847-48, 1849-50 *Rochester City Directory*, Monroe Co., NY Library System, online directories, https://roccitylibrary.org/digital-collections/rochester-city-directories/rochester-city-directories-by-decade. 1850 U.S. Census, Rochester, Monroe Co., M432-531, 341, #458.

[419] 1855 NYS Census, Rochester, Monroe Co., Ward 3, 107, #217. *Rochester Daily Democrat*, 8 Sept. 1849, 3:3, *Rochester Newspapers Index, 1818-1850*, http://www3.libraryweb.org/research. Dorothy Porter Wesley & Constance Porter Uzelac, eds, *William Cooper Nell: Selected Writing, 1832-1874* (Dorothy Porter Wesley Research Center, Inc. 2002), 20. "Report of Colored Citizens of Rochester," *Frederick Douglass' Paper*, 1 Sept 1854, transcription, www.accessible.com. George S. Conover, ed., *History of Ontario County, New York* (Syracuse, NY, Mason & Co., 1893), Part II, *Family Sketches*, 274.

[420] *Navy Survivors' Certificates, 1861-1910,* Benjamin F. Cleggett (Landsman, U.S. Navy), Cert.#22.872, online images, www.fold3.com. "Benjamin F. Clegget Dies", *Rochester Democrat & Chronicle*, 13 Jan 1917, www.fultonhistory.com. Ontario County Surrogate Court Records, Probate File, Benjamin F. Cleggett.

[421] *Navy Survivors' Certificates, 1861-1910*, Charles Shorter (Landsman, Steerage Steward, U.S. Navy), Cert. #15.686, online images, www.fold3.com; *U.S., Naval Enlistment Rendezvous, 1855-1891*, Charles Shorter, database, www.ancestry.com.

[422] *U.S. General Land Office Records, 1776-2015*, online database, www.ancestry.com.

[423] Grover, 22. 1840 U.S. Census, Huron, Wayne Co., NY, 118. 1850 U.S. Census, Huron, Wayne Co., NY, M432-613, 395B, #209. 1860 U.S. Census, Arlington, Van Buren Co., MI, M653-562, 756, #556. Wayne Co., NY Deed Book 58/442. *Michigan Deaths, past 1897*, Nicholas Gayton, 1909, www.seekingmichigan.com.

[424] 1840 U.S. Census, Manchester, Ontario Co., NY, M704, 66; 1850 U.S. Census, Manchester, Ontario Co., NY, M432-572, 322A, #311. 1860 U.S. Census, Unadilla, Livingston Co., MI, M653-552, #18; online images, www.ancestry.com.

[425] CWMR, Albert O. Grayson, Charles H. Grayson, John W. Grayson, Harry Grayson, (Co. H. 102nd USCT), RG94-USCT-Box 23, online images, www.fold3.com.

[426] Letter from Griffin Paddock to Hon. Comm. of Pension, 7 Nov 1871, Civil War Pension, Charles H. Grayson (Musician, Co. H, 102nd USCT), Lucy A. Grayson, Mother's Pension, Cert. #111.157.

[427] Civil War Pension, Charles H. Grayson (Musician, Co. H, 102nd USCT), Lucy A. Grayson, Mother's Pension, Cert. #111.157.

[428] Civil War Pension, Albert O. Grayson (Pvt., Co. H, 102nd USCT), Emily F. Grayson, Widow's Pension, Cert. 836.453. *Cook Co., IL Death Certificates*, Lucy A. Grayson, Reg. #23694.

[429] Civil War Pension, Harry Grayson (Pvt., Co. H, 102nd USCT), Cert. #116.832. *Michigan Deaths and Burials, 1800-1995*, online database, www.familysearch.org.

[430] CWMR, Allen and Nicholas Gayton (Co. B, 102nd USCT), RG94-USCT-102-Bx 21, www.fold3.com.

Conclusion

[431] Rampersad, Arnold and David Roessel, eds. *The Collected Poems of Langston Hughes,* (Vintage, New York, 1994), 147-48.

Bibliography

Books

Adams, Virginia M. Adams, ed. *On the Altar of Freedom: A Black Soldier's Civil War Letters from the Front*. Boston. University of Massachusetts Press. 1991.

Addeman, J. M. *Reminiscences of Two Years with The Colored Troops*. Providence. N. Bangs Williams & Co. 1880.

Blackett, R.J.M., ed. *Thomas Morris Chester: Black Civil War Correspondent, His Dispatches from the Virginia Front*. Reprint, New York. Da Capo Press. 1991.

Bristol, Douglas Walter. *Knights of the Razor: Black Barbers in Slavery and Freedom*. Baltimore. The Johns Hopkins University Press. 2009.

Brown, Catherine S. *Abel Brown, Abolitionist*, Edited by Tom Calarco. Jefferson, NC. McFarland & Co., Inc. 2006.

Chenery, William H. *The Fourteenth Regiment Rhode Island Heavy Artillery (Colored)*. Providence. Snow & Farnham. 1898.

Clark, Lewis H. *Military History of Wayne County, New York*. Sodus, NY. Lewis H. Clark, Hulett & Gaylord. 1883.

Coddington, Ronald S. *African American Faces of the Civil War: An Album*. Baltimore. Johns Hopkins University Press. 2012.

Conover, George S., ed. *History of Ontario County, New York*. Syracuse, NY. Mason & Co. 1893.

Cook, Thomas. *Palmyra and Vicinity*. Palmyra, NY. *Palmyra Courier-Journal*. 1930.

Cornish, Dudley Taylor. *The Sable Arm: Black Troops in the Union Army, 1861-1865*. University Press of Kansas. 1987.

Cross, Whitney R. *The Burned-over District: The Social and Intellectual History of Enthusiastic Religion in Western New York, 1800-1850*. Ithaca, New York. Cornell University Press. Reprint. 1982.

Dyer, Frederick H. *A Compendium of the War of the Rebellion*. Des Moines, Iowa. The Dyer Publishing Co., 1908.

Emilio, Louis F. *A Brave Black Regiment: The History of the 54th Massachusetts, 1863-1865*. Reprint, Da Capo Press. 1995.

Field, Phyllis F. *The Politics of Race in New York: The Struggle for Black Suffrage in the Civil War Era*. Ithaca, New York. Cornell University Press. 1982.

Fox, Charles B. *Record of the Service of the Fifty-Fifth Regiment of Massachusetts Volunteer Infantry*. Boston. 1868.

Glatthaar, Joseph T. *Forged in Battle: The Civil War Alliance of Black Soldiers and White Officers*. New York. The Free Press. 1990.

Goodwin, Doris Kearns. *Team of Rivals: The Political Genius of Abraham Lincoln*. New York. Simon & Schuster. 2005.

Green, A. Wilson. *Breaking the Backbone of the Rebellion: The Final Battles of the Petersburg Campaign*. Mason City, Louisiana. Savas Publishing Company. 2000.

Greene, Robert Ewell. *Swamp Angels: A Biographical Study of the 54th Massachusetts Regiment*. BoMark/Green Publishing Group. 1990.

Grover, Kathryn. *Make A Way Somehow: African-American Life in a Northern Community, 1790-1965*. Syracuse University Press. 1994.

Higginson, Thomas Wentworth. *Army Life in a Black Regiment*. Reprint. Mineola, NY. Dover Publications. 2002.

Hill, Isaac J. *A Sketch of the 29th Regiment of Connecticut Colored Troops*. Baltimore: Daugherty, Maguire & Co. 1867.

Kennedy, Joseph C. G. *The United States in 1860; Compiled from the Original Returns of the Eighth Census Under the Direction of the Secretary of the Interior*. Washington, D.C. Government Printing Office. 1864.

Kimmel, Ross M. and Michael P. Musick, *"I Am Busy Drawing Pictures": The Civil War Art and Letters of Private John Jacob Omenhausser, CSA*. Annapolis. Friends of the Maryland Archives. 2014.

LaBarre, Steven M. *The Fifth Massachusetts Colored Cavalry in the Civil War*. Jefferson, NC. McFarland & Company. 2016.

Lisarelli, Daniel Francis *The Last Prison: The Untold Story of Camp Groce, C.S.A.* Universal Publishing/uPUBLISH.com 1999.

Marcotte, Robert. *Where They Fell: Stories of Rochester Area Soldiers in the Civil War*. Rochester, NY. Q Publishing. 2002.

Manning, Chandra. *What This Cruel War Was Over: Soldiers, Slavery, and the Civil War*. New York. Vintage Books. 2007.

Matthews, Harry Bradshaw. *African American Freedom Journey in New York and Related Sites, 1823-1870: Freedom Knows No Color*. Cherry Hill, NJ. Africana Homestead Legacy Publishers. 2008.

McPherson, James M. *Marching Toward Freedom: Blacks in the Civil War, 1861-1865.* New York. Facts On File. 1991.

McPherson, James M. *The Negro's Civil War: How American Blacks Felt and Acted During the War for the Union.* New York. Vintage Books, A Division of Random House, Inc. 1993.

Murdock, Eugene Converse. *Patriotism Limited, 1862-1865: The Civil War Draft and the Bounty System.* Kent State University Press. 1967.

Newton, Alexander H. *Out of the Briars: An Autobiography and Sketch of the Twenty-Ninth Regiment Connecticut Volunteers.* Philadelphia. A.M.E. Book Concern. 1910.

Norton, Oliver Willcox. *Army Letters, 1861-1865.* Chicago. O.L. Deming. 1903.

O'Connor, Bob. *The U.S. Colored Troops at Andersonville Prison* Infinity Publishing. 2009

Phisterer, Frederick. *New York in the War of the Rebellion, 1861 to 1865.* Albany. Weed, Parsons and Company. 1890.

Quarles, Benjamin. *The Negro in the Civil War.* Reprint. New York. Da Capo Press. 1989.

Redkey, Edwin S., ed. *A Grand Army of Black Men: Letters from African-American Soldiers in the Union Army, 1861-1865.* Reprint. Cambridge University Press. 1993.

Salvatore, Nick. *We All Got History: The Memory Books of Amos Webber.* Reprint. Urbana and Chicago. University of Illinois Press. 1996.

Schubert, Irene and Frank N. *On the Trail of the Buffalo Soldier: 1866-1917.* Rowman & Littlefield, 2nd ed., 2004.
Scott, Donald, Sr. *Images of America: Camp William Penn.* Charleston, SC. 2008.

Scott, Donald. *Camp William Penn, 1863-1865: America's First Federal African American Soldiers' Fight for Freedom.* Atglen, PA. Schiffer Military History. 2012.

Smedley, R.C. *History of the Underground Railroad in Chester and the Neighboring Counties of Pennsylvania.* Lancaster, PA. John A. Hiestand. 1888.

Thomsen, Brian M., ed. *The Civil War Memoirs of Ulysses S. Grant.* Reprint. New York. Tom Doherty Associates, LLC. 2002.

Trudeau, Noah Andre. *Like Men of War: Black Troops in the Civil War, 1862-1865*. Boston. Little Brown and Company. 1998.

Trudeau, Noah Andre. *The Last Citadel: Petersburg, Virginia, June 1864-April 1865*. Boston. Little, Brown and Company. 1991.

Trudeau, Noah Andre, ed. *Voices of the 55th: Letters from the 55th Massachusetts Volunteers, 1861-1865*. Dayton, Ohio. Morningside House, Inc. 1996.

Urwin, Gregory J. W., ed. *Black Flag Over Dixie: Racial Atrocities and Reprisals*. Southern Illinois University. 2004.

Wellman, Judith M. *Uncovering the Freedom Trail in Auburn and Cayuga County, New York*. Cayuga County Historian. 2005.

Wesley, Dorothy Porter & Constance Porter Uzelac, eds. *William Cooper Nell: Selected Writing, 1832-1874*. Dorothy Porter Wesley Research Center, Inc. 2002.

Westwood, Howard. *Black Troops, White Commanders and Freedmen during the Civil War*. Carbondale. Southern University Library Press. 1992.

Wilson, Keith P. *Campfires of Freedom: The Camp Life of Black Soldiers during the Civil War*. Kent State University Press. 2002.

Wisnoski, Donald M. *The Opportunity Is at Hand: Oneida County, New York Colored Soldiers in the Civil War*. Schroeder Publications. 2003.

Zubritsky, John. *Fighting Men: A Chronicle of Three Black Civil War Soldiers*. Boston. Branden Publishing Co. 1994.

Pamphlets

Record of the Action of the Convention Held at Poughkeepsie., July 15th and 16th, 1863 For the Purpose of Facilitating the Introduction of Colored Troops into the Service of the United States. New York. Francis & Loutrel Steam Printers and Stationers 1863.

Report of the Finance Committee of the House of Representatives, on Bounty Frauds, etc. Providence, Rhode Island. H.H. Thomas & Co., Printers to the State. 1865.

Union League Club. *Report of the Committee on Volunteering, October 13, 1864*. New York. Union League Club. 1864.

Articles/Chapters

Suderow, Bruce A. "The Civil War's Worst Massacre." In *Black Flag Over Dixie: Racial Atrocities and Reprisals* edited by Gregory J. W. Urwin. Southern Illinois University. 2004.

Arenson, Adam. "African North Americans and the War." *New York Times*, "The Opinionator", 3 April 2013. https://opinionator.blogs.nytimes.com/2013/04/06/african-americans-and-the-war/.

National Archives and Records Administration

> *Compiled Service Records, United States Colored Troops* (Record Group 15)
> Civil War Pension Files (Record Group 94)

Digital Collections

Accessible Archives, www.accessible.com.
Adventist Digital Library, https://adventistdigitallibrary.org.
Ancestry.com, www.ancestry.com.
Chronicling America, Library of Congress, http://chroniclingamerica.loc.gov.
Family Search, www.familysearch.org.
Fold3, www.fold3.com.
Fulton History, www.fultonhistory.com (Newspapers)
Genealogy Bank, www.genealogybank.com. (Newspapers)
Google Books, https://books.google.
Internet Archive, http://archives.org.
Library of Congress, www.loc.gov/collections/civil-war.
Massachusetts Historical Society, www.masshist.org/library.
Monroe County (NY) Library System, https://libraryweb.org.
New England Historic Genealogical Society, www.americanancestors.org.
New York GenWeb, www.nygenweb.com.
New York Genealogical & Biographical Society, www.newyorkfamilyhistory.org.
New York Historic Newspapers, www.nyhistoricnewspapers.org.
New York Military Museum, http://dmna.ny.gov.
Newspapers, 1700s-2000s, www.newspapers.com.
Our Documents Initiative, www.ourdocuments.gov.
Seeking Michigan, www.seekingmichigan.com.

U.S. Army Heritage and Education Center,
http://ahec.armywarcollege.edu.
University of Rochester, www.lib.rochester.edu.

Websites

African American Civil War Memorial Museum,
www.afroamcivilwar.org.
American Civil War, https://americancivilwar.com.
American Battlefield Trust, www.battlefields.org.
Battle of Charleston, www.battleofchas.com.
Battle of Olustee, www.battleofolustee.org.
Civil War Prisoners, www.civilwarprisoners.com;
www.nps.gov/civilwar/search-prisoners.htm.
Find A Grave, www.findagrave.com.
Lest We Forget, www.lestweforget.hampton.edu.
National Parks Service, www.nps.gov/civilwar.
The Siege of Petersburg Online, www.beyondthecrater.com.

National Archives and Records Administration

Compiled Service Records, United States Colored Troops
(Record Group 15).
Civil War Pension Files (Record Group 94).
United States Census Records, 1790-1940.

APPENDIX

Chronology

1861

March 4	Abraham Lincoln Inauguration.
April 12	Fort Sumter in Charleston Harbor, South Carolina attacked by Confederate forces.
April 14	Federal forces at Fort Sumter surrender.
April 15	President Lincoln calls for 75,000 volunteers.
April 19	First troops leave New York to join Union Army
May	Frederick Douglass urges recruitment of African American soldiers
July 21	First Battle of Bull Run.
July 26	African American leaders apply to New York Governor Morgan for permission to raise three regiments of black troops.

1862

February	Frederick Douglass speaks at Cooper Institute in New York City urging enlistment of black soldiers.
September 22	President Lincoln issues preliminary Emancipation Proclamation, declaring his intent to free all slaves in territory controlled by the Union Army.

1863

January 1	Emancipation Proclamation issued, freeing all slaves held in states "in rebellion" and authorizing enlistment of African American soldiers into the army.
January	Massachusetts' Governor, John A. Andrew and Rhode Island's Governor William Sprague receive permission to raise regiments of black soldiers. Only Massachusetts takes immediate action.
February 23	African American leaders from New York write to President Lincoln about their desire to organize regiments of black troops.
March 3	Passage of Civil War Military Draft Act.
May 22	United States Colored Troops (USCT) established by War Department as branch of United States Army.

May 28	54th Massachusetts, first black regiment raised in the North, leaves Massachusetts for service in Union Army.
June 22	55th Massachusetts mustered into service.
July	Camp William Penn, outside Philadelphia, begins to receive recruits for the USCT.
	Rhode Island revives effort to raise a black regiment.
July 1-3	Battle of Gettysburg.
July 13-16	New York City Draft Riots.
July 15-16	Convention of Colored Citizens meets in Poughkeepsie, New York, to plan for recruitment of black troops in New York State.
July 17	Draft in the Western Division of New York State gets underway.
July 18	Assault on Fort Wagner, South Carolina
September 9	Rhode Island given permission to recruit black troops for a full regiment of heavy artillery.
November 23	Massachusetts receives permission to recruit black soldiers for the 5th Massachusetts Cavalry regiment.
December 3	Union League Club of New York City receives permission from War Dept. to recruit in New York for the 20th USCT.

1864

January	1st and 2nd Battalions of 14th Rhode Island Heavy Artillery (later known as 11th USCHA) sent to Dept. of the Gulf for service on the Mississippi River.
January 4	Union League Club receives permission to recruit for 26th USCT.
January 16	8th USCT leaves Camp William Penn for New York City and transported to South Carolina.
February 20	Battle of Olustee, Florida.
March 5	20th USCT leaves New York
March 27	26th USCT leaves New York
April 3	3rd Battalion of 14th Rhode Island leaves camp to join the regiment in the Dept. of the Gulf.
May	5th Massachusetts Cavalry leaves Camp Meigs.
May 4	Beginning of Virginia Campaign, designed to capture Richmond.
June 13	Congress passes Army Appropriations Bill to equalize pay between black and white troops
June 15	Siege of Petersburg and Richmond begins.

	Battle of Baylor's Farm, Virginia.
July 30	Battle of the Crater, Petersburg, Virginia.
August 1	War Dept. issues orders, instructing implementation of equal pay for black troops.
November 15	General Sherman's army begins its March to the Sea
December 3	Formation of 25th Army Corps, comprised of all black troops – 32 infantry units and one cavalry regiment, total 13,630 men. Maj. Gen. Godfrey Weitzel commander.
December 21	Surrender of Savannah, Georgia to General Sherman.

1865

January 31	Passage of 13th Amendment to the U.S. Constitution, ending slavery.
February 18	Surrender of Charleston, South Carolina.
April 2	Fall of Petersburg, Virginia.
April 3	Fall of Richmond, Virginia.
April 9	General Lee surrenders to General Grant at Appomattox, Court House, Virginia.
April 26	General Johnston surrenders to General Sherman near Durham, North Carolina.
June	25th Army Corps sent to Texas.
August 20	54th Massachusetts mustered out at Charleston, South Carolina.
August 28	26th USCT mustered out at Hilton Head, South Carolina.
August 29	55th Massachusetts mustered out at Charleston, South Carolina.
	20th USCT mustered out at Millikin's Bend, Louisiana.
October 2	14th Rhode Island Heavy Artillery (11th USCHA) mustered out at New Orleans, Louisiana.
October 10	5th Massachusetts Cavalry mustered out at Clarksville, Texas.
November 10	8th USCT mustered out at Brownsville, Texas.
November 11	31st USCT mustered out at Brownsville, Texas.

African American Soldiers from Western New York

SURNAME	FIRST NAME	REGIMENT	ENLISTED	BIRTH PLACE
Adams	William H.	26th USCT	1864/01/02	Genoa, NY
Addison	George N.	54th Mass.	1863/03/29	Elmira, N.Y.
Adkins	George A.	8th USCT	1863/10/05	New York
Alby	Morris	26th USCT	1863/12/03	Madison Co., N.Y.
Alexander	George	54th Mass.	1863/04/21	So. Carolina
Alexander	George	8th USCT	1863/07/17	Steuben Co., N.Y.
Alexander	William	20th USCT	1864/09/22	Steuben Co., N.Y.
Allen	George H.	8th USCT	1863/07/17	Newburgh, N.Y.
Allen	Thomas N.	20th USCT	1864/08/16	Pennsylvania
Anderson	Andrew J.	11th USCHA	1863/10/06	Canada
Anderson	Charles H.	11th USCHA	1863/10/02	Oswego, N.Y.
Anderson	William P.	11th USCHA	1863/10/06	Virginia
Armstrong	David	11th USCHA	1863/10/30	Watertown, N.Y.
Armstrong	George H.	11th USCHA	1863/10/08	Brownsville, N.Y.
Armstrong	Wesley R.	54th Mass.	1863/04/08	Pennsylvania
Atkins	Charles G.	54th Mass.	1863/04/09	Livingston Co., N.Y.
Babcock	Sydney M.	26th USCT	1864/01/04	Yates Co., N.Y.
Bagby	Alexander	8th USCT	1863/08/25	Virginia
Bailey	Frederick	20th USCT	1864/09/14	Campton, N.Y.
Baker	Elijah	29th Conn.	1864/01/09	Scipio, N.Y.
Beames	Stephen F.	26th USCT	1864/01/04	Cecil Co., Va.
Bennett	Jackson	8th USCT	1863/08/08	New Haven, Conn.
Bias	James	43rd USCT	1864/08/23	Maryland
Blackman	Paul G.	8th USCT	1863/08/19	Missouri
Blake	Alexander	31ST USCT	1863/12/21	New York City
Bland	John	11th USCHA	1863/12/05	Geneva, N.Y.
Bliss	George	20th USCT	1864/09/02	Steuben Co., N.Y.
Bogart	Benjamin F.	20th USCT	1864/08/17	Ontario, N.Y.
Bogart	George W.	11th USCHA	1863/12/09	Walworth, N.Y.
Boyer	Frank	54th Mass.	1863/04/08	Danville, Pa.
Boyer	William	8th USCT	1826/07/20	Lycoming, Pa.
Brainard	Dorsey	8th USCT	1863/09/26	Maryland
Breed	George F.	11th USCHA	1863/10/31	Norwich, N.Y.

Brewster	Alfred	11th USCHA	1863/11/14	Elmira, N.Y.
Broadit	Robert	11th USCHA	1863/11/18	Rochester, N.Y.
Brooks	William	8th USCT	1863/07/16	Pennsylvania
Brown	Edward	8th USCT	1863/08/05	Rochester, N.Y.
Brown	Glenalvin	8th USCT	1863/07/28	Maryland
Brown	James	25th USCT	1864/12/22	Canada
Brown	John E.	11th USCHA	1863/10/17	Rochester, N.Y.
Brown	Joseph	54th Mass.	1863/03/29	Cazenovia, N.Y.
Brown	Lewis	8th USCT	1863/07/25	Washington, D.C.
Brown	Thomas	8th USCT	1863/07/23	Maryland
Brown	William	5th Mass. Cav	1864/01/12	Rochester, N.Y.
Brown	William R.	54th Mass.	1863/04/08	Clinton Co., Pa.
Brushell	Jonathan E.	11th USCHA	1863/11/23	Norwich, N.Y.
Bryant	Beverly	20th USCT	1864/09/15	Virginia
Buck	Joseph R.	8th USCT	1863/07/19	Broome Co. N.Y.
Bulah	Joseph P.	11th USCHA	1863/12/21	Albany, N.Y.
Burke	Richard	8th USCT	1863/08/08	Virginia
Burns	Harvey	26th USCT	1864/01/01	Angelica, N.Y.
Burns	Sylvester	11th USCHA	1863/12/06	Schenectady, N.Y.
Burton	Ferdinand	8th USCT	1863/08/08	Erie Co., N.Y.
Butler	Alfred W.	5th Mass. Cav	1863/12/24	Manchester, N.Y.
Butler	George	54th Mass.	1863/12/03	Kent, N.Y.
Butler	George	8th USCT	1863/07/16	Pennsylvania
Butler	James	8th USCT	1863/07/24	Maryland
Butler	John	26th USCT	1864/01/04	Washington, D.C.
Butler	Stephen	8th USCT	1863/07/24	Maryland
Carpenter	George	11th USCHA	1863/12/05	Oswego Co., N.Y.
Carpenter	Samuel	20th USCT	1864/08/22	Onondaga Co., N.Y.
Carr	Amasa	20th USCT	1863/12/24	Oneida Co., N.Y.
Carr	George H.	20th USCT	1864/01/04	Oneida Co., N.Y.
Carter	Jacob	54th Mass.	1863/03/29	Syracuse, N.Y.
Carter	Levi	54th Mass.	1863/04/08	Washington, D.C.
Casey	Reuben D.	11th USCHA	1863/12/23	Genesee Co., N.Y.
Casey	William M.	11th USCHA	1863/12/23	Genesee Co., N.Y.
Castles	James	11th USCHA	1863/09/16	Rochester, N.Y.
Cezar	Garnet G.	54th Mass.	1863/03/17	Buffalo, N.Y.
Champlin	Charles E.	11th USCHA	1863/10/06	Watertown, N.Y.

Champlin	George H.	11th USCHA	1863/10/30	Brownsville, N.Y.
Champlin	Richard	11th USCHA	1863/11/16	Brownsville, N.Y.
Chancellor	Richard	8th USCT	1863/07/27	Virginia
Charles	Nelson	8th USCT	1863/09/25	North Carolina
Charles	William F.	8th USCT	1863/08/08	Madison Co., N.Y.
Clark	George W.	26th USCT	1864/01/04	Ontario Co., N.Y.
Clark	James	20th USCT	1864/01/04	Maryland
Clark	Stephen W.	8th USCT	1863/07/29	Essex Co., N.J.
Clark	Thomas C.	26th USCT	1863/12/26	New Jersey
Clark	William H.	11th USCHA	1864/01/06	Palmyra, N.Y.
Clause	Abram	26th USCT	1864/01/05	Rochester, N.Y.
Cleggett	Benjamin F.	Navy	186410/04	Oswego Co., N.Y.
Cleggett	James H	Navy	1863/03/19	Rochester, N.Y.
Cleggett	William T.	11th USCHA	1864/01/13	Rochester, N.Y.
Cleveland	Abram	54th Mass.	1863/03/29	Syracuse, N.Y.
Cleveland	Francis	29th Conn.	1863/12/23	Sacketts Harbor, NY
Cole	William	20th USCT	1864/09/02	Maryland
Collins	James W.	5th Mass. Cav	1863/12/22	Ithaca, N.Y.
Collins	Theodore	8th USCT	1863/08/08	New York
Comback	Oliver C.	20th USCT	1863/12/09	Pennsylvania
Condol	Arthur	26th USCT	1863/12/31	Middletown, Conn.
Cone	William A.	11th USCHA	1864/01/06	Brockport, N.Y.
Conrad	Andrew B.	11th USCHA	1863/11/23	Mexico, N.Y.
Conway	Jeremiah	26th USCT	1864/01/21	Auburn, N.Y.
Cook	Abram	26th USCT	1863/12/25	Manchester, N.Y.
Cook	Henry H.	20th USCT	1864/08/23	Eaton, N.Y.
Cooley	Henry	20th USCT	1864/09/29	Virginia
Cooper	Charles H.	8th USCT	1863/07/24	Sodus, N.Y.
Copes	William T.	26th USCT	1863/12/28	Sussex Co., Del.
Cornish	Alford	54th Mass.	1863/04/08	Binghamton, N.Y.
Cortright	George W.	11th USCHA	1863/12/23	Huron, N.Y.
Cortright	John W.	11th USCHA	1863/12/12	Huron, N.Y.
Cortright	Prime	11th USCHA	1864/01/06	New Jersey
Cortright	William F.	38th USCT	1865/03/26	Huron, N.Y.
Coy	John	8th USCT	1863/08/22	Virginia
Craig	Thomas	20th USCT	1863/12/28	Oneida Co., N.Y.
Crampton	Samuel A.	11th USCHA	1863/12/11	Washington, D.C.

Creamer	Charles L.	54th Mass.	1863/03/29	Syracuse, N.Y.
Croger	Amos	20th USCT	1864/08/29	Chemung Co., N.Y.
Croger	George A.	54th Mass.	1863/04/08	Cayuga Co., N.Y.
Culbert	William	20th USCT	1863/12/18	Maryland
Dade	Emanuel	8th USCT	1863/07/23	
Darrow	Charles W.	26th USCT	1863/12/24	Tompkins Co., N.Y.
Davis	Alfred	20th USCT	1864/08/29	Virginia
Davis	Frank	54th Mass.	1863/04/08	Chemung Co., N.Y.
Davis	Gabriel	26th USCT	1864/01/02	Montezuma, N.Y.
Davis	Hannibal F.	11th USCHA	1863/10/30	Montezuma, N.Y.
Davis	John	20th USCT	1864/09/20	Mississippi
Davis	John E.	55th Mass.	1863/05/27	Buffalo, N.Y.
Davis	John E.	54th Mass.	1863/03/18	
Davis	Lyman	11th USCHA	1863/11/07	Elmira, N.Y.
Davis	Thomas	54th Mass.	1863/03/18	Oswego, N.Y.
Davis	William	20th USCT	1864/10/24	Canada
Davis	William H.	11th USCHA	1863/11/07	Elmira, N.Y.
Day	Solomon	54th Mass.	1863/04/09	Canandaigua, N.Y.
Decker	John	54th Mass.	1863/03/29	Syracuse, N.Y.
Deforest	Andrew	54th Mass.	1863/03/29	Syracuse, N.Y.
Deforest	James N.	11th USCHA	1864/01/14	Syracuse, N.Y.
Demann	Webster	11th USCHA	1863/12/05	Waterloo, N.Y.
Demun	Aaron	20th USCT	1863/12/22	Springport, N.Y.
Denning	Charles A.	31ST USCT	1863/12/18	Chemung Co., N.Y.
Dennis	Henry F.	54th Mass.	1863/04/29	Ithaca, N.Y.
Dennis	Samuel	8th USCT	1863/08/05	Maryland
Dennison	Asa	11th USCHA	1863/12/05	Sullivan, N.Y.
Dennison	Jesse	11th USCHA	1863/11/18	Stockbridge, N.Y.
DePuy	Hugh	11th USCHA	1863/12/05	New York
DePuy	John	26th USCT	1864/01/21	Auburn, N.Y.
Derby	Charles H.	11th USCHA	1863/11/14	Geneva, N.Y.
Dewey	David	20th USCT	1863/12/21	Schenectady, N.Y.
Dickinson	William	29th Conn.	1863/12/11	Phoenix, N.Y.
Dixon	Henry	11th USCHA	1863/10/27	Geneva, N.Y.
Dixon	Hezekiah Jr.	11th USCHA	1863/12/02	Rochester, N.Y.
Dorsey	Francis	31ST USCT	1864/07/16	Geneva, N.Y.
Dorsey	George W.	54th Mass.	1863/04/23	Geneva, N.Y.

Dorsey	Henry W.	20th USCT	1864/09/13	Pennsylvania
Dorsey	Thomas	11th USCHA	1863/11/26	Syracuse, N.Y.
Dorsey	Thomas	11th USCHA	1863/11/26	Syracuse, N.Y.
Dorsey	William T.	8th USCT	1863/07/24	Sodus, N.Y.
Douglas	Henry	20th USCT	1864/09/09	Virginia
Douglass	Charles R.	54th Mass.		Massachusetts
Douglass	Charles R.	5th Mass. Cav	1864/03/26	Massachusetts
Douglass	Louis F.	54th Mass.	1863/03/25	Massachusetts
Dover	John H.	54th Mass.	1863/03/18	Buffalo, N.Y.
Drake	Nathan	8th USCT	1863/07/29	Wayne Co., N.Y.
Drenshaw	William	8th USCT	1863/08/18	Ohio
Duffin	Charles J.	11th USCHA	1864/01/06	Geneva, N.Y.
Duffin	Theodore	8th USCT	1863/07/29	Wayne Co., N.Y.
Dunkerson	Nelson	11th USCHA	1863/09/21	Canada
Elebeck	William	5th Mass. Cav	1863/12/29	Buffalo, N.Y.
Enty	Gabriel	5th Mass. Cav	1864/02/09	Cayuga Co., N.Y.
Fayette	James	8th USCT	1863/07/31	Pennsylvania
Fields	Henry	11th USCHA	1863/12/23	Chatham, N.Y.
Fisher	Franklin	11th USCHA	1863/11/28	Ithaca, N.Y.
Fletcher	Charles M.	26th USCT	1864/01/19	Ontario Co., N.Y.
Fletcher	David R.	11th USCHA	1864/02/04	Batavia, N.Y.
Fletcher	George	31ST USCT	1864/02/11	Bath, N.Y.
Fletcher	Martin V.	26th USCT	1863/12/21	Greece, N.Y.
Fletcher	Roderick S.	11th USCHA	1864/02/04	Ontario Co., N.Y.
Fletcher	Samuel	11th USCHA	1863/11/28	Bath, N.Y.
Ford	Joseph	8th USCT	1863/08/18	Virginia
Foster	Andrew R.	20th USCT	1864/08/17	Brooklyn, N.Y.
Fountain	George	8th USCT	1863/07/29	New York
Francis	Charles L.	11th USCHA	1863/12/05	Oswego Co., N.Y.
Frank	Alonzo	29th Conn.	1863/12/05	Rome, N.Y.
Frank	Milton	8th USCT	1863/08/26	Oneida Co., N.Y.
Freeland	Augustus	26th USCT	1863/12/18	Ontario Co., N.Y.
Freeman	Amos G.	11th USCHA	1863/11/21	Utica, N.Y.
Freeman	Charles E.	26th USCT	1864/01/13	Auburn, N.Y.
Freeman	Charles H.	26th USCT	1864/01/04	Ontario Co., N.Y.
Freeman	Ephraim	55th Mass.	1863/06/08	Buffalo, N.Y.
Freeman	George E.	11th USCHA	1863/10/26	Auburn, N.Y.

Freeman	John	20th USCT	1864/09/05	Pennsylvania
Freeman	John W.	11th USCHA	1863/12/05	Auburn, N.Y.
Freeman	Lewis H.	11th USCHA	1863/10/30	Auburn, N.Y.
Freeman	William LG	11th USCHA	1863/10/04	Steuben Co., N.Y.
Fryman	Edgar J.	8th USCT	1863/08/04	Columbia Co., N.Y.
Gardinier	Ira W.	54th Mass.	1863/03/17	Rochester, N.Y.
Garner	George H.	54th Mass.	1863/07/14	Rochester, N.Y.
Garthen	John W.	20th USCT	1864/09/01	Canadice, N.Y.
Garthen	William	20th USCT	1864/09/09	Canadice, N.Y.
Gayton	Aaron	26th USCT	1863/12/23	Geneva, N.Y.
Gayton	Allen	102nd USCT	1863/10/21	Wayne Co., N.Y.
Gayton	George	20th USCT	1864/01/16	Ontario Co., N.Y.
Gayton	Nicholas	102nd USCT	1863/10/21	Wayne Co., N.Y.
Gayton	Samuel	26th USCT	1864/01/22	Geneva, N.Y.
Gayton	Walter	54th Mass.	1863/03/29	Geneva, N.Y.
Gayton	William C.	26th USCT	1863/12/24	Geneva, N.Y.
Gibbs	James E.	25th USCT	1865/01/10	Canada
Gilbert	Edward P.	31ST USCT	1864/02/22	Steuben Co., N.Y.
Goodman	Richard D.	54th Mass.	1863/04/8	New York City
Goodman	William H.	20th USCT	1863/12/17	Elmira, N.Y.
Graham	Simon L.	20th USCT	1864/08/26	Rochester, N.Y.
Graves	George L.	20th USCT	1863/12/17	Virginia
Graves	John G.	11th USCHA	1863/10/17	Pennsylvania
Gray	Chester	11th USCHA	1863/10/28	Auburn, N.Y.
Gray	George	11th USCHA	1863/10/30	Auburn, N.Y.
Grayson	Albert O.	102nd USCT	1863/12/05	Ontario Co., N.Y.
Grayson	Alexander	26th USCT	1864/08/08	Palmyra, N.Y.
Grayson	Amos	102nd USCT	1864/09/01	Ontario Co., N.Y.
Grayson	Charles H.	102nd USCT	1863/12/29	Ontario Co., N.Y.
Grayson	John W.	102nd USCT	1863/12/29	Ontario Co., N.Y.
Grayson	Harry	102nd USCT	1863/12/30	Manchester, N.Y.
Green	Henry	26th USCT	1863/12/25	Virginia
Greene	George H.	11th USCHA	1863/09/17	Rochester, N.Y.
Gregor	Abraham	43rd USCT	1864/08/27	Sodus, N.Y.
Gregor	Bradley	8th USCT	1863/07/25	Wayne Co., N.Y.
Gregor	David J.	11th USCHA	1863/12/12	Montezuma, N.Y.
Gregor	Elijah	8th USCT	1863/07/24	Wayne Co., N.Y.

Gregor	Samuel D.	11th USCHA	1863/12/23	Sodus, N.Y.
Groff	Joseph	11th USCHA	1863/10/29	Maryland
Gulliver	Samuel	29th Conn.	1863/12/03	Corning, N.Y.
Hall	George W.	11th USCHA	1863/10/26	Oneida Co., N.Y.
Hall	Henry	8th USCT	1863/08/26	Oneida Co., N.Y.
Hall	Mathew	20th USCT	1864/10/04	Canada
Hamilton	Alfred	54th Mass.	1863/04/09	New York
Hamilton	Thomas	54th Mass.	1863/03/28	Delaware
Hammit	Harrison	20th USCT	1863/12/26	Yates Co., N.Y.
Harding	Cornelius	54th Mass.	1863/04/09	Maryland
Hardy (1)	Charles H.	11th USCHA	1863/12/05	Geneva, N.Y.
Hardy (2)	Charles H.	11th USCHA	1863/09/21	New York
Hardy	John	26th USCT	1864/01/04	Geneva, N.Y.
Hardy	John A.	8th USCT	1863/09/01	Geneva, N.Y.
Harrison	John F.	54th Mass.	1863/03/19	
Hart	Thomas	20th USCT	1864/08/11	Maryland
Hawkins	Isaac S.	54th Mass.	1863/12/12	Ridgeway, N.Y.
Haymer	Jacob	8th USCT	1863/07/27	Troy, N.Y.
Hazel	Allen	11th USCHA	1863/11/18	Camden, N.Y.
Hazel	Henry W.	11th USCHA	1863/10/22	Camden, N.Y.
Henry	Alexander	54th Mass.	1863/03/29	Syracuse, N.Y.
Henry	James F.	11th USCHA	1863/12/08	Bath, N.Y.
Henry	Richard T.	11th USCHA	1863/11/04	Petersburg, N.Y.
Henry	William	20th USCT	1864/10/13	Canada
Hersey	Samuel E.	54th Mass.	1863/03/29	Churchville, N.Y.
Hill	Charles	8th USCT	1863/08/19	Stockbridge, N.Y.
Hill	John G.	11th USCHA	1863/11/21	Columbia Co., N.Y.
Hodges	Joseph	20th USCT	1864/08/23	Virginia
Holland	Adam	31ST USCT	1863/12/17	Gorham, N.Y.
Holland	Isaac	26th USCT	1863/12/19	Ontario Co., N.Y.
Holmes	George	54th Mass.	1863/04/8	Pennsylvania
Holmes	William A.	11th USCHA	1863/11/28	Dresden, N.Y.
Howard	Henry	11th USCHA	1863/10/15	Maryland
Howland	George	11th USCHA	1863/12/30	Ontario Co., N.Y.
Hurley	Nathaniel	54th Mass.	1863/03/29	Rochester, N.Y.
Jackson	Edward	31ST USCT	1863/12/31	Ontario Co., N.Y.
Jackson	John	11th USCHA	1863/11/16	Canada

Jackson	John L.	29th Conn.	1863/12/28	Oswego, N.Y.
Jackson	William	5th Mass. Cav	1864/01/30	Buffalo, N.Y.
Jackson	William G.	11th USCHA	1863/11/25	Maryland
Jameson	James	54th Mass.	1863/04/29	Ithaca, N.Y.
Jeffrey	Nathan C.	54th Mass.	1863/03/18	Rochester, N.Y.
Johnson	Alexander	54th Mass.	1863/04/08	Steuben Co., N.Y.
Johnson	Birney S.	54th Mass.	1863/04/08	Mt. Morris, N.Y.
Johnson	Ephraim S.	5th Mass. Cav	1864/01/20	Painted Post, N.Y.
Johnson	Festus	45th USCT	1864/06/29	Seneca Falls, N.Y.
Johnson	Garret S.	20th USCT	1864/09/12	Geneva, N.Y.
Johnson	George H.	5th Mass. Cav	1863/12/26	Olean, N.Y.
Johnson	James P.	54th Mass.	1863/04/08	Pennsylvania
Johnson	Sidney W.	11th USCHA	1864/01/06	Fulton, N.Y.
Johnson	Walter E.	11th USCHA	1863/12/05	Geneva, N.Y.
Johnson	William	11th USCHA	1864/01/06	Rochester, N.Y.
Johnson	William	5th Mass. Cav	1864/01/27	Rochester, N.Y.
Johnson	William	26th USCT	1864/01/04	Washington, DC
Johnson	William H.	11th USCHA	1863/12/05	Geneva, N.Y.
Johnson	William R.	26th USCT	1863/12/29	Geneva, N.Y.
Johnston	Jacob	26th USCT	1863/12/25	Rochester, N.Y.
Jones	Benjamin	11th USCHA	1863/12/23	New Jersey
Jones	Nelson	20th USCT	1864/08/25	Virginia
Jones	Thomas	8th USCT	1863/07/29	Canada
Jubiter	Harvey A.	20th USCT	1863/12/19	Ontario Co., N.Y.
Jupiter	Benjamin.	26th USCT	1863/12/18	Geneva, N.Y.
Jupiter	Dwight	8th USCT	1863/07/28	New York
Kane	Charles	54th Mass.	1863/03/27	Illinois
Kane	William	26th USCT	1863/12/24	Maryland
Kinney	Nathaniel	8th USCT	1863/07/28	New York
Labiel	William H.	11th USCHA	1863/12/05	Oneida Co., N.Y.
Lane	James	54th Mass.	1863/04/21	Pennsylvania
Lee	George H.	54th Mass.	1863/02/22	Geneva, N.Y.
Lee	James	8th USCT	1863/07/25	Green Co., N.Y.
Lee	John	11th USCHA	1863/11/14	Elmira, N.Y.
Lee	John A.	20th USCT	1863/12/18	Elmira, N.Y.
Lee	Joseph	5th Mass. Cav	1864/01/27	Oswego, N.Y.
Lee	Manuel	54th Mass.	1863/04/21	Ohio

Lee	William R.	54th Mass.	1863/05/1	Maryland
Lenison	Phillip	11th USCHA	1863/10/29	Syracuse, N.Y.
Leonard	Joseph	11th USCHA	1863/10/06	Jefferson Co., N.Y.
Leonard	Simon A.	11th USCHA	1863/10/06	Jefferson Co., N.Y.
Lester	William H.	8th USCT	1863/07/25	Maryland
Lewis	Charles J.	11th USCHA	1863/12/05	Salina, N.Y.
Lewis	Edward	11th USCHA	1863/11/26	New Jersey
Lewis	Lorenzo T.	54th Mass.	1863/04/23	Seneca Co., N.Y.
Lewis	William O.	8th USCT	1863/07/25	Catharine, N.Y.
Lincoln	William	11th USCHA	1863/10/26	Geneva, N.Y.
Linyer	Henry	20th USCT	1864/09/04	Tennessee
Lloyd	Thomas	8th USCT	1863/07/23	Wayne Co., N.Y.
Low	Dennis	8th USCT	1863/07/20	Maryland
Lucas	George	54th Mass.	1863/03/27	Kent Co., Del.
Lucas	William H.	11th USCHA	1863/12/09	Corning, N.Y.
Lukes	Edwin	54th Mass.	1863/03/18	
Lunn	Amos	11th USCHA	1863/09/16	Crawford, N.Y.
Lush	Thomas N.	20th USCT	1863/12/18	Tompkins Co., N.Y.
Mann	Robert W.	8th USCT	1863/07/17	Steuben Co., N.Y.
Mann	William H.	11th USCHA	1863/12/11	Steuben Co., N.Y.
Marshall	James	8th USCT	1863/07/20	Pennsylvania
Mason	James G.	5th Mass. Cav	1864/01/26	Rochester, N.Y.
Mathews	Clinton	20th USCT	1864/08/31	Maryland
Mathews	Peter	20th USCT	1864/08/10	Cayuga Co., N.Y.
Mathews	Thomas	1st USC Cav	1864/09/16	Springport, N.Y.
McDonald	William H.	11th USCHA	1863/11/28	Rochester, N.Y.
McKenzie	Lloyd S.	8th USCT	1863/07/29	Canandaigua, N.Y.
McQuarter	Peter	11th USCHA	1863/11/26	New York
Middleton	Augustus L.	39th USCT	1863/12/24	Ovid, N.Y.
Miller	Andrew	54th Mass.	1863/04/08	Union Co., Pa.
Miller	Benjamin	11th USCHA	1863/10/27	Utica, N.Y.
Moore	Charles H.	11th USCHA	1863/12/30	Rochester, N.Y.
Moore	George	11th USCHA	1864/01/13	Saratoga Co., N.Y.
Moore	John W.	54th Mass.	1863/03/17	Ontario Co., N.Y.
Moore	Miles	54th Mass.	1863/04/29	Ithaca, N.Y.
Morgan	Jerome G.	11th USCHA	1863/10/23	Syracuse, N.Y.
Morton	Alfred	8th USCT	1863/08/17	Maryland

319

Moshroe	George W.	54th Mass.	1863/04/08	Steuben Co., N.Y.
Murray	Abraham	11th USCHA	1863/12/02	Rochester, N.Y.
Murray	Henry	8th USCT	1863/07/25	Seneca Co., N.Y.
Myers	Aaron C.	11th USCHA	1863/12/30	Monroe Co., N.Y.
Nelson	James	54th Mass.	1863/03/21	Buffalo, N.Y.
Nelson	John	5th Mass. Cav	1863/12/26	Batavia, N.Y.
Netson	William J.	54th Mass.	1863/04/04	Niagara, N.Y.
Newport	William	29th Conn.	1864/01/02	Sodus, N.Y.
Nichols	John	29th Conn.	1863/12/03	Oneida, N.Y.
Nixon	Samuel H.	26th USCT	1864/08/08	Pennsylvania
Noyes	Henry	29th Conn.	1864/01/09	Wayne Co., N.Y.
O'Neal	John R.	54th Mass.	1863/03/17	Maryland
Palmer	Irenas J.	5th Mass. Cav	1863/12/26	Hinsdale, N.Y.
Palmer	Levi	11th USCHA	1863/10/22	Whitestown, N.Y.
Patterson	Abraham	8th USCT	1863/07/31	Pennsylvania
Pell	John	11th USCHA	1863/11/14	Whitestown, N.Y.
Perry	John	20th USCT	1864/09/01	Steuben Co., N.Y.
Pertilla	William H.	11th USCHA	1863/10/30	Owego, N.Y.
Pertiller	Richard	54th Mass.	1863/04/08	Tioga Co., N.Y.
Peterson	Edward	26th USCT	1863/12/31	Leicester, N.Y.
Peterson	James H.	31ST USCT	1863/12/21	Angelica, N.Y.
Peterson	John	26th USCT	1864/01/05	Leicester, N.Y.
Peterson	John S.	5th Mass. Cav	1863/12/26	Pennsylvania
Peterson	Peter	26th USCT	1863/12/31	Leicester, N.Y.
Peterson	Solomon	5th Mass Cav.	1863/12/26	Scio, N.Y.
Philips	William	31ST USCT	1864/01/11	Maryland
Phillips	John	20th USCT	1863/12/18	Maryland
Pollett	Reuben	43rd USCT	1864/09/01	Virginia
Porter	John W.	8th USCT	1863/08/21	Maryland
Postley	George	8th USCT	1863/07/13	Delaware Co., N.Y.
Postley	James	54th Mass.	1863/04/08	Chemung Co., N.Y.
Potter	James A.	1st USCT	1864/09/03	Hillsdale, N.Y.
Powell	James H.	54th Mass.	1863/04/08	Pennsylvania
Preston	Levi A.	8th USCT	1863/09/01	New York
Price	James F.	54th Mass.	1863/04/21	Pennsylvania
Price	John P.	54th Mass.	1863/04/08	Maryland
Prime	Aaron	11th USCHA	1863/10/26	Auburn, N.Y.

Prime	William E.	11th USCHA	1863/12/19	Watkins, N.Y.
Prince	Festus	20th USCT	1863/12/18	Geneva, N.Y.
Prue	Daniel	8th USCT	1863/07/28	Geneva, N.Y.
Prue	Nathan	26th USCT	1863/12/29	Geneva, N.Y.
Ray	Albert	20th USCT	1863/11/30	Cayuga Co., N.Y.
Ray	David H., Jr.	11th USCHA	1863/11/16	Canandaigua, N.Y.
Reader	Robert	11th USCHA	1863/11/07	Bath, N.Y.
Reason	Charles K.	54th Mass.	1863/03/29	Syracuse, N.Y.
Redder	Jacob W.	11th USCHA	1863/11/19	New Jersey
Reed	Nelson T.	26th USCT	1863/12/31	Moscow, N.Y.
Reese	Edward	11th USCHA	1863/12/03	Maryland
Renkins	Alexander	54th Mass.	1863/03/19	Pennsylvania
Reynolds	George	54th Mass.	1863/04/14	Corning, N.Y.
Riggs	Amos	26th USCT	1864/01/04	Jerusalem, N.Y.
Riggs	Thomas P.	54th Mass.	1863/03/21	New York
Robbins	Albert O.	55th Mass.	1863/06/03	Peterboro, N.Y.
Robbins	Laban	55th Mass.	1863/06/03	Peterboro, N.Y.
Roberts	Augustus	8th USCT	1863/08/19	Maryland
Robinson	Alfred	8th USCT	1863/07/25	Binghamton, N.Y.
Robinson	Samuel J.	55th Mass.	1863/05/26	Canada
Robinson	Samuel J.	54th Mass.	1863/03/18	Canada
Robinson	William R.	11th USCHA	1863/10/30	Ogdensburg, N.Y.
Rose	Aury	20th USCT	1863/12/07	Perinton, N.Y.
Russell	Gerrit S.	8th USCT	1863/07/31	Madison Co., N.Y.
Russell	Henry	8th USCT	1863/07/28	Geneseo, N.Y.
Russell	Richard S.	8th USCT	1863/08/24	Maryland
Sampson	William H.	11th USCHA	1863/12/05	Corning, N.Y.
Sarsnett	Edward	11th USCHA	1863/09/08	Phelps, N.Y.
Schenck	Anthony	54th Mass.	1863/04/29	Ohio
Schuyler	George	11th USCHA	1863/12/14	Medina, N.Y.
Sesor	Oscar	55th Mass.		Rochester, N.Y.
Sesor	Oscar	54th Mass.	1863/03/17	Rochester, N.Y.
Shears	George	3rd NY Batt.	1864/09/03	Manchester, N.Y.
Shears	Henry	26th USCT	1864/01/04	Maryland
Shears	Theodore S.	126th NY	1862/08/08	Manchester, N.Y.
Shorter	Alfred	26th USCT	1864/02/10	Cayuga Co., N.Y.
Shorter	Charles	Navy	1864/09/14	Seneca Co., N.Y.

Shorter	John	54th Mass.	1863/04/09	Clyde, N.Y.
Shorter	William	102nd USCT	1863/12/26	New York
Skank	Samuel	8th USCT	1863/07/28	Herkimer Co., N.Y.
Smith	Augustus	26th USCT	1864/01/12	Maryland
Smith	Edward C.	54th Mass.	1863/04/29	Ithaca, N.Y.
Smith	George	54th Mass.	1863/04/08	Chemung Co., N.Y.
Smith	James	8th USCT	1863/08/07	Virginia
Smith	John	26th USCT	1864/02/01	Pennsylvania
Smith	Joseph	8th USCT	1863/07/25	Pennsylvania
Smith	William	11th USCHA	1863/11/18	Annsville, N.Y.
Snowden	Philip	54th Mass.	1863/04/08	Pennsylvania
Sprague	Nathan	54th Mass.	1864/09/13	Maryland
Squires	William H.	8th USCT	1863/08/19	Camillus, N.Y.
St. Clair	James	20th USCT	1864/08/29	Columbia, PA
Steadman	George	26th USCT	1864/01/04	Geneva, N.Y.
Steadman	Samuel	26th USCT	1864/01/04	Ontario Co., N.Y.
Stephenson	Robert	20th USCT	1864/09/29	Pennsylvania
Steward	Henry F.	54th Mass.	1863/03/29	Horseheads, N.Y.
Stewart	George H.	54th Mass.	1863/04/09	
Stewart	John	20th USCT	1864/08/21	Virginia
Story	Chauncey	8th USCT	1863/08/19	New York
Suesbury	Samuel B.	11th USCHA	1863/12/17	Elmira, N.Y.
Sullivan	John	11th USCHA	1863/10/30	Maryland
Sullivan	Robert	5th Mass. Cav	1864/06/22	Steuben Co., N.Y.
Suzey	Frank	11th USCHA	1863/12/05	Geneva, N.Y.
Suzey	Sylvester F.	8th USCT	1863/09/01	Geneva, N.Y.
Swails	Stephen A.	54th Mass.	1863/04/09	Pennsylvania
Swan	Elisha S.	26th USCT	1863/12/29	Albany, N.Y.
Taylor	Charles F.	11th USCHA	1863/12/15	Rochester, N.Y.
Taylor	Charles W.	26th USCT	1863/12/29	Geneva, N.Y.
Taylor	Ebenezer	11th USCHA	1863/12/12	Fishkill, N.Y.
Taylor	James H.	11th USCHA	1863/10/17	Auburn, N.Y.
Taylor	Lewis	11th USCHA	1863/10/02	Geneva, N.Y.
Tenike	Philip	20th USCT	1864/09/01	Ulster Co., N.Y.
Thomas	George W.	54th Mass.	1863/04/08	Racine, Wisc.
Thomas	James	20th USCT	1864/08/11	Canandaigua, N.Y.
Thomas	James C.	11th USCHA	1863/10/17	Otsego, N.Y.

Thomas	Walter	11th USCHA	1863/11/28	New York
Thompson	Albert	8th USCT	1863/07/23	Oneida Co., N.Y.
Thompson	Albert D.	54th Mass.	1863/03/17	Oswego, N.Y.
Thompson	Henry	8th USCT	1863/07/24	New Jersey
Thompson	Henry	11th USCHA	1863/11/30	Oswego, N.Y.
Thompson	Henry D.	25th USCT	1864/08/10	New York
Thompson	Isaac	29th Conn.	1863/12/28	Sacketts Harbor, NY
Thompson	Jeremiah	11th USCHA	1863/11/30	Oswego, N.Y.
Thompson	John	8th USCT	1863/08/14	Pennsylvania
Thompson	Orange L.	8th USCT	1863/08/26	Madison Co., N.Y.
Thornton	Lawrence	20th USCT	1864/09/05	Virginia
Van Hazen	Calvin	8th USCT	1863/07/25	Oneida Co., N.Y.
Van Horn	Cornelius	26th USCT	1863/12/18	Ovid, N.Y.
Van Horn	Daniel	31ST USCT	1864/02/22	Ontario Co., N.Y.
Van Horn	William	20th USCT	1864/09/01	Palmyra, N.Y.
Van Horn	Winfield B.	11th USCHA	1863/12/03	Rochester, N.Y.
Van Schaick	Amos	8th USCT	1863/08/19	Brutus, N.Y.
Van Schaick	George	8th USCT	1863/07/23	Cayuga Co., N.Y.
Van Schaick	James	26th USCT	1864/01/04	Brutus, N.Y.
Van Schaick	William	20th USCT	1864/08/15	Auburn, N.Y.
Vincent	Chauncey	11th USCHA	1863/12/03	Troy, N.Y.
Waller	John	8th USCT	1863/07/20	Delaware
Warren	George C.	5th Mass. Cav	1864/01/26	Syracuse, N.Y.
Washington	David A.	54th Mass.	1863/04/08	Buffalo, N.Y.
Washington	George	54th Mass.	1863/03/29	Syracuse, N.Y.
Washington	Peter	20th USCT	1864/09/05	Virginia
Waters	Joseph	26th USCT	1863/12/28	Venice, N.Y.
Waters	William	26th USCT	1863/12/23	Venice, N.Y.
Watkins	Edwin J.	20th USCT	1864/08/23	Manchester, N.Y.
Watkins	Stephen L.	11th USCHA	1864/01/21	New York
Watson	Richard R.	29th Conn.	1863/12/21	Camden, N.Y.
Watson	William	54th Mass.	1863/04/01	Maryland
Watts	George H.	31ST USCT	1863/12/17	Michigan
Weir	James S.	54th Mass.	1863/11/26	Buffalo, N.Y.
Wells	James M.	11th USCHA	1863/10/30	Frankfort, N.Y.
Wesley	Charles H.	55th Mass.	1863/06/05	Elmira, N.Y.
West	Peter	54th Mass.	1863/04/21	Buffalo, N.Y.

White	Anthony T.	11th USCHA	1863/11/20	Ontario Co., N.Y.
Whiten	Charles	54th Mass.	1863/03/29	Syracuse, N.Y.
Whitmore	Harvey	8th USCT	1863/07/21	Cayuga Co., N.Y.
Whitney	George	20th USCT	1863/12/18	Ontario Co., N.Y.
Wickop	George	26th USCT	1863/12/24	Cayuga Co., N.Y.
Wigden	Cyrus B.	11th USCHA	1863/11/28	Geneva, N.Y.
Wigden	Martin	20th USCT	1864/09/01	Steuben Co., N.Y.
Wigden	William A.	11th USCHA	1863/11/28	Geneva, N.Y.
William	Whorton A.	54th Mass.	1863/02/24	Utica, N.Y.
Williams	Charles	29th Conn.	1863/12/11	Geneva, N.Y.
Williams	Charles H.	11th USCHA	1863/10/26	Auburn, N.Y.
Williams	George L.	11th USCHA	1863/12/14	New York
Williams	James A.	29th Conn.	1864/01/02	Madison, N.Y.
Williams	James R.	8th USCT	1863/08/11	Missouri
Williams	Joseph	20th USCT	1863/12/17	Geneva, N.Y.
Williams	Peter	26th USCT	1863/12/23	Auburn, N.Y.
Willis	Charles J.	54th Mass.	1863/03/29	Syracuse, N.Y.
Wilson	Frank	11th USCHA	1863/12/07	Missouri
Wilson	George	26th USCT	1863/12/25	Rochester, N.Y.
Wilson	James H.	54th Mass.	1863/04/08	Livingston Co., N.Y.
Wilson	William H.	8th USCT	1863/08/25	Virginia
Wilson	William W.	31ST USCT	1864/07/30	New York
Wise	William	54th Mass.	1863/04/09	Maryland
Wooby	Porter	29th Conn.	1864/01/02	Clyde, N.Y.
Wooby	William	29th Conn.	1864/01/02	Sodus, N.Y.
Woodlin	William P.	8th USCT	1863/08/20	Louisiana
Wright	George	8th USCT	1863/08/22	Wyoming Co., N.Y.
Wyatt	John	20th USCT	1864/09/03	Virginia
Wycoff	Thomas A.	11th USCHA	1863/10/31	Hector, N.Y.
Zinn	Alfred D.	8th USCT	1863/07/18	Maryland

Note: *A Compendium of the War of the Rebellion* by Frederick H. Dyer is a valuable resource, providing brief regimental histories and summaries of battles and casualties. (http://archive.org.) Names have been standardized to match text. More detailed information can be found in Compiled Military Service Records.

Acknowledgments

No research project is successful without many persons willing to share, offer encouragement, and make suggestions. There is no way that I will be able to give a complete accounting of all those who have helped along the way, nor is it possible to convey to them how thankful I am for their help.

First on my list would be my husband, George Perez, who over the years has been supportive and patient as we made multiple visits to the National Archives, battlefields, and National Cemeteries. Thanks also go to son and daughter-in-law Michael and Helen Beebe-Perez, who generously provided a home base and wonderful company on our many trips to Washington, D.C.

The archivists, librarians, town clerks and local historians, who are the custodians of invaluable collections in the many small historical societies, museums, town offices and public libraries of Western New York, need a special thank you. I regret that I have not fully explored many of their resources, but other researchers should be encouraged to tap into these collections.

The explosion of resources now available on the internet made much of this research possible. The digitizing of books by Google and Internet Archive made it possible to access material that ten years ago would have required trips to university libraries. Genealogical research has been revolutionized by sites such as Ancestry.com, Fold3, and Familysearch.org. The digitized newspaper collections and academic journals are phenomenal resources for all researchers.

Lastly, there is a long list of other researchers who have inspired me, shared their research and expertise, offered encouragement and support. I am sure to leave someone out, but even if you don't see your name, know I appreciate your contribution to this project: Ruth Rosenberg Naparsteck; Dr. Judith Wellman; Dr. David Anderson; Preston Pierce; Mary Jo Lanphear; Jim and Ruth Chatfield; Bette, Susan and Janet Wallace; Sandra Simmons Newport; Bertha Newport; Martha Newport Swan and her daughters, Eva (Swan) Miller and Bette (Swan) Lattimore; Judyth Scott Gilbert; Dr. Stanton F. Biddle; Aife Murray; and Sarah L. H. Gronningsater.

About the Author

George and Marjory Allen Perez

George and I have collaborated on a wide variety of projects over the years, with George providing artwork, photography and encouragement, while I did the research and writing. None of those projects spanned as many years as this one, which took us to the National Archives for multiple visits and to Civil War battlefields, museums and National Cemeteries – too many to count.

One of our more humorous adventures had us wandering around in circles in Virginia countryside trying to follow the route Grant's Army took in June of 1864, prior to setting up the siege lines around Petersburg and Richmond. After we had passed the same church for the third time we gave up and went looking for a place to have lunch.

George's often asked question, "What are you going to do with all this material?" has finally been answered with the publication of *Freedom, A Shared Sacrifice!*

The above photo was taken at about the half-way point of the journey. We are much older, but not necessarily wiser, as we are already thinking about the next project.

Marjory Allen Perez

Index

Duffin
  Charles, 164
  Charles J., 163, 164, 165,
    167, 168
  James W., 164
  John, 164
  Mary Ann, 164
  Susannah, 164
  Theodore, 82
Dunham
  Sarah, 34
Eaton
  Rev. Horace, 192
Elebeck
  Junius H., 69
  Mary A., 69
  William, 60, 69
Elmira, N.Y., 183
Emancipation Proclamation,
  2, 4, 13, 73
Emilio
  Capt. Luis, 35, 45, 49
Engley
  James C., 123, 127, 128,
    130
English Turn, Louisiana, 136
Farragut
  Adm. David G., 258
Fayette
  James, 90
  James L., 90
  Martha, 90
Fields
  Henry, 127
Finegan
  Gen. Joseph, 37, 93
Fisher
  Ellen, 147
  Franklin, 147
Fitzhugh
  Peregrine, 80, 193
Fletcher
  Archelaus, Jr., 147, 204
  Archelaus, Sr., 147, 205
  Charles Morris, 147, *182*,
    204

David R., 146, 147, 148,
  204
Emily, 147
Mahasca, 147
Martin Van Buren, 147,
  182, 204
Mary E., 147
Roderick S., 131, 148, 204
Samuel, 151, 204
Florence Prison, *33*
Foland
  A. J., 188
Folly Island, S.C., 16, 25, 26,
  27, 35, 47
Forbes
  John, 180
Ford
  Joseph, 93, 96
  Susan, 257
Fort Experanza, 135
Fort Fisher, 241
Fort Jackson, 138, 139, 150
Fort Jefferson, 155
Fort Wagner, 27, 33
  Assault, 36
  Siege, 36
Foster
  Andrew R., 190, 192, 193
  George Harvey Dwight, 108
  Harriet, 108, 210
Fountain
  George, 76
Frank
  Alonzo, 224, 225, 226, 227
  Milton, 105
  Robert, 105
Freedmen's Bureau, 42
Freeland
  Augustus, 182
Freeman
  Charles H., 182, 203
  Eliza, 203
  Emeline J., 117
  Ephriam, 26
  Henrietta, 203
  William L. G., 133

Fremont Legion, 170, 172, 173
Fribley
  Col. Charles W., 81, 115
Frost
  Lt. Frank Frost, 143
Fryman
  Edgar, 82
Fyler
  Asa, 34
  Polly, 34
Gannett
  Lt. William, 25
Garnet
  Henry Highland, 197
Garrison
  William Lloyd, 133, 264
Garthen
  John W., 186
  Sarah, 186
  William, 186
Gaton. *See* Gayton
Gayton
  Aaron, 182, 208
  Allen, 271
  Eva, 23
  George, 182, 208
  Harriet Hardy, 23
  Henrietta, 23
  Judah, 271
  Maria, 190
  Nicholas, 271
  Samuel, 208
  Samuel., 182
  Thomas, 23, 265, 266, 271
  Walter, 23
  William C., 182, 208, 209
Geneva Gazette, 76
Geneva, N.Y., 182
Gibbs
  James, 235
  Mary E., 235
  Redding, 235
Gillam
  Adalaide, 181
  Harriet, 181

Joseph, 181,189
  Mary. 181
  Philip, 181,189
Gillmore
  Gen. Quincy A., 37
Gloucester
  Rev. J. N., 170, 172
Goff
  Delly, 163, 166
Goodman
  William, 183
Goodrich
  Lucius, 225
Gould
  Israel, 229
  William E., 229, 230
Graham
  Simon, 188
Grant
  Gen. Ulysses S., 109
Graves
  Catharine, 159
  Jeremiah, 159
  John C., 157, 159
  Rosella, 159
Grayson
  Albert O., 266, 267, 270
  Amos, 266
  Charles H., 266, 267, 269
  Charlotte, 266
  Congo, 265
  EmilyFrances, 270
  Esther, 265
  Harriet, 266
  Harry, 266, 267, 270
  John W., 266, 267
  Judah, 266
  Judson, 265, 266, 267, 269
  Lucy Ann, 265, 266, 267, 268, 269, 270
  Mary Jane, 266
  Pompey, 253
  Willard C., 266
Greeley
  Horace, 170

Holmes, 35
    Charles M., 187
    George, 34, 35
    John, 35
    Mary A., 35
    Rebecca, 35
Howard
    James, 151
Howland
    George, 150
    Slocum, 188
Hurley
    Nathaniel, 29, 33
Jackson
    David, 218
    Edward, 218, 219
    Fanny L., 151
    Maria, 258
    Mary A., 35
    Mary J., 249
    Moses, 29
    Susan, 218
    William, 70
Jacobs
    Clarissa, 222
    Tilman, 252
Jeffries
    Augustus, 180
Jenness
    J. Francis, 82
Johnson
    David, 224
    Ephraim, 61, 70
    Garret Smith, 187
    George H., 60
    Hannah E., 224
    Ida, 249
    James P., 54
    Marcella, 228
    Maria, 224
    Mary Louise, 224
    William, 152
    William R., 182
Johnston
    Gen. Joseph E., 244

Jones
    Benjamin, 137
    Martha, 90
    Rufus Sibb, 98, 103, 116
Jubiter. *See* Jupiter
Jupiter
    Alfred, 211
    Anthony, 209, 210
    Benjamin, 205
    Benjamin W., 182, 209,
       210, 211, 212, 213
    Dwight, 108, 209
    Harriet, 108
    Harvey, 108, 182, 184, 209
    Jane, 210, 214
    Mary Jane, 108
    Susan, 209, 210
Kane
    Charles, 33
    Elias K., 33
    Rebecca, 34
Kenny
    Phillis, 189
Key
    Jane, 54
Ku Klux Klan, 42
Lay
    Robert, 91
Le Vere
    George W., 184
Lee
    Elva Josephine, 34
    Estella Frances, 34
    Gen. Robert E., 54
    George H., 21, 23
    H. I., 126
    Hannah, 22
    John, 150
    John A., 183
    Joseph, 70
    Katy, 22
    Mary Ann, 34
    Mary Lucinda, 22
    Molly, 79, 80
    Thomas, 22, 23
    William Freeman, 34

William R., 21, 34
Willis, 22
Lemunyon
William F., 253
Lenison
Philip, 136
LeVere
George W., 175
Lewis
Emiline, 94
Jane (Key), 54
Lorenzo T., 53
Peter, 94
Robert, 54
William T., 93, 94
Libby Prison, 218
Liberator, 264
Lincoln
Abraham, 13
Lloyd
Charles W., 20
Jane, 193
Sophia Matilda, 166
Thomas, 91, 222
William Thomas, 92
Lodine
Hannah, 107
Loguen
Jermain W., 95, 172
Low
Dennis, 113
Susan, 113
Lukes
Edwin, 24
Lunn
Amos A., 135, 150
Charles, 150
Helen E., 150
Lush
Thomas N., 183
Mann
Robert T., 82
Susan, 148
William H., 148
Marshall
James, 107

Mason
James A., 70
Judah, 266
Matagorda Island, 135, 138, 153, 184
Mather
Lt. Col. A. E., 185
Mathews
Amy, 249
Peter, 249, 252
Thomas, 249, 250, 251

Mayberry
Mary E., 203
McGonigal
Ethel, 228
Henry, 228
Mary, 228
McKenzie
Lloyd, 76
McKinney
Richard, 248
McWilliams
J. A., 183
Miller
Andrew, 21, 50, 55
Peter, 143, 144
Miller, George. *See* Shears, George C.
Moore
Ardelle, 20
Charles H., 150
David, 19
David M., 19
Elizabeth, 19
George, 149
John W., 29
Maria, 149
Miles, 19, 20
William A., 19, 162
Morris Island, 20, 27, 33, 35, 43, 54, 55
Moshroe
George W., 29, 32
Murray
Henry, 111

341

Wells
Charity, 44
Wesley
Charles H., 26
Whedon
Ezra, 94
Sylvester, 94
Whitaker
Helen, 104
White
Anthony, 151
Mayor Jonas, 75
Whitney
George, 180, 181, 187
Wigden
Martin, 187
Permilia, 187
Wilberforce University, 110
Williams
Joseph. *See* Gillam, Joseph
Wilson
Ida, 220, 229
James, 229
James A., 220
Sarah Elizabeth, 220
Sarah J., 220, 229
William, 220, 228, 229,
230, 231

Wooby
Bessie, 224
Clara Belle, 224
Clarissa, 222
Frederick, 224
Hannah E., 224
Hannah Louise, 224
James, 224
John, 222
Mary, 222
Mary (Newport), 247
Mary Ellen, 224
Mary Louise, 224
Porter, 222, 224
William, 222, 224
Woodlin
Alice, 117
Emeline J., 117
William P., 82, 83, 84, 85,
88, 98, 99, 102, 103,
105, 108, 110, 111, 115,
116, 117, 118
Wright
Maj. Thomas, 215, 217
Wycoff
Thomas A., 131, 150
Yellow Bluffs, Fla., 97, 100,
203
Young
Thomas, 81

343